The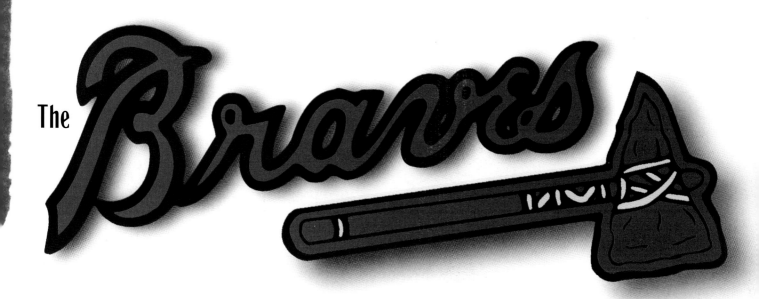

1914 Boston Braves.

1957 Milwaukee Braves.

1991 Atlanta Braves.

The

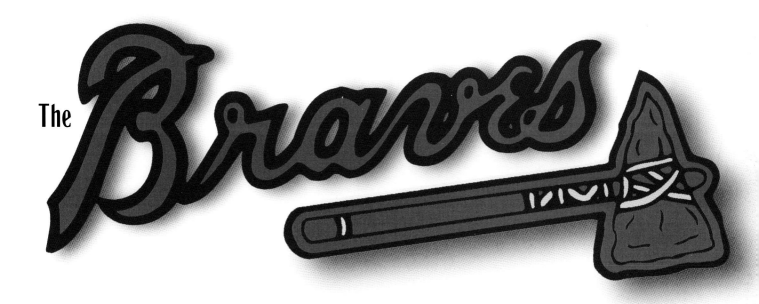

An Illustrated History
of America's Team

by

Bob Klapisch &
Pete Van Wieren

Turner Publishing, Inc.
ATLANTA

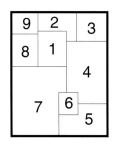

Front cover legend:
1. Hank Aaron. (Atlanta Braves Public Relations)
2. Davey Johnson (middle). (Atlanta Braves Public Relations/C. W. Skinner)
3. Bill Bruton (left), Warren Spahn. (Bettman/UPI)
4. David Justice. (Atlanta Braves Public Relations/Joe Sebo)
5. Sid Bream (sliding). (Chris Hamilton)
6. Babe Ruth. (National Baseball Library and Archive, Cooperstown, NY)
7. Rabbit Maranville. (National Baseball Library and Archive, Cooperstown, NY)
8. Dale Murphy. (Atlanta Braves Public Relations/Joe Sebo)
9. Braves fan. (Atlanta Braves Public Relations/Joe Sebo)

Back cover, top: National anthem, Braves Field, Boston. (Sporting News)
Back cover, bottom: National anthem, Atlanta-Fulton County Stadium, Atlanta. (Atlanta Braves Public Relations/Marty Moore)

Published by Turner Publishing, Inc.
A Subsidiary of Turner Broadcasting System, Inc.
1050 Techwood Drive, N.W.
Atlanta, Georgia 30318

Library of Congress Cataloging-in-Publication Data
Klapisch, Bob.
The Braves: an illustrated history of America's team/Bob Klapisch
and Pete Van Wieren. —1st ed.
        p.   cm.
ISBN 1-57036-170-3 (Hardcover)
ISBN 1-57036-207-6 (Paperback)
1. Boston Braves (Baseball team)—History. 2. Milwaukee Braves
(Baseball team)—History. 3. Atlanta Braves (Baseball team)—History.
I. Van Wieren, Peter.   II. Title.
GV875.B59K53 1995
796.357'64'0973—dc20   94-40194
                                                         CIP

Distributed by Andrews and McMeel
A Universal Press Syndicate Company
4900 Main Street
Kansas City, Missouri 64112

Editorial: Kevin Mulroy, Katherine Buttler, and Lauren Emerson
Design: Robert Zides
Photo Editor: Dianne Joy
Production: Anne Murdoch

First Edition
10 9 8 7 6 5 4 3 2 1

Printed in the U.S.A.

contents

introduction

When we are first attracted to baseball, it is usually because of a team. The home team. It is only after this first connection that we begin to identify our favorite players and begin building our own treasure trove of unforgettable moments and become baseball fans.

As fans, we take on a collective identity that often mirrors the history of the team we follow. New York Yankees fans, for instance, display an arrogance and confidence that comes from supporting a team with a long winning tradition. Boston Red Sox supporters, on the other hand, are a group plagued by frustration and the vexation that accompanies so many near-misses. And then there are the Chicago Cubs fans, baseball's eternal optimists.

Braves fans are not as easy to categorize. Geographically scattered, this family of fans has pulled for a team whose history is filled with incredible peaks, deep valleys, and everything in between. This family has lived in the Northeast, the Midwest, the Southeast, and today, anywhere cable television is available.

There are still Braves fans in Boston who fondly recall the era of "Spahn and Sain, then pray for rain." There are still Braves fans in Milwaukee who will proudly tell you how their team interrupted a decade of dominance by the Yankees-Dodgers-Giants triumvirate. There are, of course, millions of Braves fans throughout the Southeast and millions more who witnessed Atlanta's worst-to-first miracle of 1991 on national cable television. And they still watch. It may have been a reach to champion the Atlanta Braves as "America's Team" in the 1980s, when TBS began broadcasting the games from coast to coast. But today, that designation rings true.

As a Braves broadcaster for the past twenty years, I have had the privilege of witnessing and recounting all of the peaks and valleys this team has taken us through in that time. In this profession, you are supposed to remain objective. But that's impossible. Like the fan watching at home, Ernie Johnson, Skip Caray, Don Sutton, Joe Simpson, and I are connected to this home team. These Braves.

As journalists, we'll call the game as honestly and accurately as we can. But inside each of us, there's a Braves fan that cheers for every Braves victory and hurts with every loss.

We don't really feel like historians, but I guess we are. At the least, we are narrators for this particular era of Braves history. I can recall being at the microphone when the Braves ended the forty-four-game hitting streak of Pete Rose in 1978, and when Bob Horner hit his fourth home run in a game against Montreal in 1986, and when the Braves clinched the National League West in 1991. At the time, they were the exciting moments that we live for in our business. But today, they are past chapters in Braves history.

The history of the Braves dates all the way back to the earliest years of professional baseball. It winds through Boston, Milwaukee, and Atlanta, and has given us more than one "miracle" season. It has produced fourteen pennant-winners and forty Hall-of-Famers. It includes over fourteen thousand games.

Are the Braves of today as good as the 1957 Milwaukee Braves? Are they better than the "Miracle" Boston Braves of 1914? Who was the better pitcher in his prime, Warren Spahn or Greg Maddux? Who was better at turning the doubleplay—Mark Lemke, Glenn Hubbard, or Johnny Evers? Should Dale Murphy make the Hall of Fame? Will anyone break Hank Aaron's home-run record?

History and tradition are the backbone of baseball. They create the thread that ties one generation of baseball fans to the next. As broadcasters, we can't help but become a part of this process. When we tell a Phil Niekro story, we are bringing back memories to the older fan, but are educating the new ones who never saw "Knucksie" pitch.

This book brings all of the Braves family together. As in any historical account, it is people, not events, that draw our attention. No team history is a mere retelling of who won or lost, but is a compilation of individual stories. The personalities of players, managers, and owners are as much a part of baseball lore as the games themselves.

The history of the Braves is filled with characters as diverse as those in any Dickens novel. Owners have displayed the generosity of Ted Turner and the tight-fistedness of Judge Emil Fuchs. Managers have shown the comical flamboyance of Casey Stengel and the stony reticence of Luman Harris. Players have exhibited the steely feistiness of Johnny Evers and the warm sincerity of Dale Murphy. It is the collection of these and other distinctive personalities that helps define the Braves during any given era.

While the history of the Braves is highlighted by Hank Aaron becoming baseball's all-time home-run king, it also includes Babe Ruth's final year as a player with the 1935 Boston Braves. And though the Braves' story must focus on the "miracle" years, it cannot ignore the long stretches of mediocrity and failure that came in between. While this story reaches to the present day with images of sold-out crowds waving their tomahawks, it reminds us that the franchise once failed in Boston, repeated that failure in Milwaukee, and nearly went under again in Atlanta. And while the future of the Braves looks bright with Greg Maddux, Fred McGriff, Tom Glavine, and David Justice, history cautions us that baseball is a game of never-ending cycles. Somewhere down the road there are valleys yet to be crossed.

That's the problem with delivering a history of an ongoing institution such as the Braves. You can't write a final chapter. Perhaps the greatest Braves star has yet to be born. Perhaps the greatest Braves moment is just around the corner.

Fifty years from now, entire chapters of this book might be reduced to a signal paragraph, so insignificant might they become. But their content will never change. History is indelible. Every pitch thrown, every at-bat, every game played merely extends it.

When you attend your next game, or listen or watch on radio or TV, you become an automatic witness to a new page of baseball history.

Pete VanWieren

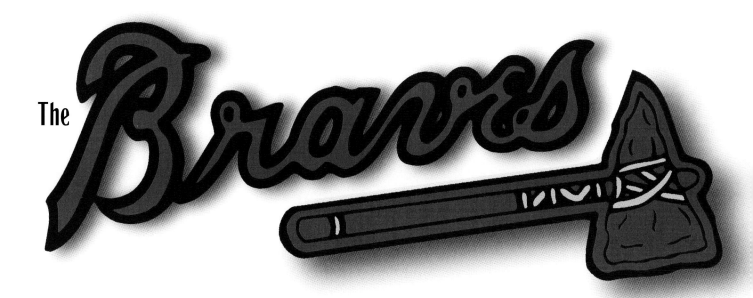

boston

1871 **1952**

Braves Field, Boston.

the birth of a franchise

1

*"Boston can now boast of possessing a
first class professional Base Ball club . . ."*
—*Boston Journal,* January 21, 1871

In the beginning they were the Red

Stockings, or more simply, the Reds—Boston's pride, its piece of America's

new pastime. Slow and awkward by today's standards, the game of baseball

was brand new in 1871, and so were the team nicknames—lacking in

imagination perhaps, but still exciting to a population that quickly fell in

love with the sport. In later years, the Red Stockings would become the

Doves, the Rustlers, the Bees, and eventually the Braves—but it never real-

ly mattered much to Bostonians what their team was called. All they want-

ed was a winner. The town watched new leagues come and go, as new rules

were introduced and old ones discarded, until, by 1900, baseball loosely

began to resemble the game we now embrace. In 1914, Boston's patience

1889 Boston Beaneaters (manager Jim Hart, center).

Kid, We Hardly Knew Ye

After winning 27 games in his first year in Boston, 1890, pitcher Kid Nichols was unstoppable. He won 30 games in 1891, 35 in 1892, 33 in 1893, and another 32 in 1894. Nichols averaged more than 400 innings a year in his prime in the 1890s, although that statistic, like most of that era, is hard to measure against modern stats. Baseball was a slower game back then, and it was easier for the standout athlete to dominate. Still, in his fourteen years, Nichols won 360 games and lost only 202. He pitched 530 complete games, winning 30 games in seven consecutive seasons, 20 or more in ten consecutive seasons. Nichols was inducted into the Hall of Fame in 1949.

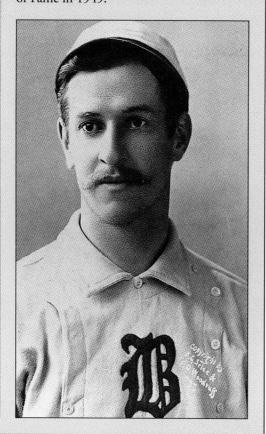

Star pitcher Kid Nichols.

was rewarded, as the Braves engineered one of the most miraculous second-half runs in baseball history, rising from last place in July to a first-place finish and capping the season with a four-game World Series sweep of the heavily favored Philadelphia Athletics. Even today, sportswriters still liken Boston's triumph to the Mets stunning the Baltimore Orioles in the 1969 World Series, or the Giants' slaying of the Brooklyn Dodgers for the National League pennant in 1951.

The road to 1914 was a long one, sometimes ugly, shaped by the many changes baseball underwent in its infancy. Before 1900, the game was played with a "dead ball," one that was loosely wound at its core and therefore not likely to travel far. The pace of the game, much slower and easier on the body, made it possible for pitchers to win 30-40 games a year without ruining their arms— therefore, historians have generally discounted all pre-1900 stats. Yet, by any measure the Braves of that era dominated the sport. "Break up the Red Stockings" was the common refrain among the team's detractors as the Reds, owned by Harry Wright, won 12 pennants out of 29, including four in a row between 1872 and 1875, a success so overwhelming the National Association of Professional Players eventually disbanded— simply because no one could compete with the nearly invincible Reds.

The Red Stockings were immensely successful in raising the energy level of the citizens of Boston. By the last quarter of the nineteenth century, America was in the midst of tremendous industrial development, and cities, especially those in the Northeast, were growing quickly. But after a long and tedious day's work in the factories or sweatshops there was little for the average citizen to do—at the time, the best form of entertainment available was a day in the park, or an evening in the saloon or the dance hall. When professional baseball became an option, the response was overwhelming. Like other Americans across the country, Bostonians, at first simply spectators to the new sport, quickly became fanatics. In 1873, Boston lost a 14-4 game to the

Lord Baltimore Nine, prompting this irate letter to the editor of the *Boston Herald*:

" . . . we have spent our last half-dollar on the Boston ground . . . and we don't believe the club exists that can fairly beat the Bostons, in even three innings, when the score is 14-4 . . . we think the Boston Club is on the make. The club of '72 is not the club of '73 and we hope they will disband before they go backward any further." An official of the Red Stockings promptly replied, offering the fan a flat $50 for every game he could prove was being fixed or thrown. Discontent soon evaporated, however, when the Red Stockings won their second straight championship.

The team's secret weapon was the son of an Illinois farmer, a pitching sensation named Albert Goodwill Spalding. The first professional ball player to win more than 200 games, Al Spalding's pitching excellence and gentlemanly manner helped improve the public's perception of baseball players. Spalding's contribution to the team was acknowledged with an $1,800 salary increase in 1873, and that winter he went to England on vacation to spend his newly earned cash. Once there, Spalding discovered cricket, the English national pastime. He conceived of the ultimate showdown—a game between the American baseball champs and the

British cricket champs—and convinced the officials of the Marylebone Cricket Club to approve a visit by two American teams, the Red Stockings and the second-place Philadelphia Athletics. The match was supposed to generate excitement in England for baseball, tweak the British in the process, and above all, make money. The experiment worked in some, but not all aspects. The Red Stockings and Athletics played each other fourteen times, with Boston winning eight games. The highest drama, however, was saved for the matches between the Reds and the British, with Boston winning five of six, thanks to the cricket backgrounds of brothers Harry, Sam, and George Wright. The American victory over Marylebone, 107-105, was described in some Boston papers as "the greatest American victory over the English since the Revolution."

The trip didn't earn the Red Stockings much cash, however—a mere $844.13. So they were happy to return to the States to the comfortable dominance they enjoyed in the National Association. In 1874, the Reds were 52-18, taking advantage of a loose league and an even looser schedule: 96 of the 232 scheduled games weren't played. Even so, Boston outraced the second-place Brooklyn Nationals by 13½ games, carrying the pennant in 1875 with an

Nineteenth-century catcher's mask, a primitive predecessor of today's high-tech design.

The Boston Red Stockings of 1873, champions of the National Association with a 43-16 record. Four future Hall of Famers played for this team: pitcher Al Spalding (top row, second from left), outfielder Jim O'Rourke (seated, far left), shortstop George Wright (seated, third from left), and player-manager Harry Wright (seated, middle). Second baseman Ross Barnes (top row, far right) won the National Association batting title in 1873 with a .402 average.

Pitcher Albert G. Spalding.

From Pitcher to Corporate Giant

"Everything is possible to him who dares."
—Al Spalding

Called "the father of the greatest sport the world has ever known," by *The New York Times* in 1899, pitching ace Albert G. Spalding was one of the best-known players of the early Boston Reds era. He was recruited in 1870 by owner Harry Wright from Rockford, Illinois, where he had pitched for the Forest Citys, winning 45 games between 1867 and 1870. He was awarded an astounding $2,500 contract by Wright, $500 of it paid up front, and it was Spalding who pitched Boston's first game, on April 6, 1871. Playing to a crowd of 5,000 curious fans, the Red Stockings won 41-10 against a hapless pick-up team. The next season Spalding went on to lead the Reds to the championship of baseball's first professional league, the National Association of Professional Baseball Players. Playing against teams from Fort Wayne, Chicago, Philadelphia, and New York, Spalding would lead the Red Stockings to three more league championships before returning to Chicago to captain the White Stockings in 1876.

In Chicago, Spalding would build a financial empire on the success of Spalding Sporting Goods, a company he started to manufacture baseballs and other equipment for the National League, and which quickly expanded to include all varieties of sporting products which the company manufactures even to this day.

incredible 71-8 record, including a 26-game winning streak between April 19 and June 3. That was also the year baseball saw the introduction of the catcher's mask, which wasn't the only change the game underwent. The National Association was coming apart, soon to be replaced by today's National League, and the changes that were taking place had everything to do with Boston. Four of the Reds' best players simply defected to a new and wealthy upstart Chicago franchise, the White Stockings. Those defectors included Spalding, seduced away by owner William Hulbert, who told the pitcher, "You're a midwesterner, Al, and you should be playing in Chicago. I would rather be a lamppost in Chicago than a millionaire in any other city." Spalding agreed and left Boston, claiming the team's outrageous winning percentages were beginning to bore him. A significant salary increase and the promise of a percentage of the gate also helped decide him in favor of Hulbert's White Stockings, who, a year later, would win the league championship.

Hulbert was successful in creating the National League, raiding National Association teams—five of whom folded rather than compete with him—often and effectively. The Red Stockings, still intact, wisely chose to join this new circuit. But there was a price to pay for leaving the comfort of the National Association, as the Red Stockings finished only fourth in the National League's first season. As an illustration of how loosely—even tenuously—assembled the National League was in 1876, the Philadelphia Athletics and New York Mutuals both failed to make their second western trip, and for that reason were expelled from the league. Boston earned the honor of being the only club to play all of its seventy regularly scheduled games.

Until 1920, the baseball used was a slower ball, nowadays referred to as a "dead ball."

so what's a beaneater?

2

*"The Bostons could have beaten any all-star nine
the league could have put together this season."*

—John Montgomery Ward, manager of the New York Giants, 1893

It took nearly two decades, but Boston

finally made its mark on the National League in the 1890s. From 1891 to

1898, they won five pennants, all under manager Frank Selee, and all were

claimed under their new nickname—the Beaneaters. As baseball's pop-

ularity grew, teams were becoming known nationally, and the Red

Stockings, realizing their name was too similar to the Cincinnati Red Legs,

changed their nickname to the "Beaneaters." The name was coined by local

sportswriters, who seized on the city's love affair with baked beans. And it

didn't hurt that Mike "King" Kelly, one of Boston's most popular players of

the pre-1900 era, pronounced one day, "I'm a bean eater, too." Kelly

was an outsider. He'd been sold to the Beaneaters from the hated Chicago

Mike "King" Kelly, a hard-hitting, hard-living star of the 1890s.

White Stockings for the outrageous price of $10,000, and in addition, Boston owner J. B. Billings agreed to pay Kelly $5,000 a season, by far the most generous salary to date. Kelly, one of the finest players of baseball's infancy, won the National League batting title in 1886 with a .388 average and was such an exceptional athlete that, despite being an average runner, he managed to steal 84 bases in his first season with the Beaneaters in 1887. Teammate Hugh Duffy, who would later play on the same clubs with Hall of Famers Nap Lajoie and Honus Wagner, was once asked to compare them to Kelly. Duffy said, "I think a pitcher would rather face Wagner than Lajoie, but it's my opinion that Mike Kelly was the greatest player ever to put on a uniform. There never was a player so outstanding."

Loud, charismatic, and a lover of the nightlife, Kelly often played with a hangover, which made him popular with some Boston fans, but not with his first baseman/manager John Morrill. Honest John, as he was known, was famous for never losing his temper and he never, ever drank. Not surprisingly, Morrill had no patience for Kelly's flamboyance, and the Beaneaters were eventually divided into two factions—those who admired Kelly and

those who professed loyalty to Morrill. Morrill lost the power struggle and was eventually sold to the Washington club.

By 1890, the Beaneaters had a new manager, and with him began their first National League dynasty. Frank Selee had done some managing in the New England League and the Northwestern League, and by the time he arrived in Boston, he had carved out a reputation as a quiet, calm man who knew his baseball. The Beaneaters of the '90s were the first team to really emphasize fundamentals: Selee had them bunting in one-run games, and he taught them the art of the hit-and-run and the importance of the stolen base. Selee was best with his younger players, and the feeling was mutual.

"If I make things pleasant for the players, they reciprocate," Selee said. "I want them to be temperate and live properly. I do not believe that men who are engaged in such exhilarating exercise should be kept in straitjackets all the time, but I expect them to be in condition to play. I do not want a man who cannot appreciate such treatment."

The result of this philosophy? Selee's team never finished lower than fifth place in his twelve years in Boston, not to mention those five pennants they gathered. In his first season, however, the Beaneaters finished fifth with a 76-57 record, although much of the blame could be laid to rest on yet another league that stole eleven players from the Beaneaters' roster, including Kelly.

The Brotherhood of Professional Baseball players, which was the first attempt to form a union, was formed by nine members of the New York Giants and was initially designed to protect players from the abuses many managers visited upon their players. Brotherhood chapters were set up throughout the National League, and at first met no opposition from owners because, if nothing else, the fraternity promoted good will among the players.

By 1887, the Brotherhood had gained enough strength to seek formal recognition from the National League and negotiate contract reform. National League elders resisted this new wave of thinking, which only stiffened the players' resolve, and by 1890, a new league, the Player's League, was born. The plan was to place franchises in seven National League cities—Boston, New York, Brooklyn, Philadelphia, Pittsburgh, Cleveland, and Chicago—with an eighth team in Buffalo. Under the Brotherhood's constitution, the players and each team's backers would share in the league's profits. It was a revolutionary concept, one that even today owners are loath to accept. The Brotherhood offered huge financial incentives for National League players to leave their teams—signing bonuses, guaranteed three-year contracts, and greater expense allowances. The National League responded with bribes, too, and was ready to offer King Kelly a flat $10,000 to leave the Brotherhood. He refused, saying, "I'd rather stay with the boys." But, unlike Kelly, many big-name Brotherhood principals returned to the National League, uncomfortable with the idea of risking a career over a well-intentioned but poorly-run experiment. After only one season, the League collapsed.

It was in 1891 that Selee's team finally found some good luck, winning 23 of 30 in September to clinch the pennant. In 1892, the first of two times in its history the National League split its season into two, the Beaneaters won the first half, and defeated Cleveland, the second-half winners, in a best-of-nine series.

By 1893, Boston dominated the League so thoroughly that Giants manager John Montgomery Ward acknowledged that, "The Bostons could have beaten any all-star nine the league could have put together this season." Because of the futuristic offense Selee had installed—Boston used the sacrifice bunt and hit-and-run long before it was commonplace—the Beaneaters were scoring runs in clusters. They collected 1,008 in all, leading the National League. They were also the first team to steal signs from the opposing catcher, as baserunners on second conceived of body-language signals to alert the batter. Tugging at a shirt-sleeve, for instance, would sound the alarm for a coming fastball, and a hands-on-hips stance would mean a curveball.

In Their League

The first major league player ever to hit four home runs in one game, Bobby Lowe had no ego about his place in the history books. One day in 1928 in St. Petersburg, Florida, Lowe, long since retired, asked Lou Gehrig and Babe Ruth for their autographs. They obliged, of course—Ruth loved to sign and would satisfy a crowd of hundreds begging for his signature—but neither one of the Yankees realized who Lowe was, and Lowe was too bashful to identify himself. He later told friends he was afraid Gehrig and Ruth wouldn't believe anyone so skinny could have been so dangerous with the bat.

After retiring with the Detroit Tigers in 1907, Lowe took up permanent residence in Detroit, finding a job with the Department of Public Works and forging a friendship with the great Ty Cobb. One day in 1922, when Cobb was managing the Tigers, he invited Lowe to his home, where a friendly argument ensued. Lowe had told Cobb that the modern-day infielders must have been awfully inept to let Cobb steal so many bases, and went on to say that he was not impressed with Cobb's ability to

Bobby Lowe.

hook slide. Cobb heatedly told Lowe he could fool him, just as he had victimized so many second basemen of his era.

So Cobb moved the furniture in his living room, used a hassock for a base, and slid in under Lowe, using one of his best hook slides. The two men argued furiously over whether Lowe had been quick enough with his hands to tag Cobb. Lowe later conceded he had been able to catch Cobb's slide only "part of the time."

Before Stan Musial There Was . . .

After winning three straight pennants, Boston saw its streak end in 1894, although that season is most remembered by historians for Hugh Duffy's .438 average, which has never been equaled. Even by today's standards, the .438 mark is almost unreachable. The last player to hit .400 was Ted Williams, who batted .406 in 1941. San Diego's Tony Gwynn made a legitimate run at the .400 mark in 1994, batting .394 before the season was cancelled due to a players' strike. But Wade Boggs, who has flirted with an average in the high .300s many times in his career, flatly believes no one will ever top .400 again. "The media just won't let it happen," he explains. "There are too many interviews to do, too many questions to answer, too many distractions for any player to withstand."

Hall of Famer Hugh Duffy.

But Duffy faced no such obstacles. In fact, a batting average didn't count nearly as much as a pennant, so when his season ended, not even Duffy was keeping track of his personal stats. "All I knew is that I led the league (in hitting) and that was the important thing," he said. For a while, Duffy mistakenly believed he had batted .428. One thing was sure, though: Duffy achieved his success in an era when the pitching was relatively good and the quality of the baseballs was still poor.

He stood only five foot six, but Duffy is still regarded as one of baseball's pioneers. For instance, he is said to be the first player to have had the presence of mind to take two bases on a sacrifice fly—scoring from second on a deep blast to center one day in 1894. The crowd at Boston's South End Grounds, not to mention the opposing team, watched in silent awe, then exploded in cheers. They realized a small piece of baseball history had just been written by this tough little Irishman.

One Beaneater who was an integral part of the team's offensive explosion was second baseman Bobby Lowe. A mere 155 pounds, Lowe nevertheless became the first player to slug four homers in one game. On May 30, 1894, Lowe smoked pitcher Elton Chamberlain of the Cincinnati Reds, going deep twice in the third inning, once more in the fifth, and yet again in the sixth. The exhilarated crowd at Congress Street Grounds in Boston showered Lowe with close to $160 worth of coins and silver in a display of their wild enthusiasm for Lowe's muscle-flexing exhibition.

In 1897 and 1898, Selee was able to guide the Beaneaters to two more pennants. But despite their .685 winning percentage in '98, attendance sagged in Boston as the nation's attention was diverted by the Spanish-American War. Even in the middle of a September pennant race, South End Grounds couldn't draw more than 1,200 or 1,400 fans. Attendance rose slightly in 1899, but for an afternoon doubleheader on Labor Day against Washington, the Beaneaters still could not draw a crowd of more than 4,000. Maybe they had grown complacent after winning so many seasons in a row, but whatever the reason, neither the team nor their diminishing fans could know that the Beaneaters' Golden Era was over—they would not have another pennant for sixteen years.

How serious was that drought? There was a third-place finish in 1902, but after that Boston failed to reach .500 until 1914. In fact, the Beaneaters—who were soon to become the Doves, then the Rustlers, and, in 1912, the Braves—lost 100 games in four straight seasons, from 1909 to 1912. The club's collapse was bad enough—their stars aged, and the new players were notoriously poor hitters—but not nearly as ominous as the emergence of yet another new league, one that meant business: Ban Johnson's American League.

Johnson, a former college player at Marietta and Oberlin, spent some time in semi-pro ball before turning to sportswriting for the *Cincinnati Commercial Gazette*. His real pas-

sion, though, was baseball administration, and he took over the reigns of the Western League in 1894. Johnson soon renamed his property the American League to give it a more national character, and he established franchises in Chicago, Cleveland, Detroit, Minneapolis, Milwaukee, Kansas City, and Indianapolis. By 1900, the league was fully operational and was a public success.

At first, Johnson had no desire to fight the National League in Boston, and was willing to forgo placing a franchise there. But the haughty elders of the National League refused to acknowledge Johnson, even threatening to resurrect the old American Association as a rival of the American League. So Johnson responded by planting a team right in the middle of Beantown. They were called the Boston Americans, and they gained instant credibility by having Connie Mack, a baseball pioneer, as one of their organizers before he began a fifty-year tenure as manager of the Philadelphia A's. The American League lured Hugh Duffy away from the Beaneaters, allowing him to manage and play center field in Milwaukee, and Duffy induced former teammate Jimmy Collins to change allegiances,

too. However, instead of following Duffy to Milwaukee, Collins instead moved to the cross-town rivals, the Americans.

The new team in Boston was smart about its public relations, creating a 25-cent section in the bleachers and letting kids in for free. No wonder the Americans' home opener against Philadelphia on May 8, 1900, drew a respectable 11,500. By comparison, the Beaneaters pulled in a mere 5,500 against Brooklyn on that same day. The Beaneaters had even lost one of their perennial drawing cards, pitcher Kid Nichols, who had won 27 games in his first year in Boston, 1890.

By the early 1900s, the Beaneaters were an awful team, and as their decline began in earnest, Frank Selee was already gone. He was dismissed by the team's owners after the 1901 season—the triumvirate of Arthur Soden, J. B. Billings, and William Conant, better known as the Triumvirs—and somehow turned into a scapegoat for a fifth-place finish. The fans couldn't understand Selee's punishment, nor could the players. "Selee should have left that city and taken one of several good chances he had," Hugh Duffy said,

SO WHAT'S A BEANEATER?

"instead of staying here at a very small salary."
Selee went on to manage in Chicago from
1902 to 1904, but resigned because of poor
health and died of consumption five years
later at age fifty. Writing about him, baseball
historian Alfred Spink noted that, "Few men
in baseball were more popular. He was generous to a degree and extremely charitable. He
had a host of friends."

Selee was replaced by Al Buckenberger, who
stuck around for only three seasons, working
his way down the ladder of success. On
Buckenberger's watch, the Beaneaters finished
third, then sixth, then seventh. In 1904, his
last year with the team, Boston lost 98 games.

As the dark ages truly descended upon this
disintegrating franchise, Boston decided its
only hope was to elevate first baseman Fred
Tenney to manager. He was a talented hitter,
but had no real credentials as a manager.
Perhaps the Beaneaters' owners understood
this. "We don't care where you finish," one of
their principals told Tenney, "as long as you
don't lose us money." Tenney was offered a
yearly bonus for every season Boston finished
in the black. That inspired him to absurd
lengths in his belt-tightening measures: It was
not uncommon in 1905, for instance, for
Tenney himself to chase down foul balls in
the stands. The Beaneaters did actually break
even on the books, but by then the team
had all but evaporated on the field. In
Tenney's three years as manager, they finished
54 ½, 66 ½, and 47 games out of first place.
Between 1908 and 1912, Boston tried six different managers—including Tenney for one
more year in 1911—but none of them had
much effect except to keep the Beaneaters
active as the National League's public joke.

South End Grounds was Boston's National League home from 1876 through May 1894, when a fire burned it to the ground. The upper deck of this early stadium was called the Grand Pavilion.

SO WHAT'S A BEANEATER?

a miracle in the making

3

"This club is a horror show."

—Manager George Stallings, assessing the 1913 Braves

In 1913, a new manager arrived, and

with him, the start of the Braves' comeback—or at least their return to respectability. George Tweedy Stallings was born in 1867, the son of a Confederate general, and attended Virginia Military Academy, where he played baseball. After graduating Stallings moved to Baltimore with plans to study medicine. While playing in a semi-pro league he was intercepted by Harry Wright, one of the original owners of the Red Stockings, who at that time was managing the Philadelphia franchise. "You're too good a baseball player to be wasting your time in school," Wright told Stallings. And with that, Stallings' future as a doctor evaporated, and what would become a lifelong career in baseball got underway. Unfortunately, Stallings' on-field

Braves catcher Hank Gowdy, hero of the 1914 World Series.

Fred Mitchell (center of wreath) was manager George Stallings' right-hand man with the "Miracle Braves." Mitchell left to manage the Chicago Cubs in 1917, but returned to Boston as Stallings' successor in 1921.

skills were never as impressive as Wright had imagined. After spending eight years moving from minor league team to minor league team, from league to league, Stallings finally found his niche in a managing job with the Nashville club in 1895. But even as a manager, he moved often: Detroit, Philadelphia, Detroit again, Buffalo, Newark, New York, and Buffalo again.

George Stallings managed the New York Highlanders in 1909 and 1910, only to lose his job to Hal Chase near the end of the 1910 season. Braves owner James Gaffney—who changed the team's name to the Braves in 1912—spotted an opportunity, asking first if Stallings was interested in piloting the Braves, and second, what Stallings thought of his new team. When Stallings told him, "This club is a horror show," Gaffney nodded calmly. Stallings was, after all, correct. Gaffney then instructed his new manager to make whatever changes were necessary. This molli-

fied Stallings somewhat, although he made sure Gaffney understood how difficult the rebuilding job would be. "I've been stuck with some terrible teams," Stallings observed, "but this one beats them all."

Stallings came to the Braves with a reputation of being a tough, almost unforgiving manager, one who wouldn't tolerate any mistakes from his players. His teams almost always overachieved, but not even Stallings could have imagined the resurrection the Braves would undergo. There was no free agency in that era, of course, and the only way to change a lineup was through trades or by purchasing the contracts of little-known minor leaguers. Teams almost never remade themselves in two years, but that's how little time it took Stallings to take the Braves to the World Series, in one of the most remarkable metamorphoses in post-1900 baseball history.

In 1913 Stallings faced the greatest challenge of his managerial career. His first move

Mind Games

George Stallings might have had an explosive temper, but he was also one of the most calculating managers of his time. In fact, he was one of the first to engage in psychological warfare, and he made the tactic work against the A's. Legend has it that Stallings assembled a group of baseball writers from both Boston and Philadelphia in his hotel room on October 7, 1914, two days before the start of the Series, and staged a mock argument with Philadelphia manager, Connie Mack, who never knew he was being set up.

According to the story, Stallings picked up the telephone and, in front of the writers, asked Mack if the Braves could work out at Shibe Park the next afternoon at 2 P.M. Stallings listened impatiently as Mack told him the A's were scheduled to use the field at that hour. The A's manager offered Shibe to Stallings at either noon or four o'clock. Stallings told Mack to keep his field, that the Braves would beat the A's without any practice at all, then furiously hung up, leaving Mack bewildered on the other end of the line. Little did the writers know that Stallings had agreed earlier in the day to use the field at noon. But he picked a fight with Mack for the sake of a good story, and he got it.

The next day, the headlines in the Philadelphia papers claimed the A's had denied the Braves use of the field, and that the outraged Stallings was boycotting any workouts at Shibe. Instead, he took the Braves to Baker Field, the National League park, explaining he wanted his players to get used to the shadows in the outfield at that hour. Of course, all Stallings wanted to do was make the A's understand the National League upstarts were not going to be intimidated by the American League champs.

Braves manager George Stallings, flanked by 1914 pitching stars Bill James (left) and Dick Rudolph (right).

Stallings may have been the most superstitious manager in baseball history. He amassed a huge collection of lucky charms, which he kept in a trunk that traveled to wherever the Braves played. He often credited the 1914 "miracle" to a lucky ten-cent piece (blessed by a Cuban witch doctor), which he had added to his collection that year.

A MIRACLE IN THE MAKING

was to recruit catcher Fred Mitchell from the Highlanders, anointing him "My Right Eye," meaning Mitchell would be the pitching coach as well as third base coach. Mitchell also helped Stallings in spin-control, since the Braves' new manager was so temperamental and believed that emotionally frail players could never succeed on the field. His players called Stallings "Chief" or "Big Daddy."

During that season, Stallings acquired most of the hard-nosed players who were to become regulars of the 1914 World Champions. In fact, of the players Stallings inherited in 1913, only Rabbit Maranville, Hank Gowdy, George Tyler, and Otto Hess were part of the 1914 miracle. Among those imported that same year by Stallings were Joe Connolly, Leslie Mann, Charles Schmidt, and Charlie Deal. They combined to lift the Braves from eighth place to fifth in 1913, from 52 wins to 69.

But Stallings could not have gained any momentum without a transfusion to his pitching staff. Two of the most important discoveries he made in 1913 were right-handers Bill James and Dick Rudolph. James, only twenty-one, had a good fastball, but like so many young pitchers who are blessed with a live arm, he could not connect with the strike zone. Though James won only six games, Stallings knew that with time, the boy would smother National League hitters.

After a successful college career at Fordham, Dick Rudolph bounced around the minor leagues, including Vermont and Connecticut, and in 1912, played in the International League, posting a 25-10 record for Toronto. As was the case with many minor league clubs in that era, Toronto had no affiliation with any of the major league franchises, and when it was time to raise money, the minor league simply sold one of its players. On May 4, 1913, Toronto sold Rudolph to the Boston Braves for $4,000. Stallings quickly learned Rudolph had in his arsenal a sharp curve, modeled after the master of that era, Christy Mathewson, and a spitball recently learned from teammate Bill James. Midway through the 1913 season, Stallings was calling

Rudolph "the smartest pitcher I've ever seen."

Other components of the rebuilt Braves included Walter James Vincent Maranville, the tough little shortstop whom Stallings called his idea of a baseball player. What distinguished Maranville from other major leaguers was his size: at 150 pounds, it wasn't long before his nickname became Rabbit.

Maranville hit only .247 in 1913, and the Braves did not really count on him for offense. Instead, it was his defense, or more precisely his defensive charisma, that so enthralled Stallings, who admired cockiness in his players. Interestingly, Maranville had to compete against Art Bues, Stallings' nephew, for the shortstop position, but he didn't lack confidence. Indeed, Maranville told his manager, "I know I haven't got much chance

After a 6-10 rookie season, Bill James went 26-7 with a 1.90 ERA for the 1914 Miracle Braves, and added two wins in the World Series, including a 1-0, two-hitter over the A's in Game Two. However, he went only 5-4 the following year, most of which he missed due to illness. James pitched in only one more major league game, receiving a decision in a relief appearance for the Braves in 1919.

going up against your family, but if you put me in there, you'll never take me out." Bues, given the starting assignment at short in spring training, soon afterward contracted diphtheria and played in only two games for Boston in 1913.

Finally, Maranville had his chance. On Opening Day 1913, he went 3-for-4 against Christy Mathewson at the Polo Grounds, and from then on, Bues' job was his. Maranville was a success with the fans, not to mention his old friends back home, who held a Rabbit Maranville Day at South End Grounds in Boston—despite his having been a major leaguer for less than an entire season. Of course, Maranville needed help to make the infield machinery work. He got it during the off-season between 1913 and 1914. In fact, the acquisition of second baseman Johnny Evers might have been the final piece of this memorable puzzle. Evers, of course, was already a famous player by the time the Braves got him from the Chicago Cubs in exchange for Bill Sweeney and cash. Evers was part of the legendary double-play equation in Chicago— "Tinkers-to-Evers-to-Chance"—that had helped the Cubs win the pennant in 1906, 1907, and 1908.

So why did the Cubs let Evers slip away? Actually, Evers was more than just a sure-handed second baseman. In 1913 he managed the Cubs, but committed the unforgivable sin of losing to the White Sox in the city series that year. Following the Cubs defeat, owner Charles Murphy sent Evers to the Braves—punishment, no doubt. How else could one interpret an exodus from pennant-contender to the National League's public whipping boys?

Of course, Evers didn't come easily to Boston. The rival Federal League was being organized, and Evers used it to squeeze an extra $25,000 bonus from the Braves—a ransom Stallings, especially, knew was worth it. Evers was thirty-two, already a twelve-year veteran in the big leagues, and although he was never considered a great hitter—he was a mere 125 pounds—he was in the same defensive class as Eddie Collins. And while

Maranville-to-Evers-to-Schmidt might not have had the same poetic dividend as Tinkers-to-Evers-to-Chance, the result was virtually the same.

With the infield now so solidly constructed, all that Stallings needed to do was find a little magic for his 1914 outfield. Without question, the Braves were weak there, and during the season, Stallings tried eleven outfielders, making wholesale changes in his lineup, depending on who was pitching against Boston. While Stallings was not the first manager to invent the platoon, he was one of the pioneers in employing an entirely new trio, based on lefty-righty matchups.

So the 1914 Braves were ready, at least on paper. Stallings made the decision to employ a three-man pitching rotation—Tyler, James, and Rudolph—and virtually the entire baseball community reacted cynically. Three pitchers for a 154-game schedule? Stallings was either insane or, worse, stupid. Initially, his critics were proven right. The Braves lost 18 of their first 22 games, and there was no reason to believe they were going to improve. Evers caught an early-season flu, and when Maranville contracted tonsillitis, the déjà vu of losing engulfed Boston. The Braves were dead and bloodless in last place.

Incredibly, Stallings kept talking the talk, if for no other reason than to convince himself. In May he told a group of writers, "Give me another month, and we'll be in first place." Everyone coughed politely, wondering whether such an inane quote even belonged in the newspaper. As late as July 4, the halfway point in the season, the Braves were still in last place, fifteen games behind the New York Giants. The low point came days later, when the Braves played a minor league club from Buffalo—and lost 15-2.

"We lost to a soap-company team," Evers said. "That's how bad we were." On the train ride for the start of a western trip, Stallings paced up and down the length of the cars, stopping long enough at each player to stare him down. Stallings was blessed with exceptionally white teeth, and his smile was an impressive sight. In fact, he used to flash those

Rabbit Maranville Cracker Jack candy card, 1924.

Johnny Evers, considered the premier second baseman of the first two decades of twentieth-century baseball. He starred for the 1914 Braves, hitting .438 in the World Series. The diminutive Evers (5-9, 125 pounds) was never very popular with his teammates: His grouchy personality earned him the nickname, "the Crab."

teeth from the dugout as part of the flurry of signs sent to base runners. But there was no smile that night. Stallings lowered his voice and asked, "You call yourselves big leaguers?" He then walked away, mumbling profanities.

Like any team in a slump, the Braves were wondering how much lower their bad luck could sink. Without any signpost, a losing streak is like a personal hell, especially with first place slipping farther and farther away. Yet, there was something about the loss to the Buffalo team that liberated the Braves. Their embarrassment was complete; nothing else could occur that could make them feel any smaller. And then, as so often happens, fate finally became generous to them.

The Braves won 9 of 12, good enough to put them within 11 games of first place by July 19. That day, Boston swept the Reds, finally moving past seventh-place Pittsburgh in the standings. The Braves scored three runs in the ninth inning of the second game, and afterward, they mobbed Stallings as if the World Series had just been won. Intoxicated by the Braves' new-found muscles, the manager said, "Now we'll catch New York. We're

playing 30 percent better ball than anyone in the league. They won't be able to stop us."

Whether Stallings actually believed this, no one will ever know, but the words sounded convincing. Right afterwards, Stallings' Big Three rotation made him look smarter than ever. Rudolph, James, and Tyler combined to throw four shutouts in a five-game series against the Pirates. Everyone was particularly impressed by Maranville's bravery in the third game, which led to a 1-0 win. Rabbit had been batting in the ninth inning of a scoreless game, bases loaded, when Stallings told him, "Get on somehow. I don't care if you have to get hit." The Pirates' Babe Adams quickly threw two strikes, and, sensing he was in trouble, Maranville leaned over the plate as another fastball hissed toward him. The ball struck Maranville on the forehead, forcing the winning run home. But umpire Charlie Moran was suspicious, and the rules permitted him to disallow any hit batsman from taking first base if, in his judgment, the batter had made no effort to evade the pitch. So Moran leaned into Maranville's ear and said, "If you can get up and walk to first base, I'll let you get away

World's Series — Braves 5, Athletics 4, 12 Innings, Fenway Park, American League Grounds, Oct.

with it." Maranville was in fact injured and later had to be helped off the field, but he walked to first base, the run scored, and the Braves came away with another unlikely victory. Gaffney was so impressed, he called every one of his players into his office and produced contracts for the 1915 season.

By mid-August, the Braves were in fourth place, locked in a tight race that still saw the Giants in the lead. After claiming three straight pennants, the Giants were not about to unravel at the sight of the Braves, but suddenly they could not help but notice the rebuilt team from Boston. Giants manager John McGraw bitterly called them "a band of misfits," further raising the temperature in the summer of '14.

Finally, the two teams had their showdown at the Polo Grounds, and any private doubts the Braves might have had about their ability to play at the Giants' level were erased after they swept New York in three straight games. The key moment in the series came when Tyler beat Mathewson 2-0 in the third game, even after the Giants had loaded the bases in the bottom of the tenth with none out. A

week later, on August 23, the Braves finally caught the Giants in the standings, a last-to-first climb that had taken only five weeks.

The Braves could not maintain that momentum indefinitely; right after sweeping the Giants, they slumped, falling not only into second place, but then third. Boston rebounded around Labor Day, taking a doubleheader from the Cardinals, and brought themselves back into a tie for first place. The Giants headed into Boston for a three-game series, and the Braves and their fans were delirious with the prospect of finally humbling McGraw and his New Yorkers. Even the Braves' cross-town rivals, the Red Sox, were caught up in pennant fever. The Sox's new owner, Joe Lannin, offered the Braves use of the newly-built Fenway Park for the rest of the Braves' home games. Braves owner Gaffney unhesitatingly agreed.

Despite the fact that Germany had just invaded France and the world was on the brink of war, Boston immersed itself in the drama of the Braves-Giants showdown. The first two games were played in a morning-afternoon doubleheader—night baseball was

Game Three of the 1914 World Series at a sold-out Fenway Park. The Boston Red Sox offered the Braves the use of their new stadium (Fenway opened in 1912) to accommodate the large World Series crowds. The Braves accepted the offer and drew nearly 70,000 for the two games played at the Red Sox's new home.

A MIRACLE IN THE MAKING

Braves first baseman Butch Schmidt slides under the tag attempt by Athletics catcher Wally Schang in the first game of the 1914 World Series, which was won by the Braves, 7-1. Schmidt hit .285 with 71 RBIs during the regular season, but defensively he was dreadful. By 1916 he was back in the minor leagues.

still twenty years in the future. In the morning, the Braves drew 36,000 fans to their new home and defeated the Giants, 5-4.

That first game sent a strong message from the Braves: they had handled Mathewson, who even then was regarded as a legend. Some of his achievements still arch an eyebrow: Mathewson's 37 wins in one season is still the National League record, and he once pitched 68 consecutive innings without a walk. He was so revered among the players of

his day, no one dared taunt him from the dugout—and this was in an era when bench-jockeying was an art form.

But the Braves were the exception to every rule, including the hands-off policy on Mathewson. "You think you can stop us, Mathewson? Not a chance," the Braves shouted from the dugout. They went as far as to make fun of Mathewson's knock-knee posture. Mathewson was very good that morning, but not bulletproof, and although the Giants

one game, the Braves told themselves, remembering they had another nine innings in the afternoon and nine more the next day.

Perhaps their adrenaline gave out, because the Giants had no problem against Tyler in a 10-1 victory that afternoon. The hostility between the two teams was undiminished, possibly because the Braves had drawn another 40,000 fans. In New York's four-run sixth inning, Tyler almost beaned center fielder Fred Snodgrass, and the two exchanged words for the rest of the inning. In the next half-inning, Snodgrass was the target of dozens of bottles from irate fans in center field—an attack so vicious that Boston mayor James Curley came onto the field, along with a Boston Police lieutenant, to discuss the situation with home plate umpire Bob Emslie. They asked Emslie to eject Snodgrass, hoping to prevent an all-out riot. Although Emslie rejected the idea, Giants manager McGraw let common sense prevail and soon replaced Snodgrass with Bob Bescher.

The deciding game was played the next afternoon, and the Braves thrived on the energy created by James' spitter. Remember, the wet ball had yet to be outlawed in that era, and it gave the pitchers a tremendous weapon against hitters. The moisture on the ball makes it slippery upon release from the fingertips, causing it to sink or sail at the last second. Although pitchers are at a loss to explain why this happens, they know the spitter is even more greatly feared by hitters than the knuckleball; it is as unpredictable as the knuckler, but is thrown much harder. In those days, most pitchers experimented with it, and some, like Bill James, were able to perfect it.

Seventeen thousand fans were there to see James throw a three-hitter in an 8-3 win over Rube Marquard, as the Braves took over first place from the Giants. By now, the entire country seemed caught up in the small miracle the Braves had pulled off against the mighty Giants. With so much psychic energy directed in the Braves' favor, what chance did the Giants—even with McGraw managing them—really have? New York catcher Chief Meyers said, "We got discouraged because

had a 4-3 lead going into the ninth inning, they were unable to hold it. Johnny Evers hit a sinking line drive to left with runners on second and third, and the Braves were winners.

The city of Boston became an outdoor asylum as nearly all 36,000 fans poured onto the field to congratulate their team. Stallings, in fact, was unable to get into the clubhouse, which was surrounded by thousands of adoring fans. Eventually, Boston police had to escort Stallings off the field. One game, just

A MIRACLE IN THE MAKING

everyone seemed to be pulling for the Braves and rooting against McGraw." Indeed, McGraw did not even leave the dugout in the third game against Boston, managing the team from the sidelines instead of his usual spot in the third-base coaching box.

The Braves smelled a pennant and proceeded to overpower the rest of the National League. From mid-July until the end of the season, Rudolph, James, and Tyler were 49-10. James was practically perfect, 19-1, and Rudolph finished September on a 12-game winning streak. With such strong pitching, the Braves ended up taking the pennant by 10½ games, constituting a 25½-game gain in the second half of the season, during which the Braves were 60-16. And they did it without much offense. The Braves had only one .300 hitter and posted a team average of .251.

So why did the Braves win? Almost unanimously they credited their manager. "Man for man, we weren't a great team," Bill James said. "We were an eighth-place team with George Stallings, and without him, we would have stayed there."

Now Boston faced an even greater foe than the Giants: the powerful Philadelphia A's, who had just won their fourth American League pennant in five years. Under the guidance of the legendary Connie Mack, the A's had won three World Series. Small wonder the A's were considered 2-1 favorites to wipe out the Braves, regardless of how thoroughly they had outplayed the Giants.

Who could blame the oddsmakers? The A's boasted future Hall of Famers Herb Pennock, Eddie Plank, and Chief Bender (a Chippewa Indian) on their pitching staff. Also on the roster was second baseman Eddie Collins and Home Run Baker on third. Stuffy McInnis played first base, where he had not made an error in 163 games.

The Braves' chances slimmed even further when they lost third baseman Red Smith to a broken ankle. Smith, who had come to Boston in mid-season, was hitting .314 and was replaced by the light-hitting Charlie Deal. Incredibly, Stallings never wavered in his belief that he could humble the A's. In

fact, he told the media, "We'll beat them in four straight." Two months earlier, Stallings would have been ridiculed. But this time—after all, Stallings had forecast the Giants' demise—he was taken seriously.

The first time the two teams stepped on the field, the bench-jockeying from the Braves dugout was intense, almost hostile. Mack himself wondered, "What have we done to get the Braves so stirred up?" The Braves were particularly harsh on Philadelphia catcher Wally Schang—who was so unnerved, he allowed Boston to steal nine bases in the course of the Series—and in the very first game, gave the A's a taste of what kind of Series it would be. Mack started Bender, who had posted a 17-3 regular season record, was 6-3 in World Series action, and had never been knocked out of post-season game. Bender was so confident of beating the Braves he did not bother to scout them in the final weeks of the regular season, despite the fact that Mack had dispatched him to New York for precisely that reason. Bender casually told Mack there was no need to make the trip because the Braves were "bush leaguers." Mack was furious, although he gave Bender a chance to redeem himself by starting him in Game One.

Bender pitched reasonably well for five innings, although he was trailing Rudolph 3-1. Boston finally knocked Bender out in the sixth inning, scoring three more runs. After this, Mack decided he had seen enough and walked slowly to the mound to take the ball out of the pitcher's hands. It was the first time Bender had ever failed to finish a World Series game, a humiliation that was compounded when Mack looked into Bender's eyes and said, "Guess they're not so bad for a bunch of bush leaguers, huh?"

If the Braves proved they could out-hit the A's in Game One, they also proved they could out-pitch them in Game Two. James and Eddie Plank engaged in a small classic, with James defeating him 1-0, although it took an acrobatic doubleplay from Maranville in the bottom of the ninth to save Boston.

With the Braves in a two-game lead, the

Braves manager George Stallings graces the cover of the 1914 World Series program.

Rabbit Maranville,
during his second tour of
duty with the Braves
(1929–35).

A MIRACLE IN THE MAKING

The Meanest Man in Boston

How tough was George Stallings? Legend has it that he so intimidated his teams, at least in the minor leagues, that one day he actually bullied a Buffalo pitcher into burning his uniform.

This happened after the pitcher had walked the bases loaded, then walked in two runs. Stallings strode to the mound and loudly commanded, "Go on to the clubhouse and burn your uniform!" The pitcher trudged off the field, and moments later smoke was seen rising from the chimney in the clubhouse. A player on the bench pointed this out to Stallings, who seemed genuinely shocked at the depth of his pitcher's remorse—and gullibility.

"What, is he really burning up his uniform?" Stallings asked in disbelief. "My God, what a bonehead. Somebody go and stop him." The uniform was saved, but the player didn't survive long on Stallings' roster.

Braves manager George Stallings.

entire city was in a frenzy. Nearly three hundred Braves fans had made the journey to Philadelphia for Games One and Two, not a small contingent considering the difficulty and cost of travel in that era. Whatever the Braves' army lacked in numbers, they made up for in arrogance as they marched through the streets of Philly chanting, "Sweep . . . sweep." Stallings fueled the hysteria by telling his equipment manager to ship all the players' road uniforms back to Boston. "We won't be coming back here," the manager brazenly said.

He was right. The Braves took Game Three in Fenway, 5-4 in twelve innings in front of 36,000. Actually, this was the only game of the Series in which the A's led, taking a 4-2 advantage in the top of the tenth. But Braves catcher Hank Gowdy, who had hit a single, double, and triple in Game One, blasted a home run off Joe Bush, a twenty-one-year-old right-hander with a good fastball. Three hits later in the inning, the score was tied again. In the twelfth inning, Gowdy's bat was a blur through the strike zone as he matched another of Bush's pitches. Once again, he beat Bush in this match-up of power, sending a double into the left-field corner. With no one out, Herbie Moran tried to bunt pinch-runner Larry Gilbert over. Bush fielded the bunt in front of the mound and threw the ball at third, but the ball went wildly past it. The Braves had won Game Three. The crowd at Fenway could taste a sweep and so could Stallings, who ordered his traveling secretary to cancel the Braves' Game Five reservations in their Philadelphia hotel. As the manager put it, "If we could win that game, then there's no way we're going to lose Game Four."

Once again, Stallings' vision of the future was prophetic. Rudolph returned after just three days' rest and smothered the A's, 3-1. The winning hit came from Evers, who hit a two-run single in the fifth off pitcher Bob Shawkey. And even though the A's Herb Pennock came back with three shutout innings, the damage was done. Philadelphia could not get close to Rudolph, and the Series was over. It was the first four-game sweep in World Series history.

The hero? Gowdy, without a doubt. He batted .545, including two home runs and a triple. No one wanted the moment to end, as the fans kept the celebration going for hours on end in the city. Even Connie Mack conceded the moment to his National League opponents. "They were a great team, one of the greatest," Mack said. "They had a great spirit and couldn't be broken." So impressed was Mack with Boston's miracle—and so dejected by his A's unraveling—that he immediately traded away the components of his $100,000 infield, and his A's teams spent the next decade losing more games than they won.

In retrospect, Mack overreacted to the loss. There are certain times in history—as the Braves themselves would learn some seventy-seven years later—that a particular season belongs to a particular team, and no power on earth can change that energy. How else to explain the Braves' two-year climb from 1912 to 1914? Or for that matter, the Braves' worst-to-first resurrection in 1991?

The 1914 Braves were remembered for nearly a half-century for their World Series accomplishment. Since 1950, of course, there have been other moments of great theater— Bobby Thomson's 1951 home run against the Dodgers, the 1969 Mets' World Series win over the Orioles, Joe Carter's series-winning homer in 1993. But in 1950, the mid-century mark, the Associated Press' poll of sportswriters asking them for the greatest upset in any sport since 1900 produced a resounding vote: the 1914 Braves, 128 votes to 53 over any other team.

Many years after his Series defeat to Boston, the Athletics' Chief Bender told a reporter, "Spirit is something you can't buy or learn. You don't know where it comes from when you have it, and you don't know where it went when it's gone. The Boston Braves had that kind of spirit in 1914. It wasn't just combativeness—it was confidence and determination. And that's a hard nut to crack."

A MIRACLE IN THE MAKING

the aftermath

4

"A squeeze play? No. Let us score runs in an honorable way."

—Judge Emil Fuchs, Braves owner, briefly serving as manager

There is a perceived affliction in

baseball called The Year After Syndrome. No one really knows its origin, or knows a remedy for it, but the hallmarks are plain enough: win a World Series one year, and the next season, something—or more often, everything—goes wrong. There are a many exceptions, of course, most recently the Toronto Blue Jays in 1992 and 1993, but for some winners, a championship means a poor follow-up season. 🪶 A once-mighty batting order can suddenly look ordinary in front of even mediocre pitching. A pitching staff that dominated the league only a few months before is ruined by injuries, or by curveballs that refuse to obey, or by fastballs that live in the upper regions of the strike zone. It is more than just baseball's law of physics

Bill McKechnie, manager of the Braves, 1930–37.

at work. In 1915, the Braves learned that greatness can come in finite doses.

The Braves failed to defend their title in 1915, finishing seven games behind the Phillies. All the elements that had worked so smoothly in defeating the Giants for the pennant and the A's in the World Series collapsed, utterly and completely. First the pitching went: Bill James, who was 19-1 down the stretch of the 1914 race, became ill early the next spring and spent most of the season at home recuperating. And Dick Rudolph, who delivered that untouchable 12-game winning streak at the 11th hour in 1914, was a 22-game winner in 1915, but he also lost 19. George Tyler showed he was only mortal, as well, posting a 10-9 record.

A good part of the Braves' pitching problem stemmed from the offense—or, rather, lack of. The team batted only .240, the lowest average in the National League that year. Not a single player batted above .300. Not that the Braves' lineup was so overpowering, but then they lost Johnny Evers. On April 18 in a game against Brooklyn, Evers badly sprained his ankle sliding into second base and had to be carried off the field. An accomplished baserunner, Evers had tried to stretch a single into a double, and was unable to negotiate the bag properly upon sliding. He jammed the ankle, and the base, refusing to yield, caused considerable damage to Evers' ligaments. Because he was in so much pain and his ankle healed so slowly, the Braves were without their second baseman until June 29, and by then they were mired in last place. In all, Evers played in only 83 games in 1915, batting just .263. Various ailments kept him to just 24 games in 1917, and he was subsequently released to the Philadelphia Phillies.

Like A's Chief Bender said during the World Series, "Attitude is everything." And without Evers for much of the first half of the season, the Braves lost not only their tough little leader, but their tough attitude as well. However, even with their good luck having dried up on them, the Braves were still able to create some second-half drama. Although

they were dead last as late as July 15, an August performance surge put the Braves in second place by September 24. They had a chance at the Phillies, too, going into a critical five-game series. But Grover Cleveland Alexander, who went 31-10 that season, threw his fourth one-hitter of the season against the Braves on September 28. The next night, the Phillies clinched the pennant, officially putting an end to the Braves' defense of their title.

In retrospect, it was not an entirely wasted season. The Braves still drew a respectable 376,000 fans—a drop of only 6,000 from the miracle comeback in 1914. Financially the franchise was healthy enough for Braves ownership to unveil its new stadium in August of 1915, Braves Field. Owner James Gaffney decided if his Braves could not hit, then no other National League team was going to do much damage in the new park, either. Each team had the authority to configure its stadiums to its choosing, so Gaffney set the foul poles 402 feet away from home plate, and placed the center-field wall in another galaxy, 550 feet away. Gaffney was intrigued by the possibility of hitting a home run without the ball leaving the park, and he went to such an extreme to realize this wish that Ty Cobb remarked, "One thing is sure, no one is ever going to hit one out of here."

Cobb was right for about five seasons, until a much livelier ball was introduced to the sport and Babe Ruth turned Americans into home-run fanatics who had no use for cavernous stadiums like Braves Field. But for those five seasons, Boston liked to think it had the perfect ballpark, and in fact, the Red

Exterior of Braves Field, Boston's new National League home in 1915. The Braves continued to play here until their move to Milwaukee in 1953. Braves Field is still in use as a part of the athletic facilities at Boston University.

Sox accepted the Braves' invitation to play their home games of the 1915 World Series at Braves Field.

The Braves may have been proud of their 1914 World Series win, and their new ballpark in 1915, but the foundation of the franchise was slowly eroding. George Stallings was still the manager, but Evers aged quickly, Hank Gowdy was in the Army, and the injuries to the pitching staff came in bunches. A second-place finish in 1915 was followed by a third-place finish in 1916 and by 1917, nearly all the momentum they had gained from beating the A's in the 1914 Series had been used up. From 1917 to 1932, the Braves finished higher than fifth only once, and in fourteen of those sixteen seasons, fell below .500.

It was only a matter of time before the Braves' collapse would consume Stallings. Without his once-exceptional pitching staff, even the miracle-maker looked vulnerable. By 1918, the Braves had fallen to seventh place. The city belonged almost entirely to the Red Sox, who since 1901 had been competing with the Braves and winning. Even in their new ballpark, the Braves could not hit much, and hence, drew only 162,000 fans in 1920. That meant two out of every three fans the Braves had attracted during the prime years from 1913 to 1917 had turned their backs on the franchise.

Stallings' disaffection with his job was not confined to the Braves' ineptitude. The club had changed ownership in 1918 and was now controlled by a New York group headed by George Washington Grant. What worried Boston's followers were the close ties Grant had with New York Giants manager John McGraw. It was McGraw who convinced Grant to buy the Braves, and once he did, the two teams completed several trades that were so one-sided—in favor of the New Yorkers— that even the Braves players must have wondered about a fix. The most conspicuous swap came in 1919, when the Braves sent right-hander Art Nehf to the Giants in exchange for four players and $40,000. Even on those terms, the Giants came out ahead:

After going 17-8 for the Braves in 1917 and 15-15 in 1918, pitcher Art Nehf was traded to the New York Giants in 1919. It was one of the most lopsided trades in Braves history: Nehf became a full-fledged star with the Giants, while none of the four players he was traded for lasted long with the Braves.

New York won four straight pennants between 1921 and 1924, and during that span, Nehf won 66 games.

At the end of the 1920 season, George Stallings' contract was about to expire, and the new Braves ownership was in no mood to keep him on the payroll. Grant had no real sense of Boston history, no understanding of the magnitude of Stallings' success in 1914. To Grant and his group, Stallings was part of ancient history, and now, in 1920, part of a decaying ball club. Of course, the decline was not Stallings' fault—there was no money for the Braves to buy fresh players, and the baseball they played was awful. On September 17, the St. Louis Cardinals had twelve straight hits against Braves' pitching, and perhaps it was at that point that Stallings agreed his run in Boston was over.

The Braves made Stallings a meager offer for a one-year contract for the 1921 season, knowing he would reject it. On November 6, Stallings resigned, and with the money he had saved and invested over the years, bought the Rochester franchise in the International League. Stallings was replaced as Braves manager by one of his former coaches, Fred Mitchell, who for the preceding four years had coached at Harvard, scouted for the Braves, then managed the Cubs to the World Series in 1918.

Although baseball's reputation was soiled by the 1919 World Series—in which it was later discovered that several members of the Chicago White Sox, including Shoeless Joe Jackson, were paid to lose to the Cincinnati Reds—the game was on the verge of becoming the nation's number-one pastime. Attendance for both leagues had totaled 56 million from 1910 to 1919, a time in which baseball experienced practically no growth. But in the next decade, nearly 93 million would attend baseball games—almost 7,500 a game. The major leagues were helped immeasurably by Babe Ruth's home runs and by the live radio accounts of almost every game, beginning in 1921 when KDKA first broadcast the game, the Pirates against the Phillies.

But while baseball flourished, the Braves struggled. Fred Mitchell actually coaxed a fourth-place finish out of the Braves in 1921, as they edged above .500 with a 79-74 record, but just as Stallings before him, Mitchell was not able to induce much long-term success out of his players. They lost 100 games in each of the next three seasons, prompting yet another sale of the franchise. This time it was Judge Emil Fuchs who bought the team, bringing to Boston the retired legendary right-hander Christy Mathewson to run the day-to-day business.

Mathewson was no stranger to Braves fans, having done so much damage in his years with the New York Giants. In his prime—which was actually most of his career, spanning from 1900 to 1917—Mathewson won 373 games, and four times did better than 30 wins in a season. Mathewson's finest year was 1908, when he was 37-11 with a 1.43 ERA and 11 shutouts. His calling card was the screwball—or fadeaway, as it was known then—and he is generally considered to have

Aerial view of Braves Field where, on May 1, 1920, the Braves and the Brooklyn Robins played more innings in one game (26) than had ever been played—a record that has not been matched since. In one of the most astounding pitching feats in baseball history, Boston's Joe Oeschger and Brooklyn's Leon Cadore each went the distance as the teams played to a 1-1 tie, until home-plate umpire McCormick called the game because of darkness.

THE AFTERMATH

one of the finest of these "scroogies" of the pre-1950 era.

Mathewson was only forty-three when the opportunity came to run the Braves, but he was in poor health. Having served in World War I, Mathewson had been exposed to chemical weapons during combat and suffered from permanent lung damage. Most of his retirement days were spent in Saranac Lake, New York, where he underwent regular medical treatment. Doctors had warned him that a return to baseball would damage his already fragile health. Nevertheless, he could not say no, and went as far as to assure Fuchs that his lungs were improving.

It was no surprise that Judge Fuchs believed him: His gentleness and willingness to see the good side in people was legendary, despite his deep-set eyes and intimidating stare. Fuchs had served as a magistrate in New York City from 1915 to 1918, then in 1922 became an attorney for Ralph Day, the federal prohibition director for the New York district. But Fuchs' real love was baseball, and on February 11, 1923, he bought the Braves from George Washington Grant along with Mathewson and James McDonough. Mathewson was the president while Fuchs, who owned most of the stock, became vice-president. Fuchs and Mathewson wasted little time in making changes. After one year of watching Mitchell manage, they fired him and gave Dave Bancroft the job.

Bancroft was actually a shortstop whom the Braves had acquired from the Giants, a once-outstanding player whose skills were beginning to fade. Included in the package was outfielder Charles (Casey) Stengel, who had just come off a dramatic World Series during which he had beaten the Yankees in two separate games with two home runs, and otherwise batted .417. But the notoriety was fleeting, as the Yankees still won the Series, and when it was over, Stengel was still the aging outfielder who had outlived his usefulness to Giants manager John McGraw.

Judge Emil Fuchs, owner of the Boston Braves from 1923 to 1936. During his tenure, the Braves finished as high as fourth only twice. Fuchs managed the team himself in 1929—that year, the Braves finished last.

Stengel was thirty-three, and in the Giants' opinion, near the end of a career that had begun in 1912 and taken him from Brooklyn to Pittsburgh to Philadelphia and then New York. In fact, even before the Series, he was being referred to as "Ancient Casey." But the Braves needed new blood, even if somewhat old blood, so they gladly accepted Stengel and Bancroft and hoped for the best. Fuchs was so confident of his powerful new arrangement—Mathewson as the brains, and Bancroft as the field general—the owner released a statement to the public that said, "We will be fighting it out with the best of them for the highest honors in baseball." Not surprisingly, Fuchs was silent at the end of the 1924 season, when the Braves finished last with another 100 losses. Stengel hit .280 but impressed no one in the field or at the plate. Clearly, Stengel's reflexes were waning, and he was batting .077 early the following season when Judge Fuchs decided Casey would be better off managing one of the Braves' minor league teams. In May of 1925, Casey Stengel's major league career ended.

Bancroft, however, did considerably better in 1925 as the Braves rose to fifth place. But at the end of the season, just as the World Series between the Pirates and Washington Senators was about to begin, there was bad news from Saranac Lake in New York: Mathewson had died, unable to defeat the infections in his lungs. Since Mathewson had never really been part of the everyday equation in Boston, as his chronic ailments kept in him in the hospital most of the time, during his absences Judge Fuchs had acted as team president. When Mathewson passed away, Fuchs assumed the position in an official capacity.

Jack Slattery began the season as the Braves' manager in 1928, an otherwise forgettable year except for the fact they were graced with Rogers Hornsby's presence. It has been argued that Hornsby was the greatest second baseman baseball has ever known—in any era. His career spanned twenty-two years, starting with the St. Louis Cardinals in 1915 and ending with the St. Louis Browns in 1937, and in between are some of the most impressive statistics the game ever produced. Hornsby hit over .400 three different times, and in each of those seasons hit at least 25 home runs. The year before he came to the Braves, Hornsby hit .361 with 125 RBIs for the Giants. Yet, they traded him to Boston for Shanty Hogan and Jimmy Welsh, and baseball's most oft-asked question in the 1927 off-season was: Why?

Rumor had it that Hornsby was engaged in a power struggle with manager John McGraw for control of the Giants. Or that Hornsby's explosive temper had gotten the best of him after a one-run loss, and he had literally thrown owner Horace Stoneham out of the clubhouse. Other rumors had it that Hornsby had had a fistfight with the team's traveling secretary, Jim Tierney.

Hornsby was no different with the Braves—as fiercely independent as any modern-day ballplayer. In fact, Hornsby might have been more difficult to manage than any player of his era—at least to a lightweight like Slattery, who was used to dealing with the proper etiquette of college players. Suddenly, he was facing the fury, not to mention the egocentrism, of the game's greatest hitter, who was not interested in being polite. It did not take Hornsby long to target Slattery as his enemy, and within weeks of the 1928 season he was telling anyone and everyone that Slattery did not have the baseball

IQ, or the emotional strength, to run a major league team.

Fuchs had some loyalty to Slattery, but not enough to withstand Hornsby's heat. Although the Judge summoned Slattery to his offices for a series of "meetings," ostensibly to work things out, by early June, when the Braves were slipping away fast, Hornsby let loose his final bombshell.

Hornsby said he would rather be traded than play for Slattery. Well, as no doubt Hornsby knew, the last item on Fuchs' agenda was trading the game's greatest second baseman. So Slattery was history, after guiding the Braves to a .355 winning percentage. Not that the Braves were any more successful under Hornsby. Their new manager inspired them to a 39-83 record, a mere .320 winning percentage, and Boston finished the season with 103 losses. Only two other Braves team have exceeded that number (the 1935 team lost 115 games, and the 1988 Braves lost 106).

Immediately upon assuming the reins as manager, Hornsby made this self-serving speech to the Braves: "I don't smoke, drink, or chew. I can hit to left, center, and right. They call me a great player. If you do like I do, you can be a great player, too."

Hornsby might have fallen short in inspirational talks, but he certainly flourished as a hitter, thanks in part to Braves Field's new dimensions. During the previous off-season, Fuchs installed an extra stand of bleachers in left and left-center fields, cutting the left-field foul line from 402 feet to 353 feet. Fuchs also made a home run to center field more reality than a fantasy, slicing it from 550 feet to 387 feet.

Hornsby prospered, but even though he won the 1928 National League batting title with a .387 average, the rap was that as the Braves slid towards 100 losses, Hornsby was more concerned with his bat than the Braves' day-to-day fortunes. On top of that, the smaller Braves park made the opposing hitters even more dangerous to Braves' pitching. It was not all that surprising that Boston lost five straight doubleheaders

Judge Emil Fuchs (right) alongside baseball's first commissioner, Judge Kenesaw Mountain Landis (left), and Christy Mathewson (center). Mathewson, one of the game's all-time pitching greats, served as Braves general manager from 1923 until his untimely death in 1925.

THE AFTERMATH

Two of baseball's legendary hitters: Lou Gehrig (left) and Rogers Hornsby (right). Hornsby's one season with the Braves (1928) was filled with confrontation, first with manager Jack Slattery and then with Judge Fuchs, who bowed to Hornsby's demand to be traded.

between September 4–9, and that the Cardinals beat the always-compliant Braves on September 16 to clinch the pennant.

After the season, Hornsby is said to have walked into Fuchs' office and asked for liberation from the Braves. Who could blame him, playing for a last-place team that wasn't even supported by its hometown fans? While the Yankees were regularly drawing over one million fans a year in the Bronx, the Braves drew only 227,000, and had long since been eclipsed by the Red Sox.

Face to face with Fuchs, Hornsby appealed to the owner's baseball common sense: "Judge, you need a young club, and I have about one year left in me. Why don't you let me make a deal for myself with Chicago. It would help everybody involved." Hornsby was stretching the truth some. He was far from losing his hand-to-eye coordination, and his bat would continue to terrorize National League pitching for many more years. In fact, after he successfully abandoned

the Braves, Hornsby hit .380 for the Cubs in 1929, leading the league with a .679 slugging percentage and 156 runs scored. No doubt, the Braves would have loved to have that offense on their side, but Fuchs allowed himself to be swindled out of the National League batting champion without getting a respectable player in return.

Instead, the Braves got Freddie Maguire, who played second base for them through the 1931 season, and Socks Seibold, a right-hander who posted losing records in each of the five years he played in Boston. Actually, the greatest benefit gleaned from the Hornsby deal was the cash—$100,000—that was used to purchase Wally Berger from the Cubs' farm team in Los Angeles. Berger went on to become a five-time All-Star.

By 1929, the Braves' universe had unraveled so much that Fuchs decided he had better manage the team himself. He actually told reporters during a press conference, "The time has gone when a manager has to chew tobacco and talk from the side of his mouth. I don't think our club can do any worse with me as manager than it has done in the last few years." Wrong, wrong, wrong. With the former magistrate running the team from the dugout, the Braves finished last for the first time since 1924, losing 98 games. But at least there was Sunday baseball for the first time in Braves history, and they were able to draw a barely respectable 372,000 fans. In 1930, Judge Fuchs wisely decided to resign his position and appointed a professional baseball man, Bill McKechnie, to take over. McKechnie had played briefly for the Braves in 1913, and although there wasn't much life in his bat, he nevertheless had played a great second base for the New York Americans. The reason for that, according to manager Frank Chance, was, "McKechnie knew more about baseball than the rest of my team put together."

McKechnie had managed the Pirates from 1922 to 1926, winning the pennant in his next-to-last season, and even beating the Senators in a seven-game World Series. He had then moved on to manage the St. Louis Cardinals, winning the pennant in 1928—but losing the Series four straight to the Yankees. That was hardly an indictment of the Cardinals or McKechnie, since Babe Ruth and Lou Gehrig were in their prime, and Ruth, in fact, had hit three home runs in Game Four to finish demolishing St. Louis.

So by 1929, McKechnie's reputation was such that Fuchs offered him a practically unheard-of three-year deal. Although the Braves never finished higher than fourth under McKechnie, he remained a fixture in Boston for eight years, and was replaced in 1937 by Casey Stengel.

If any one player distinguished himself in the McKechnie era, it was Wally Berger. In his rookie year in 1930, Berger hit .310, but more importantly, he crushed 38 home runs, more than anyone in the Braves' history. He also set a National League record for a rookie, and set new marks for a first-year player with 119 RBIs. A right-handed hitter, Berger made no pretense of his love of home runs.

Every at-bat was a potential muscle-flexing exhibition, although he struck out only 69 times in 555 at-bats.

Berger was the most impressive rookie the Braves had acquired since Rabbit Maranville and Hank Gowdy joined the team in 1912. And he was quick to make an impression on the win-starved fans: on Memorial Day, 1930, the lanky outfielder smoked a home run over the fence in left-center, a blast that carried the ball close to 500 feet.

But Berger's finest moment in those dark years probably came in the 1933 season, when McKechnie's Braves pulled themselves into the first division for the first time since 1921. Remember, these were the days of eight-team leagues—and no divisions, no playoffs. So to finish fourth meant something: the first division. Never mind that Boston was still nine games out of first place at season's end. An 83-71 record was a moral victory, a small miracle, and Bostonians actually took the Braves seriously for most of the summer. They drew more than 500,000 fans, the third straight season in which a McKechnie-led team topped the half-million mark. And Berger was a large part of that mini-resurrection.

As late as August 31, the Braves were only

Boston National League Official Score Card, 1929.

Wally Berger set a rookie record for home runs in a season, with 38 in 1930. The record stood until 1987, when Oakland's Mark McGwire hit 49 in his debut season. Berger finished his career with 242 home runs.

THE AFTERMATH

What's In a Name?

I t might require a scorecard just to keep track of the different nicknames the Braves have used over the years. They were first introduced to baseball as the Red Stockings—or the Reds—in 1876, and kept that moniker for six years. In 1882, as the popularity of the Cincinnati Reds grew, Boston sportswriters sought a separate identity for their team and soon renamed the team the Beaneaters. They remained the Beaneaters until 1906, when the team was purchased by two brothers, George and John Dovey, who gave the team their own name. The Boston Doves lasted until 1910, at which time the team was sold to a business syndicate headed by William Hepburn Russell—and was renamed the Rustlers. Russell died of heart failure in November of 1911, after his team lost 107 of 151 games. The team was subsequently purchased by James Gaffney, a New York political contractor with strong connections to Tammany Hall. Tammany—a political society dating back to the American Revolution—had taken the name of a Delaware Indian chief, Tamanend, and through history, Tammany elders had been known as chiefs. Gaffney's players became his Braves.

The Braves kept their white uniforms and red stockings, but now wore an old-English "B" on their jerseys as well as the profile of an Indian. They remained the Braves until 1936, when the franchise, nearly bankrupt after the Depression and a string of losing seasons, sought a new public image. General manager John Quinn conducted a fan poll in search of a nickname, and the winner was "Bees." Six years later, a new group of owners headed by Louis Perini heartened fans by restoring the old Braves nickname, which has followed them from Boston to Milwaukee and on to Atlanta.

Sherry Magee of the 1915 Boston Braves.

six games behind the first-place Giants when they hosted the New Yorkers for a six-game series. Dreams of the impossible flashed through everyone's mind that week: beating the powerful Giants six straight times, claiming first place, a wonderful déjà vu of the 1914 comeback that had left manager John McGraw so devastated.

In the first game of the series, Berger hit his 25th home run of the season, and the Braves were 7-3 winners. The next day, more than 50,000 fans showed up for a doubleheader that was the start of the Braves' fast and final decline in 1933. Carl Hubbell won the first game, and the Giants won the nightcap, too, as New York reliever Dolph Luque got the decision by lacing the game-winning double to left in the ninth inning.

The Giants won the fourth game of the series. They won the fifth game. And they probably would have won the sixth game had it not been stopped because of darkness with the score tied, 4-4. Judge Fuchs praised his Braves, and all that was left for the team was the honor of finishing in the first division.

They went on a 23-game road trip after the massacre by the Giants, going 12-11 but losing ground to the Cardinals.

Wally Berger was not even supposed to play in the finale of 1933, having caught a severe cold during an earlier road trip to Pittsburgh. Advised by doctors to remain in Pittsburgh for at least two to three weeks, Berger did manage to stroll over to Forbes Field while the Phillies were in town. There he scouted a rookie pitcher, Reginald Grabowski, who threw a tight little curveball which today would be known as a slider.

Berger returned to Boston just as the Braves—who were in fifth place, one game out of fourth place and the first division— were finishing the season against the Phillies. In the seventh inning, with the Phillies leading, 1-0, the still-weakened Berger stuck his head out of the clubhouse to see who was smothering the Braves' offense. There, before Berger's eyes, was Grabowski, throwing his miniature curveball.

Berger returned to the clubhouse and threw his uniform on. The bases were loaded, and he told McKechnie he wanted one at-bat against Grabowski, just one. "If he throws that curveball over the plate, I'll hit it out of the park," he announced to the dugout. That was Berger's receipt for the prediction, making it public.

Grabowski had no idea that he had been so thoroughly scouted by Berger. He threw that curveball once, and Berger took it for a strike. Innocently, Grabowski tried it again, and this time Berger hit the ball on a line over the left-field fence. It was a grand slam, giving the Braves a 4-1 lead that meant everything to them.

Not only did Boston win the final game of the season, but thanks to Berger's 27th home run of the season, the Braves climbed into fourth place. By finishing in the first division, every player earned an additional $242. That was a handsome bonus in 1933—so pleasing to the Braves that Rabbit Maranville planted a kiss on both of Berger's cheeks at home plate.

Maranville would soon find out how mean-spirited the fates could be, though. In the following spring training, he broke an ankle in an exhibition game against the Yankees. Rabbit was already thirty-nine, naturally losing the war with time, and the injury cost him the entire 1934 season, and, effectively, his career.

Maranville spoke valiantly of returning to the Braves, and whenever someone asked how he was healing, he would weave a little fiction and say he was doing fine. The bones in Rabbit's ankle never properly fused, however, and all that was left for the tough little infielder in 1935 was to be Babe Ruth's partner in decline.

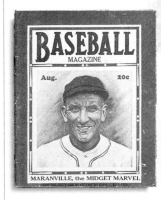

Rabbit Maranville, shown here near the end of his twenty-three-year major league career, was still a cover boy. For fifteen of those twenty-three seasons, Maranville wore a Braves uniform.

welcome to an old and tired legend

5

"You have been a great asset to baseball . . . your greatest value to a ball club would be your personal appearance on the ball field."

—Judge Emil Fuchs, in a letter welcoming Babe Ruth to the Braves, February 23, 1935

In 1935, in the midst of the Great

Depression, Bostonians had fewer recreational dollars than ever, and even an afternoon at the ballpark was a costly expense. Judge Fuchs was not immune to the nation's economic catastrophe, either. Like so many monied Americans whose wealth rested in the stock market, Fuchs was practically broke by 1935, and his franchise close to bankruptcy. The Braves' financial situation had grown so serious that Fuchs made public a plan to install a dog-racing track in the outfield and run races there when the Braves were on the road. The National League, rightfully horrified by Fuchs' desperation, ruled against the idea. In fact, there was an internal power struggle, led by the governor of Massachusetts, to take over control of the Braves.

The Braves' acquisition of Babe Ruth in 1935 was publicity driven.

Boston Braves pennant.

It took enormous financial maneuvering, but Fuchs eventually satisfied the league elders that he could sustain the Braves for at least one more year. Yet, Fuchs needed money. He needed fans. He needed—a savior. He turned his attention toward New York, where the game's greatest player was ready for retirement.

Or was he? Babe Ruth had announced at the end of the 1934 season, not long after slugging his 700th home run, that he was through as an everyday player. Although the forty-one-year-old Babe still had not lost the grace of his long, powerful swing, that was the only weapon nature had not stolen. Ruth had gained a tremendous amount of weight, and atop his spindly legs, he was practically useless in the outfield. Running was a personal torture for Babe, and the little nagging injuries seemed to pile up, one after another, taking forever to heal. Yet Ruth could not let go of the game. He had asked over and over if there would be an opportunity to manage the Yankees, who had become so fearsome to opposing pitchers they were now known as the Bronx Bombers. Ruth was pitiful in his stubbornness, unable—or at least unwilling—to see that owner Jacob Ruppert had no intention of giving Ruth the reins to his Yankee team.

Ruth finished the 1934 season quietly, batting a weak .288 with only 22 home runs. Everyone assumed he was making his farewell tour of the American League, and it was in Boston that Ruth received the fondest send-off. There was strong sentiment that the Babe should finish his career where he started it in 1914, with the Red Sox, and owner Tom Yawkey was leaning toward making the Babe his manager. Yet Red Sox general manager Eddie Collins opposed the move and succeeded in hiring Joe Cronin from the Washington Senators.

None of these machinations were lost on Fuchs, who asked Ruppert and Barrow if a deal could be arranged to sell the great Babe Ruth to the Braves. The Yankee principals were more than ready to get rid of Ruth, who had become a nuisance in his pursuit of manager Joe McCarthy's job. Ruppert had once said he would never let the Babe play for another club, but he had long since changed his mind. When Fuchs called, all that remained in this drama was to arrange the money. Fuchs knew exactly what to say: he would pay Ruth $25,000, make him an assistant manager to Bill McKechnie, and offer him a limited partnership in the franchise. That meant Ruth would share in the club's profits. And of course, the game's most prodigious home-run hitter could play as often as he wanted, depending on how his body felt.

Ruth could not resist Fuchs' proposal, especially the strong hints about taking McKechnie's job in a year or so. Nevertheless, Ruth made one last inquiry to the Yankees, asking how long they were committed to McCarthy as manager. Barrow told Ruth that McCarthy was staying, and that if he were smart, he would take the Braves up on their offer. So Ruth accepted, and on February 24, 1935, his fifteen-year association with the Yankees was over. He traveled to Boston for the formal signing, the requisite press conferences, and to try on the Braves uniform, which everyone agreed looked clownish on the Babe after so many seasons in the classic Yankee pinstripes.

Of course, Ruth had been a home-run factory during his career as a Yankee. But in a Braves uniform he looked more mortal than ever, some days even feeble. He showed up in spring training so fat he was practically immobile in the outfield, and although he played a little first base in Florida, even there he looked unsure. Yet there was no turning back on this plan, not when Fuchs had generated so much publicity.

More than 25,000 fans showed up on Opening Day to see Ruth, some of them too young to remember his first tenure in Boston. Back in 1914, Ruth had been a lean left-hander with an angry fastball. He did not hit many home runs in those days, mostly because the ball had not been juiced yet, but even as a twenty-year-old, Ruth had a special on-field charisma. Perhaps the Babe's greatest gift was his ability to make people notice him.

He knew what was expected of him the minute he stepped into the batter's box in 1935, and even though Ruth was unable to deliver as he aged, there were still moments when he could defeat time.

Opening Day was one of those instances. The Braves were facing Carl Hubbell and the Giants, perhaps the best pitcher and the best team of the mid-'30s. Ruth made the day his, slamming an RBI single in the first inning, and later crashing a two-run homer in the fifth, giving Boston the room it needed for a 4-2 win over the mighty Hubbell. Of course the city was delirious with nostalgia, thankful to be able to travel in this time tunnel with Ruth, and wondering how long the journey would last.

The mirage could only last so long. Even Ruth admitted his Day One theatrics were, "just a flash." A month earlier, during the exhibition season, Ruth observed, "Kids were striking me out or getting me to pop up on pitches I would have hit out of the park a few

years earlier. And it was more and more of an effort to move at first base or run the bases. It was just torture."

In the next month, Ruth proved just how on-target he was in his self-assessment. He had only two hits the rest of April with one RBI and just one more home run. Besides missing a dozen games with a bad cold, not once did he play an entire game. Clearly Ruth would not—or in reality, could not—last the season. The only question was how he could leave the game with grace. Ruth's relationship with Braves management soured quickly, once he realized Bill McKechnie was not about to retire or be promoted to general manager. And Fuchs was proving to be no more than an opportunist, trying desperately to cash in on Ruth's dwindling on-field presence. On May 12, Ruth told McKechnie and Fuchs he was finished. No more baseball, no more autograph sessions, no more hope of someday managing. The Babe had finally accepted the

Boston Braves
program, 1935.

By the time Babe Ruth joined the Braves, fans saw only a semblance of the player he had once been. There were a few heroic moments left, but by June of 1935, the Babe had had enough and retired.

fact that it was time to begin another life, a new life, away from baseball. But Fuchs was not about to let go of his prize possession easily.

More than anything else, Fuchs had wanted Ruth to attend promotional events in Boston, where he had been promised around town to sign autographs at local stores. In return for his presence, merchants were required to purchase Braves tickets in bulk—not a bad idea on Fuchs' part, except that he had counted on Ruth's cooperation.

It might have been different if Ruth were hitting a little, or if Ruth did not feel like he had been duped into thinking he could make a profit on the Braves' profit. True, he was given franchise stock as part of signing bonus, only to discover it was an empty currency. The Braves were broke, and their stock was barely worth the paper it was printed on. So when Ruth said he was finished, he meant it.

Undeterred, Fuchs begged Ruth to stay with the Braves as an active player, at least until the conclusion of the team's trip through the western half of the league. As the Judge put it, "Those cities are all waiting to see you. They've had big ticket sales for our games. They've got Babe Ruth Days planned. You can't quit now."

Ruth relented, but still told the local papers he planned to quit after the road trip. Publicly embarrassed, Fuchs was forced to admit if Ruth's performance didn't improve, then he would retire to pinch-hitting and coaching. To no one's real surprise, Ruth's average fell to .155, and the end loomed. Incredibly, though, there were still a few flashes of greatness in the man's bat.

In Pittsburgh, Ruth hit three home runs in one game. In the first inning, he beat Red Lucas deep to right-center. In the third, Ruth faced the Cubs' Guy Bush. It was a slow, decrepit Ruth that Bush was facing, but on this day, a dangerous one as well. Ruth homered against Bush in the third inning, hit an RBI single in the fifth, and in the seventh homered again, his third home run of the day.

Years later, Bush told reporters, "I never saw a ball hit so hard, before or since. Ruth was old and fat, but he still had that great swing. Even when he missed, you could hear the bat go swish. I can't remember anything about the first home run he hit off me that day. I guess it was just another homer. But I can't forget that last one. It's probably still going."

Bush was right: Ruth had hit the ball completely out of Forbes Field. No one had ever put on such a display of power—an estimated 600 feet. This, from a forty-one-year-old man who was admittedly washed-up. That was Ruth's 714th home run, and in a perfect world, it would have been a perfect setting for retirement. The great Babe was 4-for-4 with three home runs and six RBIs.

But Ruth was a man of his word, and he had already promised Fuchs he would remain on the active roster while the Braves finished the road trip in Philadelphia and Cincinnati. By the time he stepped to the plate at Crosley Field, the energy had vanished from his bat. In front of another huge crowd, he was 0-for-3, striking out all three times.

The next day against the Reds, Ruth was 0-for-2, and he ended the series by leaving in the fifth inning with a bad knee. In Philadelphia, where he was presented with an impressive floral bouquet, he struck out twice. The next day he struck out in the first inning, and hurt his knee in the bottom half going after a fly ball. He took himself out of the game, and that was Babe Ruth's final game appearance.

Even then, it did not end that smoothly. Fuchs still wanted Ruth on the active roster, even though the Babe was asking repeatedly to be placed on the voluntary retired list. The idea was to squeeze an extra week out of Ruth, with the Giants and Dodgers both coming to town. The opportunity to see Ruth on the same field against his former New York rivals was one Fuchs did not think Bostonians would pass up.

But Ruth had other ideas. As part of America's celebrity society, he had been invited to the reception for the ocean liner *Normandie*, which was due to arrive in New York that week. In 1935, an ocean liner's docking was a chance for the social heavyweights to be seen and mingle, and this was where Ruth's heart was—at least after struggling as he had with the Braves. The two egos were on a collision course. When Ruth told Fuchs he was leaving for New York, since his knee was too stiff to play, the now-furious Judge demanded he stay. Ruth then took the dispute public, telling reporters in the Braves

clubhouse that he had quit and calling Fuchs "a dirty double-crosser."

Fuchs responded by releasing Ruth on the spot and calling him "a poor sport." The Judge told reporters, "He says I double-crossed him. I wrote him a letter saying I had lost a large sum of money on the Braves, which is true. Ruth would have been the manager some day if he had been a good soldier, and hadn't asked for extra privileges."

To this, Ruth shook his head and said, "I don't think it's fair that after twenty-one years in baseball and after what I have given to the game for Judge Fuchs to question my sportsmanship. I'll match my record in baseball against his any day." Fuchs made sure the relationship could never be repaired, issuing one final statement blaming Ruth for the Braves' sorry 10-27 record, including the ongoing slump that saw Boston lose 12-of-13.

Fuchs, of course, was looking for any scapegoat he could find, and an aging, recalcitrant Ruth was as a good target. But there was no masking the Braves' ineptitude. After Ruth left—beginning a retirement that was filled mostly with golf and bowling—the Braves finished a staggering season in which they lost 115 games. They were the worst National League team of the century, winning fewer games than even Casey Stengel's 1962 Mets.

It was only a matter of time before Judge Emil Fuchs finally ran out of money. Unable to meet the obligations on his numerous outstanding loans, Fuchs stepped down as president of the Braves after ten years of running the day-to-day operations following Christy Mathewson's death. By then, the Braves had endured a public humiliation—a 15-game losing streak in July, and dropping 28 of 30 games between August 18 and September 14.

The remaining partners of the franchise reorganized and named Bob Quinn, formerly the business manager of the Brooklyn Dodgers, as the new president. Quinn's first order of business was to change the Braves' name to the Bees in response to a fans' poll. After the 1937 season, another dreary summer under Bill McKechnie, Quinn decided the

In Casey Stengel's six years as Boston manager, the team never finished higher than fifth place. But while with Boston, the engaging personality that was to lead the Yankees' dynasty of the '50s was emerging.

team needed a new manager, too. Actually, McKechnie wasn't bad at his job—his 1936 Braves won 71 games, a 32½-game improvement over the previous years, which still ranks as tied for the third-best won-lost turnaround in major league history. But time is always a manager's worst enemy. Sooner or later, the years consume them all. After '37, it was McKechnie's turn to leave, and he was replaced by Casey Stengel.

The Old Professor, as he was to be known later in his baseball life, was living in Texas, working the oil business, when Quinn called. He had been released from managing the Dodgers at the end of a three-year contract. Under Stengel, Brooklyn finished sixth in 1934, fifth in 1935, and seventh in 1936. When Bob Quinn left for Boston, Stengel became a casualty of the franchise's in-fighting.

Casey had made a great deal of money in Texas oil in 1937—his initial $10,000 investment paid off handsomely, making him financially secure for the rest of his life—yet he missed the Dodgers, he missed baseball. "If the game is your work, and you ain't doing it," he said, "you miss it, right?"

Quinn wanted Stengel to manage, and he wanted some of Casey's newfound money, too. He offered Stengel a chance to invest in the newly named Bees, which Casey agreed to. Thus, twelve years after he ended his major league career in Boston, Casey was back in Beantown. Those with good memories remembered Stengel as a showman in the mid-1920s, when he was the Braves' center fielder. One time, during the national anthem, Stengel took off his cap, letting a sparrow fly out. And during an exhibition game, Stengel disappeared down a manhole in the outfield while chasing a fly ball.

Unfortunately, there was not much magic Stengel could work for the Bees as their manager. After a fifth-place finish in his first year, Boston finished seventh in four straight seasons. And as colorful as Stengel was with the fans, not to mention the press, the gate count dropped below 300,000 in his second year and never rose above that in his remaining years in Boston.

The bigger problem, of course, was World War II, and the talent drought it created in baseball. Both leagues were enduring a shortage of athletes, as many established players were being drafted, and the rookies of the future were being taken into military service before they even reached the big leagues. Casey did have an outstanding player in Ernie Lombardi, though, and he held a special affection for him. The heavy-legged catcher, who played only one year in Boston, was a fine hitter, but one of the slowest men in baseball history. Stengel made it a personal project to get Lombardi a stolen base.

One afternoon against the Giants, Lombardi was on first base, utterly ignored by the defense. No one was holding him on, and the pitcher was working from a full windup. For any other player, that would have been an open invitation to take second base. But not Lombardi, who was too embarrassed by his lack of speed to dare try it. Or was he? From the dugout, Stengel yelled, "Steal it, Lom!" and that was all he had to hear. Lombardi lumbered to second, a millisecond ahead of the throw and tag, and he looked into the dugout, right at Stengel, beaming.

Stengel also had great respect for Paul

Waner, who had been a legendary outfielder with the Pirates for fifteen years, but was close to retiring by the time he landed in Boston. Casey had the honor of managing Waner in 1942 when he got his three-thousandth career hit, and the idea was to let the thirty-nine-year-old Waner leave the game gracefully, mostly as a pinch-hitter. But Casey was desperate for talent in 1943, and age did not matter. So he used Waner day in and day out, literally running him into the ground.

The Bees were in the middle of a stretch of doubleheaders in August, and Stengel, short of outfielders, played Waner in all of them. Inning after inning, the Bees were pounded, and the line drives were like blurs into the gaps. Waner got so tired chasing down the doubles and triples that he finally surrendered. A base hit rolled past him, and Waner's legs gave out. He fell down and stayed there. Even though the ball stopped rolling only a few feet away, Waner was too exhausted to get up.

There were two schools of thought about Stengel's managerial career in Boston. Those who admired his success with the Yankees say Casey left the Bees too soon, that sooner or later, an influx of talent would have arrived and then he could have revealed his true baseball genius. Others disagreed, almost vehemently, insisting Stengel was a comedian, reliant on gimmicks, and that without on-field talent, he was no more than an ordinary manager, if that.

Either way, Stengel's days in Boston were numbered after spring training. That's when Lou Perini, one of the team's new investors, attended an exhibition game and asked Casey afterward what had happened when the Bees bunted into a doubleplay. Even though Perini's curiosity was sincere, not malicious, Stengel was offended by the question, and he gave Perini a long-winded, convoluted answer, purposely designed to confuse the baseball outsider. Perini, confused by Stengel's reply, bluntly asked that he explain himself again. One more time, Stengel took Perini through an oratorical maze, the kind that usually left most Casey observers laughing. But Perini was not amused. As he later said, "This man can't really know much about baseball if he isn't able to explain a simple play."

Just before the start of the 1943 season, Stengel was hit by a car, suffering a badly broken leg. He was in the hospital for several weeks and in physical therapy for many weeks beyond that. Frankie Frisch, then Pittsburgh's manager, had always kidded Stengel about his awful teams. So Frisch sent Stengel a note in the hospital that said, "Your attempt at suicide fully understood. Deepest sympathy you didn't succeed."

Stengel got a laugh out of that, but that was about the only reason to smile that summer. The Bees improved only slightly, finishing sixth. Soon after, Perini, along with Guido Rugo and Joseph Maney—all heavyweights in the Boston construction industry—bought out the remaining partners in the Bees franchise. And with the coup came the inevitable facelift. Perini wanted Stengel out, firing him as manager and buying out his percentage of the stock. Stengel knew he had had his run in Boston, and accepted the release gracefully.

In a formal letter, Casey said, "Whenever a new group purchases control of a corporation, they have the right to dictate policy. And in order that there be no embarrassment on the part of this group, I hereby tender my resignation." Casey went home to Glendale, California, to take care of his leg—and his ego. He had failed to finish in the first division even once while in Boston. He was

Paul Waner was known as "Big Poison" during his twenty-year major league career. But like Babe Ruth, by the time Waner joined Boston, his best years were behind him.

WELCOME TO AN OLD AND TIRED LEGEND

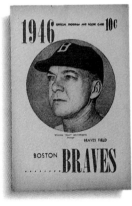

1946 Braves program.

fifty-three. He was tired. And Boston was tired of him. The parting shot from Beantown was a bitter one. Dave Egan of the *Boston Record* wrote, "The man who did the most for Boston in 1943 was the motorist who ran Stengel down two days before the opening game and kept him away from the Braves for two months."

Perini chose Bob Coleman, who had been one of Casey's coaches, as the replacement for Stengel. Coleman was a good-natured man— not clownish like his predecessor, and not given to some of Casey's darker moods, either. But like Stengel, Coleman's roster was stripped clean of talent. The war had taken most of the major league's best players, and the ones that remained—older and out-of-shape athletes—knew there was no one to take their place. So they had attitudes, too.

In fact, the only memorable moments in 1944 were the physicals administered by the U.S. Army and the inevitable sense that no matter how well a young Brave was doing on the field, sooner or later he would have a gun in his hand and a helmet on his head.

Connie Ryan was a prime example, a sec-

ond baseman who in only his second full year was named to the National League All-Star team. But at twenty-four he was ripe for the armed forces, and soon after the National League's 7-1 win over the American League, Ryan was a GI. The shuttle to the induction office was so busy, the Braves tried ten different men at third base during the summer of '44; in all, the team saw twenty-seven men go off to war.

And as usual, the Braves had trouble attracting fans. They drew only 208,691 that summer, the lowest attendance figure in either league. Nevertheless, throughout the worst of the summers in '44 and '45, Perini predicted the Braves were about to resurrect.

As the war ended, changes were coming to Boston. Soon there would be night baseball. And a tough right-hander named Johnny Sain would be getting out of the Navy Air Corps. Along with him was Warren Spahn, a left-hander who decided not to grow old, and whose body—and arm—somehow listened.

By 1948, Perini's words became prophecy.

From the Playing Field to the Battlefield

Major league baseball played on during WWII, but the talented pool of players was drained. Nearly five hundred players were called to military duty from 1942 to 1945, leaving major league rosters with mostly average, underage, or draft-ineligible players. Many of those who were called were assigned to touring All-Star teams, which helped boost morale among American soldiers. Among those on this 1942 All-Star team: Cleveland Indians pitching great Bob Feller (middle row, fifth from left), Hall of Fame catcher Mickey Cochrane (middle row, sixth from left), and future Braves coach Ken Silvestri (top row, far left). In all, thirty-one Braves players were called to duty, including such future stars as Warren Spahn and Johnny Sain.

1942 Service All-Stars.

1942 SERVICE ALL-STARS *in Service Uniforms*

© 1942 - THE SPORTING NEWS PUB. CO.

a return to october

6

"Miracle Manager my eye.
[Billy Southworth] gets the credit we deserve."
—Owner Lou Perini, after the 1948 World Series

The creation of the 1948 Braves did

not happen overnight. In fact, it took careful planning and some smart trades over a two-year period before the team was ready to compete for the National League pennant. One of the most important components was the new manager, Billy Southworth, who was hired away from the St. Louis Cardinals in 1946 after winning three pennants in six years. Lou Perini was so impressed with Southworth's work in St. Louis, he offered him $35,000 as a base salary with $5,000 for finishing fourth, $10,000 for finishing third, $15,000 for finishing second, and $20,000 for winning the pennant. The Cardinals could not match that money, and so Southworth became Boston's property, bringing with him a new philosophy for the near-dead

The 1948 National League champions hoist Billy Southworth high.

Pitcher Bill Voiselle (13-13, 3.63 in 1948) wore his uniform number as a tribute to his hometown, Ninety-Six, South Carolina.

Braves: real rules, real penalties, real fines. Southworth also established a midnight curfew and prohibited second-guessing in the clubhouse. Few modern-day managers would dare be so rigid—curfews are practically unheard today—but Southworth's credo worked for his team. The Braves won 81 games in 1946, and although they finished fourth, it was their best performance in twelve years. The following year they were led by Bob Elliott, who had been acquired in a trade from the Pirates and had promptly won the National League's Most Valuable Player Award. He hit .317 with 22 home runs and 113 RBIs, and moved then-Cardinals manager Eddie Dyer to say the deal for Elliott was "the greatest trade of all time."

Johnny Sain and Warren Spahn each won 21 games in 1947, and the duo became so dominant that by 1948, the Braves' motto "Spahn and Sain, then pray for rain" was born. The team pitched in a four-man rotation. The Braves' best hope for success rested with Spahn pitching the first day, Sain the second. If it rained the next two game days, the rotation would start over again with Spahn, who would have had three days of rest, and the third and fourth pitchers would not have to be used. The question was: Who was No. 1 on the Braves' pitching staff? Spahn was about to embark on an incredible streak of 20-win seasons, winning 20 or more 13 times from 1947 to 1963. But in 1948, he was merely 15-12 with a 3.71 ERA. Sain, by contrast, was already at his peak, having won 20 games in 1946, 21 in 1947, and posting his finest numbers in the 1948 championship season: 24-15 with a 2.60 ERA, leading the National League in wins, 28 complete games, and 315 innings. And above all, he was unflawed under pressure. In a 19-day period from September 3–19, when the pennant was being decided, Sain won 6 games, allowing only 10 runs. And as a tuneup for the World Series, a day before the season ended Sain threw five shutout innings against the Giants and was the winner in a 2-1 decision.

Of course there was more to the Braves' pitching staff in 1948 than just Sain and Spahn. On the days they weren't on the hill, manager Southworth used Bob Voiselle and Vern Bickford, and the two combined to win 24 games. In fact, the Braves looked complete enough to actually take the Series, and all Southworth had to do at times was close his eyes and imagine the magical season coming to a stunning conclusion.

The Braves even had the chance to watch their cross-town enemies, the Red Sox, lose to the Indians in a one-game playoff at Fenway Park. Most of the Braves were in attendance that day, and while a Braves-Red Sox World Series would have made for an intense week of baseball, most of the Braves were glad to see the Sox's hearts broken. That's how strong the rivalry had become between these two teams.

The Braves might have thought the Indians

Braves Field.

were a tired, emotionally spent team, but the truth was, as strong as Boston's pitching might have been, Cleveland simply had more pitching talent.

The Indians had a fine hitter in shortstop Lou Boudreau, who hit .355 with 106 RBIs, and second baseman Joe Gordon and third baseman Ken Keltner both hit over 30 homers and 100 RBIs. But the Indians' real muscle came from pitching ace Bob Feller. He was by far the hardest thrower in the major leagues, and he had the numbers to prove it. By 1948, Feller had already won 20 games five times, including a 27-win season in 1940, a 25-win

A RETURN TO OCTOBER

The Pitching Scientist

For all his on-field excellence, Johnny Sain might best be remembered as the game's wisest pitching coach. Not only could this man pitch, but he understood the philosophy of pitching and was able to teach it. After his retirement in 1955, Sain worked with Yankee pitchers in the early '60s, and was so effective, Jim Bouton was prompted to say, "Johnny Sain is the greatest pitching coach—ever.

"He taught me everything I know, how to put on sanitary socks, how to negotiate a contract. I admire him more than any man I've ever met. All players like him: white, black, conservative, liberal, loud, quiet, they all do. Johnny Sain gets a pitcher's allegiance before any manager."

Pitcher Jonny Sain, 1948.

The reason for that was Sain's absolute devotion to pitching. He was intense, composed, almost eerily locked-in when on the mound. Sain once told a reporter, "A pitcher has to be mature beyond his years. A pitcher is not like any other ball player. The very nature of his job sets him apart. There are only two men on the diamond who cannot lose their composure, who must remain above things. Those are the manager and the pitcher. A batter can kick and scream and fielders can get mad. But when a manager or a pitcher loses his composure, the advantage swings to the other side. Pitching is only partly physical skill. There is so much of it that's psychological. I can't stress enough how important that is."

season in 1941, and another 26 wins in 1946. In each of those five seasons—1939, 1940, 1941, 1946, and 1947—Feller led the American League in innings pitched and strikeouts. It was Feller's fastball that made him so special. Because there were no radar guns in that era, and opposing hitters and scouts could only guess at his velocity, it is generally believed Feller's heater could top 95-mph.

And he had the strikeouts to prove it. In 1946, his best year ever in dominating hitters, Feller struck out 348 to go with his league-leading 10 shutouts. He seemed almost unstoppable in 1948, too, and even though he failed to reach 20 wins, he was 19-15 for the Indians with a 3.56 ERA. The only concession Feller made to time—he was approaching his thirtieth birthday during the World Series—was in strikeouts. Feller punched out a mere 164 in 280 innings, although he continued to be productive for many more seasons. In fact, at the age of thirty-two in 1951, Feller again won 20 games, going 22-8.

What all this meant was the Braves had their hands full in Game One of the Series. It was a matchup of pitching skill against pitching power; a control specialist against a strikeout deity; Sain against Feller. Who could ask for better theater in what was already promising to be a fine October showdown?

A standing-room-only crowd of 40,000 fans packed into tiny Braves Field, expecting to see a classic, and what they got was a terrific Game One. For 7½ innings, Sain and Feller matched zeroes, as neither pitcher allowed a runner to reach third base. One by one, hitters came to the plate, watched a few fastballs on the corner, and moments later headed back to the dugout, defeated. No one, it seemed, could challenge either pitcher. But then came the fateful eighth inning that left the Indians enraged by a call made by second-base umpire Bill Stewart. Leading off the inning, Braves catcher Bill Salkeld drew a walk from Feller, prompting Southworth to play chess. Salkeld was replaced by Phil Masi on the bases. Masi took second on a bunt. Eddie Stanky drew an intentional walk, as the

In Game Six of the 1948 World Series, Warren Spahn (21) looks on as Cleveland's Thurman Tucker (38) is tagged out at home by Braves catcher Bill Salkeld. The Indians, however, edged the Braves, 4-3, to win the Series four games to two.

Indians were logically poising for a double play. But Feller had an even faster way out of trouble. He and Boudreau timed a pickoff play perfectly, as the shortstop slipped in behind Masi and gained the advantage in reaching second base a half-second before the pinch-runner.

What Feller and Boudreau had done was initiate the "daylight" play. Its execution requires perfect timing, but the moment the pitcher sees the shortstop has surprised the baserunner, he knows a quick pickoff throw will likely be successful. And in this case, Boudreau and Feller were in synch. The throw to second beat the stunned Masi, who slid directly into Boudreau's waiting tag. To everyone watching, the Indians had defused the Braves' rally and were on their way to wriggling out of the inning.

In fact, all of Braves Field was resigned to another scoreless inning—until umpire Stewart called Masi safe. The Indians were enraged as they argued—correctly, as game-films have shown through the years—that

Masi slid right into Boudreau's tag. But there was no swaying Stewart, who had given the Braves the chance to keep the inning alive. Later, Stewart defended his decision, insisting, "Masi's hand was on the base when Boudreau tagged him on the shoulder."

That was all the Braves needed. Sain—who batted for himself since Southworth had decided it was Sain's game to win or lose—flied out to right for the second out. But Tommy Holmes singled through the Indians' infield, and the Braves were on their way to a

Bill Salkeld (left) and Phil Masi (right), the Braves' catching platoon of 1948.

A RETURN TO OCTOBER

The 1948
National League Champion
Boston Braves

Front row (left to right): Phil Masi, Clint Conatser, Sibby Sisti, coach Bob Keely, coach Johnny Cooney, manager Billy Southworth, coach Freddie Fitzsimmons, Tommy Holmes, Warren Spahn, batting practice pitcher Johnson, Alvin Dark, clubhouse attendant Shorty Young. Batboy in front.

Middle row: Trainer Lacks, Red Barrett, Mike McCormick, Connie Ryan, Bill Voiselle, Vern Bickford, Johnny Antonelli, Bobby Hogue, Nels Potter, Bob Elliott.

Back row: Ernie White, Clyde Shoun, Johnny Sain, Frank McCormick, Earl Torgeson, Al Lyons, Bobby Sturgeon, Bill Salkeld, Jeff Heath.

A RETURN TO OCTOBER

controversial Game One, 1-0 win over the American League champions.

With Warren Spahn readying himself for Game Two, and the Braves already having defeated the Indians' ace, the Braves and their fans entertained wild thoughts of winning the Series, and maybe even marching toward a sweep. The odds were against it, but there were still many Braves fans who remembered the miracle of 1914, and how the A's were not supposed to have had any problem with George Stallings' upstarts.

But this was not 1914. The Indians took Spahn apart in Game Two in a 4-1 defeat that was more one-sided than the score indicated. Spahn was given a 1-0 lead in the first inning against Bob Lemon, thanks to Bob Elliott's RBI single that scored shortstop Al Dark. But Lemon was unhittable after that point, shutting down the Braves on eight hits.

By contrast, Spahn got weaker as the game progressed. He allowed two runs in the fourth inning, and the Indians took a decisive 3-1 lead in the fifth on a single by Boudreau to center. That was the last pitch Spahn threw for the day.

The Braves left Boston with a split of the first two games, knowing they not only had to deal with the Indians on their home field for Games Three, Four, and Five, but the enormous Municipal Stadium crowds, too. Game Three, for example, drew over 70,000—and that crowd was dwarfed by the 81,000 who showed up for Game Four, and the 86,288 fans who packed the ballpark for Game Five.

With that home-field advantage, it was no surprise that Cleveland took Game Three, 2-0, giving them a 2-1 Series advantage. What might have raised a few eyebrows, however, was the pitching of rookie left-hander Gene Bearden, who threw a five-hit shutout against Boston. Twenty-seven-year-old Bearden was one of the Indians' secret weapons in 1948: he was 20-7 and led the American League with a 2.43 ERA. Before beating the Braves, he had defeated the Red Sox in the one-game playoff that decided the American League pennant.

Even though the Indians had trouble with Vern Bickford's sinker—they totaled only five hits in the entire game—they made their opportunities count. Cleveland took a 1-0 lead in the third inning when Al Dark threw wildly to first, attempting to complete the back end of Larry Doby's grounder to second. With the ball sailing past first base, Bearden, who had led off the inning with a double, scored all the way from second base.

The Indians made it 2-0 an inning later when Jim Hegan's single to center scored Eddie Robinson, and that was the beginning of the end for Bickford. Manager Southworth knew his Braves would not score many runs against Bearden, so a two-run deficit seemed enormous, and all Boston could hope for was perfection from the bullpen. Actually the relief did its job, shutting the Indians down the rest of the way, but Bearden was too difficult for Boston hitters. They never scored a run off him, and were left as 2-0 losers.

When knuckleballer Steve Gromek outpitched Sain in Game Four, leading the Indians to a 2-1 win, who could blame Cleveland fans for believing the Braves were about to expire? After all, Gromek—a mere nine-game winner during the regular season—had just outperformed the National League's best pitcher, not to mention the Braves' ace. In the third inning, Sain was beaten by Doby's 410-foot home run to center. Although he was masterful in the final six innings, allowing only one man to reach base, the Braves had left six runners stranded in another miserable offensive performance. In the first four games of the Series, Boston had managed only three runs, and no one in Municipal Stadium expected the Series to go back to Boston.

But in the first inning of Game Five, the Indians' Bob Feller shocked everyone when he allowed Bob Elliott a three-run home run. Elliott then proceeded to take Feller deep in the third inning, too, as the Braves ran out to a 4-1 lead. Incredibly, though, the Indians exploded for four runs in the fourth inning, after Jim Hegan's three-run home run off Nelson Potter—now, finally, they sensed the Braves were ready to melt. But as Boston tied the score in the sixth inning on Salkeld's solo

Ticket to Game One of the 1948 World Series.

World Series, Game Five, 1948. Bob Elliott is greeted by teammates Tommy Holmes (1), Marv Rickert (4), and Alvin Dark (2) after hitting a first-inning, three-run homer off Cleveland's Bob Feller. The catcher is Jim Hegan.

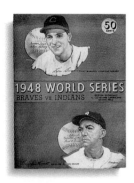

home run, once more they were stunned to see Feller unravel. The Braves scored six runs in the seventh inning, wiping out any possibility of the Indians winning the Series at home. The Braves beat up on Feller—knocking him out before he retired even one batter in the seventh—and punished relievers Eddie Klieman and Russ Christopher. As the Braves were held scoreless in the eighth and ninth innings, it took the Indians' forty-two-year-old Satchel Paige to end the carnage, and in the process, Paige became the first black pitcher to appear in a World Series game.

The Braves returned to Boston, 11-5 winners in Game Five, and all at once, the specter of a miracle returned. The task that lay ahead of the Braves was not enviable, yet it was uncomplicated: all they had they to do was solve Bob Lemon and give Bill Voiselle a few runs. Spahn later said Game Six was "the best-played game of this Series," even though it was the Indians who edged by to a 4-3 win.

Voiselle pitched well, keeping the Indians to just three runs in seven innings. But unfortunately, the Braves still could not hit much for the first seven innings (scoring only one run), by which time Cleveland had added a crucial fourth run off Warren Spahn, who was now pitching in relief of Voiselle. Singles by the Indians' Ken Keltner, Thurman Tucker, and Eddie Robinson made it 4-1, just enough breathing room to withstand the Braves' rally in the eighth.

Outfielder Tommy Holmes led off that rally with a single, an uprising that eventually loaded the bases with one out against Lemon. That's when Boudreau replaced Lemon with—who else?—Bearden. The Indians were hoping, actually, praying for a little more of Bearden's pitching magic, but just like Feller in Game Five, Bearden showed he was only human.

Clint Conatser blasted a long sacrifice fly to narrow the Indians' lead to 4-2, and Phil Masi, pinch-hitting for Salkeld, doubled off

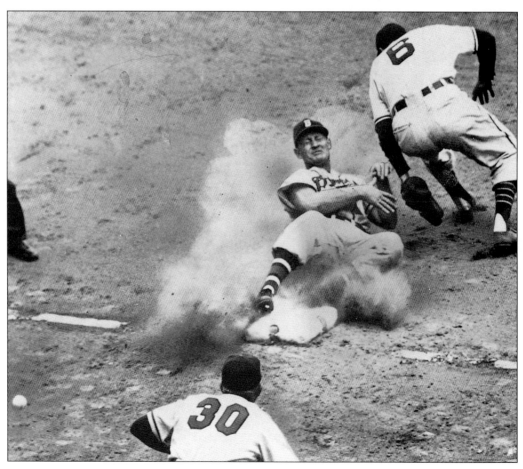

The Braves' romp in Game Five of the 1948 World Series continues as Larry Doby's throw eludes Cleveland third baseman Ken Keltner (6). Bob Elliott was waved home by Braves manager Billy Southworth (30). The Braves won easily, 11-5, but still trailed Cleveland in the Series, three games to two.

The 1948 World Series crowds at Cleveland's Municipal Stadium set new attendance records. The Game-Five crowd of 86,288 remains an American League record.

the left-field fence. In a sequence that cost the Braves the game, and essentially the Series, only Earl Torgeson scored on the hit, as Bob Elliott only advanced from second to third. When Mike McCormick hit a routine ground ball to short, the rally died.

Eddie Stanky drew a lead-off walk from Bearden, and was immediately replaced by pinch-runner Connie Ryan. That brought Sibby Sisti to the plate, and with him, the Braves' best chance for a sacrifice bunt. Everyone in the ballpark knew a sacrifice was coming. But Sisti fouled off the first pitch, and his second attempt was even worse. He popped the ball in front of the plate, allowing Jim Hegan plenty of time to whip off his catcher's mask and catch it. Worse, Hegan's throw to first base beat Ryan back to the bag—hence, a double play—and one out later, the Braves were dead.

Sisti was so distraught over his failure he approached Billy Southworth in the clubhouse after the game and said to his manager, "I let you down today. I let you down." Southworth patted his player on the shoulder and said, with as much conviction as he could muster, "You're still the best bunter in the league."

As Warren Spahn put it a few years later, "The 1948 team was a conglomeration of experienced players in the twilight of their careers. It was strictly a one-shot proposition, and nobody talked much about repeating the next year. The owners at that time were going all out to give Boston a pennant: they hired Billy Southworth, who'd led the Cardinals to three pennants, and picked a bunch of players who they'd hoped would have one big year left."

In one sense, it was a big year. The Braves drew 1.45 million and presented owner Lou Perini and his partners with a healthy profit for the summer. Management raked in an additional $210,000 in World Series revenues, while the Braves each collected $4,570 for the six-game showdown. Perini credited Southworth—not Johnny Sain and Warren Spahn and Bob Elliott, et al—with bringing the pennant to Boston. That much was evident in the way Braves management conducted its contract negotiations, since none of the Braves received much extra cash in 1949.

It was difficult for the Braves to believe their season was over. Spahn was right, of course: the Braves were built as a one-year pennant-contender, and when they failed to win it all, decay set in. Only, no one expected it to be so fast or so ugly.

Braves property manager Shorty Young paints pennants on all the Braves' trunks.

A RETURN TO OCTOBER

packing the suitcases

7

*"I have a difficult announcement to make.
We are moving the Braves to Milwaukee."*
—Owner Lou Perini, March 14, 1953

When the new season was unveiled,

Southworth was running a quasi-boot camp. He decided to work out the Braves twice a day in spring training—sessions that sometimes lasted six hours—stuck to a strict timetable, and otherwise supervised the exhibition season with a clipboard in hand. Like most pennant-winners, the Braves considered spring training a six-week vacation, a reward for the previous season's success. While everyone understood there were exercises to do, batting-practice sessions to attend, and drills to be run, no one on a championship team wants to be bothered by a manager with a stop-watch. In essence, Florida—or Arizona—becomes a place to fatten the egos, and smart managers have never intruded on this credo.

The end of an era—the Braves' final day in Boston.

The Braves' 1950 program.

Little wonder that Southworth was met with open rebellion in 1949. Before one exhibition game, he ordered his pitchers to run their sprints in the outfield, then run poles—a longer, but still-brisk jog from the left-field foul pole to the right-field pole. The pitchers complied—after all, this was the minimum workout for even the most easygoing teams—and afterward went directly to the clubhouse to shower and dress. But Southworth was not finished with them. He ordered them back on the field, insulted that they had taken it upon themselves to conclude the workout after the last pole.

Southworth's pitchers refused—a blunt, absolute no. They remained in the clubhouse, having decided they had completed enough sprints and poles for the day. After the exhibition game, Southworth told his coaches, "That's the last time anybody will put anything over on me." It did not seem like anyone was trying to trick the manager; if anything, it was an in-your-face message the pitchers were delivering to him. But it showed the rift that had grown, and Opening Day was still three weeks off.

Southworth went so far as to begin midnight curfew checks on the road, enlisting equipment manager Shorty Young as his lieutenant. Young was indiscriminate in enforcing Southworth's laws, pounding on hotel doors, caring little if he woke the milder-mannered players who had no history of curfew abuse and would already be asleep. The atmosphere became so tense that rumors began circulating that Southworth's job was in jeopardy.

Even though he had three years remaining

As the 1950s began, the Boston Braves' fortunes faded. The team returned to mediocrity, attendance dwindled, profits disappeared. Even marketing efforts such as star-studded off-season banquets failed. (Left to right: Giants manager Leo Durocher, comedian Lou Costello, Braves general manager John Quinn, Braves owner Lou Perini.)

on his contract, at $50,000 a year, the gossip of the day had it that the popular infielder Eddie Stanky was about to replace Southworth, a rumor that proved to be incorrect. Meanwhile, the Braves were able to claim first place, and in fact, led the National League as late as June 4. But then came a slew of injuries that all but ruined the summer. Earl Torgeson suffered a separated shoulder on May 14 as he slid into Jackie Robinson, trying to break up a double play. Phil Masi, mired in an awful slump, was traded to the Pirates. And perhaps worst of all, Johnny Sain suffered from arm problems and, although he pitched through the pain, posted a disappointing 10-17 record.

So began a slow, insidious slide down the standings, which ultimately left the Braves in fourth place by season's end, a full twenty-two games behind the Dodgers. If ever there was an example of The Year After Syndrome, the 1949 Braves were proof of it. Everything that could have faltered, did. The crisis raged so fiercely that Bill Southworth temporarily left the team in mid-August because of poor health. Some speculated that he was wilting under the pressure of second-guessing and clubhouse mutiny. Other rumors were even crueler, insisting that Southworth—who was already fighting a war with the press—was on the verge of an emotional collapse.

The *Boston Globe* noted as much in a late-August editorial: "The Braves were an old club, crabby, bitter, set in their ways. Players who could no longer deliver blamed their ineptness on Southworth. Victory, which sugarcoated the bitterness underneath last season, eluded the crippled Braves and left bare the acrid taste of defeat, futility and animosity.

"Southworth, one of the great managers, could not cope with the situation. Perhaps he was too aloof, too domineering, too cocky, and while he did not respect the friendship of his players, even he could not afford to lose their respect."

There was no mistaking the tidal wave of antipathy that resulted in Southworth's departure. When it came time for the Braves to split the monies awarded for their fourth-

Billy Southworth, Braves manager from 1946 to 1951. After leading the St. Louis Cardinals to three consecutive pennants, Southworth led the Braves to a 1948 National League title. But his dictatorial style began to wear thin and Southworth resigned in June of 1951. He was replaced by Tommy Holmes.

place finish, the players decided he would only get a quarter-share. While Southworth was gone, Perini named coach Johnny Cooney as the interim manager. Meanwhile, Braves ownership was faced with a brutal decision: fire Southworth and preserve the core of a once-powerful team, or simply trade away the renegades?

Perini opted for the latter option, mostly likely because he still owed Southworth two more years on his contract and some $100,000. So Eddie Stanky and Alvin Dark were dispatched to the Giants for shortstop Buddy Kerr, right-fielder Willard Marshall, third baseman Sid Gordon, and pitcher Sam Webb. With a new lineup, Southworth returned in 1950 and was strengthened by a pitching staff that was once again close to being untouchable.

Spahn was nearing his prime now, going

21-17, and Bickford was almost as good, picking up 19 wins. Most dramatically, Sain recovered from his arm troubles to become a 20-game winner again. Thanks to all this fine pitching, the Braves were in first place in mid-July, and it appeared as though Southworth's return and the decision to jettison Stanky and Dark was paying off. But August was a merciless month, and by the time September arrived, the Braves were in fourth place. They finished eight games behind the Phillies, only slightly buoyed by the fact that Sam Jethroe—the first black player in Braves history—was voted the National League's Rookie of the Year for 1950.

As it turned out, Southworth never really recovered from his illnesses and never recaptured any good kinship in the clubhouse. A majority of the players had been openly opposed to him since the end of the 1948 World Series, and even Southworth must have known that it was only a matter of time before he was replaced—a fate that eventually comes to every manager. On June 19, 1951—with the Braves slogging along in fifth place—Southworth decided that he would avoid the inevitable firing by resigning first. He cited reasons of health, despite having a

Sam Jethroe became the first black to play for the Boston Braves, in 1950. Voted National League Rookie of the Year in 1950, Jethroe led the National League in stolen bases in each of his first two seasons. Brooklyn's Jackie Robinson became the first black baseball player to break the color barrier in the twentieth century, when he made his major league debut at Ebbets Field against the Braves on April 15, 1947.

year and half remaining on his contract.

The popular Tommy Holmes was asked to replace Southworth, as Perini reasoned if the Braves could not win, at least they could win a public relations war against the Red Sox. And in continuing his efforts to draw more fans and keep the loyal ones happy, Perini decided to broadcast all the Braves' games on radio—both home and away—and Braves Field was given a neater, more pleasing appearance with the removal of all but one of the billboards from center field.

Did any of the marketing gimmicks work? Not one. Perini and Holmes learned one of the enduring lessons in baseball enterprise: Nothing beats a winning team. The 1951 Braves were on their way to a 76-78 season and a fourth-place finish that left them a staggering 20½ games behind the Giants. The worst possible news for Perini was the disappearing fan support. Since the '48 season, when it had peaked at 1.45 million, attendance declined steadily—the Braves drew 1.08 million in 1949, only 944,000 in 1950, and then a scant 487,000 in 1951. The descent seemed to gain speed as Johnny Sain aged before the Braves' eyes. He was thirty-three and had lost the anger in his fastball. With a 5-13 record, the Braves finally cut their emotional bond to Sain, trading him to the Yankees for Lew Burdette, and although Sain experienced a mild rebirth in the Bronx—winning 31 games in the next three seasons, helping the Yankees win three straight World Series—his presence was soon forgotten. Only twenty-four when the Braves acquired him, Burdette quickly blossomed, turning into a 15-game winner within two seasons. But by the time Burdette was truly dominating hitters, the Braves would be long gone from Boston, playing in front of friendlier, livelier crowds in Milwaukee.

Surely, Perini must have known his franchise was dying by the end of the 1951 season. The only question was how long could the Braves hold out in the war of attrition with the Red Sox? The club had lost almost $700,000 in 1950–51, all but wiping out the profit from the resurgence of 1947–49. One

more losing season—both on the field and in ticket sales—and it was possible that Perini would be history, at least in Boston.

It did not take long for 1952 to reveal itself as the low point in the Braves' Boston era. The Braves coughed and wheezed to a 13-21 start, which ended Holmes' brief tenure as manager, a job he had only made more difficult by insisting on serving as third-base coach as well. Even Perini was forced to admit publicly, "Maybe we were too hasty in giving Holmes the job." Holmes was replaced by Charlie Grimm, who had been managing the Braves' successful farm affiliate in Milwaukee.

Even Warren Spahn's performance reflected the disintegration of the team. He posted a 2.98 ERA and led the National League with 183 strikeouts, but was unable to break .500, finishing with a 14-19 record. Perhaps the only bright mark on an otherwise forgettable season was the performance of third baseman Eddie Mathews, a rookie who hit 25 home runs. His left-handed swing fascinated baseball observers immediately, and in fact moved

Ty Cobb to say, "I've only known three or four perfect swings in baseball. This kid has one of them." Other than that, 1952 was so awful that the Braves drew only 281,278 fans and lost almost $600,000. The newspapers were choked with rumors about an impending defection from Boston. But where could the Braves flee to? Milwaukee seemed the logical answer. The city had just built a stadium, ostensibly for its popular minor league franchise, the Brewers, but in reality to attract a major league club.

Perini's Braves were not the only club on which Milwaukee had its eye. Bill Veeck's St. Louis Browns were an appetizing possibility: perennial losers in the American League and just about out of cash. But first Perini prohibited Veeck from occupying Milwaukee—as was his right since the city was the home of the Brewers, the Braves' minor league affiliate—and then the American League stopped Veeck from moving to Baltimore, all but ensuring the Browns' collapse into bankruptcy. In effect, since he had long ago promised

Boston Braves program, 1951.

The Braves arrive in Milwaukee in 1953. (Left to right) Luis Marquez, coach Bob Keely, Jim Pendleton, coach Bucky Walters, Vern Bickford (leaning), Ernie Johnson, Lew Burdette, and Max Surkont. Equipment manager Shorty Young supervises the arrival.

never to stand in the way of Milwaukee acquiring a major league franchise, Perini's hand had been forced. Now he had no choice but to take his Braves there, or else risk a legal battle with Milwaukee city elders, some of whom were talking about canceling their lease with the Brewers.

Publicly, Perini maintained a business-as-usual posture, obtaining Andy Pafko from the Dodgers in exchange for Roy Hartsfield and cash, and later trading Earl Torgeson for Joe Adcock. And the Braves-to-Milwaukee rumors seemed to dissipate when Perini said during that winter, "We'll give Boston fans two more years to support the Braves." By March 1, the team was in spring training, with every public intention of returning to Boston by Opening Day. But the *Sporting News* reported on March 15 that the Braves would be moving to Milwaukee before Opening Day, and to the utter shock of Bostonians, Perini would neither confirm nor deny the report. The very next day, he called a press conference and said that the Boston Braves would from that point on be known as the Milwaukee Braves.

Of course, Perini uttered all the proper apologies afterward—to the fans, the employees at Braves Field and their families, even to the baseball writers who would be left without a team. But he was only telling the truth when he said Boston could not—and would not—support two baseball teams, and that there was only room for the Red Sox. "Maybe someday I'll be back in Boston," Perini said, half-joking. "Maybe someday Tom Yawkey will sell the Red Sox and I'll buy them."

Fellow National League owners had no real problem letting Perini escape. After all, they suffered with the Braves' marginal attendances, too, since National League teams shared the gate revenues. As the Giants' Horace Stoneham put it, "We never took a nickel out of Boston." The Reds' Gabe Paul did not even need that much rationale for his yes vote. "How could I vote against the Braves?" he asked rhetorically. "Lou is such a good fellow."

So the Braves were history in Boston, as the

club's equipment truck being loaded in Florida now needed a new set of directions for Milwaukee. What awaited the Braves in their new city could not be any grimmer than the last two seasons had been in Boston.

Milwaukee mayor Frank Zeidler announced a week of celebration when the news of the Braves' defection became public. The town did not need much prodding; excited fans had already been flocking to the newly-built County Stadium just to gawk at it. It was still March, and the weather was predictably raw, but that did not stop some 10,000 people from driving by the ballpark on the day of its unveiling, March 15, 1953.

There were some, of course, who would miss the old Brewers, a team that had given Milwaukee respectable baseball in previous years. In 1951, the Brewers won their league playoffs, and the '52 team included two-time Minor League Player of the Year Gene Conley, as well as Don Liddle and Billy Bruton. Right until the day before the Braves'

stunning announcement, the Milwaukee Brewers talked about repeating as league champions, and were just as stunned as anyone in Boston to learn they had been displaced. As it turned out, the Brewers were leased to the city of Toledo, where they were still the property of the Braves, and continued to flourish.

But as attached as Milwaukee might have been to its minor leaguers, the town was quick to embrace the newcomers. Fans from all over Wisconsin mailed away for season tickets, and local merchants were delirious from the marketing possibilities. Everyone, it seemed, was ready to clean the Braves' uniforms for free, offer them new-car deals, free soft drinks, free beer . . . on and on the honeymoon went, ready to last forever.

Wisconsin considered itself great baseball country—even though most of the state's residents had never attended a major league game. There were plenty of semi-pro and amateur leagues around, but in order to see real major leaguers, one had to travel to

Chicago. The Cubs and White Sox did draw from Wisconsin, but primarily from the southeastern part of the state. The rest of the residents had to rely on newspapers and radio.

Milwaukee's residents were laborers, and the biggest employers were the breweries. Television, a relatively new phenomenon, served as the greatest source of entertainment to this stay-at-home culture, but all that seemed to change when major league baseball arrived. It was time for Braves' mania: fans—new fans—from all over Wisconsin flocked to Milwaukee to see the new ballpark and order season tickets. The crowds were so huge that massive traffic jams formed around the city, and cops were assigned to the streets and intersections to stave off gridlock. Little Wisconsin towns bought tickets in bulk—2,000 or 3,000 at a time, just so they could have a day in the town's honor at a Braves game.

Small wonder the Braves caused a near-riot when their train from Florida finally arrived in Milwaukee on April 8. More than 12,000 cheering fans were waiting for them at the train depot, and the ensuing parade attracted more than 60,000 in downtown Milwaukee. So what if these fans had never seen Warren Spahn pitch or knew who Andy Pafko was? It was baseball that was coming to town, and that was initially more important than the players who were on the field.

Because it was the Braves—the franchise—who were putting Milwaukee on the baseball map, the city immediately set out to prove Perini had made the right choice. Just so America would be clear on this point, the *Milwaukee Journal* ran a daily attendance thermometer, comparing the Milwaukee draw with the previous year's Boston draw. Well, that was hardly a problem: it took all of twelve home dates in County Stadium to do that. So the *Journal* decided to replace the 1952 draw with the Braves' 1948 draw, the year they won the National League pennant and set a franchise record of 1.45 million. Again, mission accomplished: the Milwaukee Braves topped the 1948 Boston Braves with a month to go in the season. Finally, the *Journal* decided to take on the greatest attendance giant the National League had ever known, the Brooklyn Dodgers.

No team in the nation had such a cult following as the Dodgers, and they routinely packed tiny Ebbets Field. There are sections of New York—and even now, an element of the population—that still have not forgiven the Dodgers for their desertion of Brooklyn in 1957. But in 1947, they were New York's deities, pulling in 1,807,439. Incredibly, the '53 Braves beat the Dodgers, too, drawing 1,826,397.

Even before Opening Day, the Braves must have known they had stumbled on a private heaven. More than 10,000 fans showed up just to watch an exhibition game against the Braves' former rivals, the Red Sox. Never mind that it was rainy and cold—the fans were there, and they wanted baseball. The game had to be stopped after two innings because of the bad weather, so everyone came back the next day. Again, Mother Nature decided against baseball, but nothing could stop the momentum Milwaukee had generated. Finally, the Braves had a home.

Plastic Braves emblem, 1952.

Traded to Boston by the New York Yankees for an aging Johnny Sain in 1951, Lew Burdette went just 6-11 for the 1952 Braves, but he would become one of pitching's brightest stars after the Braves moved to Milwaukee.

PACKING THE SUITCASES

milwaukee

1953 **1965**

County Stadium, Milwaukee.

the inauguration

8

"This is only the beginning of good times for Milwaukee."
—Commissioner Ford Frick, 1953

After opening the season with a 2-0 whitewashing of the Reds at Cincinnati, the Braves headed for Milwaukee and the home opener at County Stadium. A sellout crowd of more than 34,000 fans squeezed into the park to watch the first National League game in Milwaukee since 1900, ready to savor every moment of history in the making. There were a wealth of firsts. First pitcher to take the mound: Warren Spahn. First batter: the Cardinals' Solly Hemus. First base hit: Del Rice. First strikeout: Steve Bilko. The fans might not have known too much about the Cardinals, or even their new hometown team, the Braves, but they were aware enough to know that Warren Spahn represented the club's spiritual backbone.

Opening Day 1953—Wisconsin Governor Walter J. Kohler, Jr.

Milwaukee Braves sticker.

Opening Day was special, and Spahn seized the moment. He had a no-hitter going into the fifth inning, but the Cardinals finally rallied with a run in the sixth. Perhaps the game's most exciting moment came in the eighth inning, with the score tied 1-1. The Cardinals had runners on second and third with two out when Stan Musial stepped up to the plate.

Staring down at Musial, Spahn must have been convinced he was already beaten. Musial was the reigning National League batting champion, and would go on to hit .337 in 1953, having compiled a .336 average the year before—his fourth title in five years. Sure enough, Musial connected, and the moment the ball left his bat, the Braves' outfield was in crisis. The line drive was like a blur in right-center, and Spahn could only watch helplessly as the ball headed for the warning track. It would mean at least one run, probably two, and spoil the homecoming party Milwaukee had thrown for its new team.

But the fans who had followed the minor league Brewers closely for the last two years knew something that not even Spahn knew. The Braves had former Brewer Billy Bruton, the rookie with legs that seemed to devour acres of territory in a single stride, in center field. Bruton could run. He could accelerate so quickly in fact that he appeared to be flying. "Watching Billy Bruton play the outfield gives me an inferiority complex," Hank Aaron would comment some years later. "I look like a Raggedy Ann doll in comparison."

Watching Bruton chase down Musial's line drive, the crowd jumped to its feet. He was gaining, gaining . . . his glove extended in what seemed like an impossible reach as he timed his leap perfectly, launching into the air, and snaring the ball in his glove. The crowd erupted in a deafening roar, and the Braves' bench went wild. Nothing like this had happened to the team in the last few years, and even though it was just one play, one out, in one game, the feeling around Milwaukee was that something truly special was about to happen in this town.

Maybe it was coincidence, maybe it wasn't, but Billy Bruton came to the plate in the bot-

tom of the eighth with two out and no one on, and worked his magic again. He hit a long triple into the wind over the head of right-fielder Enos Slaughter. The Cardinals' Gerry Staley soon loaded the bases, and when Braves cleanup hitter Sid Gordon topped a slow roller down the third base side, no mortal's legs were quick enough to reach the ball before Bruton had scored. But even with Milwaukee's 2-1 lead, Bruton wasn't finished.

The Cardinals tied the game in the top of

April 14, 1953. Milwaukee welcomes major league baseball. A sell-out crowd packs County Stadium for the home opener between the Braves (left) and the St. Louis Cardinals (right). This marked the beginning of a thirteen-year stay in Milwaukee which saw the Braves win two National League pennants and one World Series.

the ninth, sending the game into extra innings. With one out in the tenth, Bruton took a massive swing at a Staley fastball. Who could have expected the ball would travel so far? Certainly not the Milwaukee masses, who were too familiar with how little hitting power Bruton had possessed as a Brewer. The way they saw it, he had hit only five home runs in 1952, and with the strong wind against him, was not about to go deep again.

But then again, this was Opening Day, when small miracles are sometimes possible. Bruton's blast took Enos Slaughter all the way to the wall in right. Slaughter stretched, his glove extended over the wall. The Cardinals' outfielder was poised to make a handsome defensive play, but the ball bounced off his glove and into the stands for the game-winning home run. As Bruton circled the bases, the crowd wildly transformed County Stadium into an open-air asylum. Were these Braves for real?

THE INAUGURATION

Rookie center fielder Bill Bruton became the Milwaukee Braves' first hero in 1953. Bruton made a game-saving catch in the season opener in Cincinnati. Then he hit a game-winning home run in the home opener. Bruton led the National League in stolen bases in each of his first three seasons.

As it turned out, 1953 was the start of a wonderful streak for the Braves. In the thirteen seasons they spent in Milwaukee, they never had a losing season. It seemed only fitting they'd be christened like this—an extra-inning home run on Opening Day, led by their strike-zone scientist, Warren Spahn.

Spahn was already recognized as someone special, not just in Milwaukee but around the major leagues. The Braves had signed him without any real competition from other teams, a situation that could never occur today. With the money clubs now investing in scouting, a hard-throwing left-hander like Spahn would have been picked up on the radar screen as early as his freshman year in high school.

But in the late 1930s, this first-year high-school student from Buffalo, New York, was being observed by just one scout. "His name was Billy Myers," Spahn recounted years later, "and he used to watch me regularly. When I got to my senior year, he offered me a contract. That was it. I never considered playing for anyone else."

Spahn plowed through the minor leagues. He threw hard, he threw strikes, and had both a virtually unhittable curveball and an effective screwball. The equation never seemed to vary much. "All I ever wanted to do was play baseball," Spahn said. "I plugged along in the minors and pretty soon they started telling me I could be one of the good ones. That's something you don't think can ever happen to you. Suddenly it does. Then you win twenty."

Almost as soon as he pitched in his first professional game in 1942 as a Boston Brave, Spahn was drafted into the Army, and ended up missing the next three and a half seasons. It didn't take long for him to succeed as a soldier, too, and he was quickly promoted from private to staff sergeant and then to second lieutenant. And unlike many major leaguers who were able to continue playing ball in the armed forces, Spahn saw real action, serving with a unit of combat engineers, and received the Purple Heart.

But even though he ended his 21-year baseball career with 363 wins—No. 1 on the all-time list for a left-hander—the question was to follow Spahn summer after summer: Just how many wins did WWII steal from this legend? It would have been easy for Spahn to imagine 400 career wins, a mark only Cy Young (511) and Walter Johnson (416) have topped. It would have been just as understandable for Spahn to feel some bitterness, or at least regret, but he never expressed either of those sentiments. Spahn was Spahn, even from the beginning a gentle, patient man who never bothered with questions that couldn't be answered. If it was his time to serve his country, then he would do so with pride.

Spahn considered himself lucky to come home alive and healthy, able to pick up his career where he left it. He was twenty-six when he pitched again—thankful for the education the Army gave him. As he put it, "I might never have been a twenty-game winner if it hadn't been for the lessons I learned in the Army. After my experiences, nothing they asked me to do in baseball, and nothing I asked of myself, seemed like a hardship."

Of all the accomplishments in Spahn's career, the one that eluded him was the perfect game. But he came close in 1953 with an August 1 game that would have become baseball history. His opponents were the Phillies, who, along with the Braves, were waging a futile battle to catch the Dodgers.

Spahn was doing his share that summer, entering the game with a 13-4 record, having previously slayed the Giants, 13-0, for his 30th career shutout. Against the Phillies, it was the usual Spahn arsenal—fastball, curve, screwball, plenty of corner strikes—while the Braves were taking apart Jim Konstanty, little by little, until they had a 4-0 lead going into the top of the ninth.

Only then did a play that had taken place in the fourth inning begin to loom large. That's when the Phillies' Richie Ashburn had hit a high bouncer to short. Waiting for the ball was rookie Jim Pendleton, who had played shortstop in the minors but never before in the major leagues. Only twenty-four hours earlier, the Braves' regular shortstop, Johnny Logan, injured his hand placing a tag on Ashburn at second base and had been forced to leave the game.

Pendleton fielded the ball cleanly enough, but when he reached into his glove to throw it to first, found the ball slippery and elusive—he couldn't get a grip on it. The delay cost him a half-second, no more, but it was just long enough for Ashburn to beat his throw. The official scorer ruled it a hit. "The play was very close," first base umpire Larry Goetz said. "Pendleton hesitated just a little too long before he threw."

Of course, no one really paid much attention to the mistake, not in the fourth inning. But by the time Spahn had finished toying with the Phillies—making it career shutout No. 31—Ashburn was the only Philly to reach base the entire game. Now Spahn was left wondering what would have happened in the fourth inning had Logan, the ground-ball master, been waiting for the ball instead of Pendleton. Still, the Braves were grateful to be facing dilemmas like this in 1953. The '53 Braves were a dramatic improvement over the 1952 version, and although they finished 13 games behind the Dodgers, they still had 92 wins and a second-place finish to present to the city of Milwaukee.

The Winningest Left-handed Pitcher in Baseball History

After more than two decades with the Braves, Warren Spahn was unceremoniously sold to the New York Mets on November 23, 1964, reuniting him with his former manager, Casey Stengel. Spahn was never particularly fond of the Old Professor, and liked to say with a half-smile that he played for Stengel "before and after he was a genius." Stengel was similarly cool to Spahn. When a reporter asked him how Spahn had done with the Mets, Stengel said, "All right, except when he pitched."

Spahn, at age forty-four, had finally lost his skills by 1965. Even in 1964, his last season with the Braves, his decline had forced him out of the starting rotation in August and into a mop-up role in the bullpen. As a Met in '65, Spahn won four games in the first six weeks, then lost eight straight decisions and was given his release by the Mets on July 14.

But his great career did not end. Five days later Spahn was signed by San Francisco, who believed his pennant race experience would be valuable in late September. Spahn started 11 games for the Giants, posting a 3-4 record. Overall, he was 7-16 with a 4.01 ERA, and finished his career with 363 wins.

Warren Spahn.

the shot heard 'round the world

9

"There's a skinny kid in the clubhouse carrying a duffel bag."

—Braves equipment man Joe Taylor to manager Charlie Grimm,
announcing rookie Henry Aaron's arrival in spring training, 1954

The Braves' front office did its share

of wheeling and dealing in the 1953 off-season. Second place was nice enough, but it was clear the Dodgers were a far, far better team, and in order to actually compete for first place the Braves needed more muscle in the lineup. A flurry of trades, some minor, others more significant, were engineered to bring Milwaukee to the brink of a pennant victory. They involved cutting the ties with a few leftovers from the Boston era, and by the time spring training arrived, pitcher Vern Bickford was traded, catcher Walker Cooper was released, and the chubby Max Surkont and Sid Gordon were dealt to the Pittsburgh Pirates. With the heavy-legged Gordon having departed, there was an immediate need for defense in left field. The Braves

Henry Aaron (1956).

also desperately required lineup protection for Eddie Mathews, who in just two seasons had established himself as a home-run-hitting factory. He slugged 25 home runs as a rookie in 1952, then led the National League with 47 homers in 1953. Mathews was a left-handed hitter, an obvious threat to right-handed pitchers, and the only remedy available to most managers was to start as many lefties as possible against the Braves.

To make opposing teams pay a price for starting a lefty, Milwaukee acquired right-handed hitter Bobby Thomson on February 1, 1954, from the Giants. Thomson needed no introduction, not even in a town where major league baseball was new. Three years earlier, Thomson, a left fielder, had hit the dramatic play-off home run against the Dodgers, guiding the Giants in one of the greatest pennant race comebacks in baseball history. The fact that Thomson's blast came in the ninth inning made it easy for newspapers to label it, "the shot heard 'round the world."

In early spring of 1954, Thomson was nearing his thirtieth birthday, but still hadn't lost his long-ball potential. He had averaged 25 home runs and 94 RBIs in the last seven seasons, and in his last year with the Giants, hit a respectable .288 with 26 homers and 106 RBIs. Then, during spring training, Thomson's luck changed. In a freak accident on March 13 in St. Petersburg, Florida, exactly one year after Lou Perini announced he was fleeing Boston, the fates descended on the Braves again as Thomson broke his ankle sliding into second base. The fracture was serious enough to keep him out of the lineup until August 22. Ultimately, Thomson's absence cost the Braves any chance of catching the first-place Giants—who, ironically, reached the pennant on the strength of the pitchers they had acquired from Milwaukee, Johnny Antonelli and lefty Don Liddle. Without Thomson, the Braves finally turned to their future. His name was Henry Aaron.

By his own admission, Aaron wasn't ready for the responsibility thrust upon him. At the moment Thomson went down, Aaron was killing time in the Braves' dugout, mingling with the major leaguers as many minor league prospects do in spring training. Recalling his oblivion to the possibilities, he remarked that "I wasn't mature enough to realize anything more than sunup, sundown, and mealtime. I

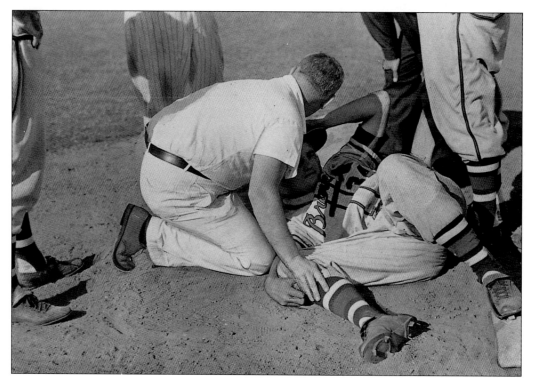

Bobby Thomson lies in agony after breaking his right ankle in a 1954 spring training game. Thomson's injury left a vacancy in the outfield, which the Braves filled with rookie Henry Aaron. Ironically, Thomson returned to the Milwaukee lineup in August after Aaron broke his ankle.

Home Run Hero

"I've seen three or four perfect swings in my time. This lad has one of them."

—Ty Cobb on Eddie Mathews

Only one player in Braves' history played in all three franchise sites, Eddie Mathews. This in itself would be enough to secure him a distinguished place in the club's legacy. But Mathews' accomplishments stand out as few others do, especially as a home run hitter.

He swatted a total of 512 home runs, and was twice the National League's home run champion. In 1953, only his second year in the majors, Mathews led the National League with forty-seven homers, and in 1959 he won his second home run crown with forty-six. Mathews still holds a league record: hitting thirty or more homers in nine consecutive seasons, 1953–61. Not only could Mathews hit, he led the National League's third basemen in assists three times.

Still, it was Mathews' swing that impressed so many in the baseball community. The Yankees so feared Mathews that they walked him four times in the 1957 World Series. Nevertheless, he won Game Four of that series with a tenth-inning home run, scoring the only run in Lew Burdette's classic win over Whitey Ford, and doubled in the first two runs in the Braves' 5-0 win in Game Seven.

Mathews once said he was motivated by the need to best every third baseman he opposed. "I wanted to beat him in every department," he insisted, "fielding, hitting, running the bases. I played that game all my life and it kept me on my toes."

Mathews eventually passed that lesson on to his players as the Braves' manager from 1972 to 1974. Sustaining his energy over a seventeen-year career—which also included brief tenures with the Astros and Tigers in 1967 and 1968—Mathews was elected to the Hall of Fame in 1978.

Eddie Mathews teamed with Hank Aaron to turn perhaps the greatest one-two home-run punch of all time. While together with the Braves, Mathews and Aaron combined for 863 homers, ranking ahead of Mays–McCovey (800) and Ruth–Gehrig (772). Mathews led the National League in home runs with 47 in 1953 and 46 in 1959.

THE SHOT HEARD 'ROUND THE WORLD

Goodbye, Bobby

The Bobby Thomson experiment of 1954 had all but collapsed in 1957, as the hero of the 1951 pennant race failed to hit for the Braves. Thomson batted .257 in 1955 with only 12 home runs and 56 RBIs, and although he improved to 20 home runs and 74 RBIs in 1956, his average sank even further, this time to .235.

There was no future for Thomson in Milwaukee, not with Hank Aaron evolving into a home-run threat as well as a high-average hitter. All that was left for general manager John Quinn was to trade Thomson and pray he would get something of value in return. In what turned out to be the steal of the year, Quinn was able to pry second baseman Red Schoendienst away from the Giants right at the June 15 deadline. The Braves got a fine half-season from Schoendienst, as he batted .310 in 93 games. Thomson, on the other hand, batted just .242 for the Giants after posting a mere .236 average with the Braves. He enjoyed a mild resurrection in 1958, playing a full season with the Cubs and batting .283 with 21 home runs and 82 RBIs.

Bobby Thomson.

certainly didn't know that when they carried Thomson by me on the way to the hospital, that was my ticket to the majors."

After graduating high school in Mobile, Alabama, in 1952, Aaron had signed as a shortstop with a black semi-pro team, the Indianapolis Clowns. His fielding left something to be desired, but a Braves scout named Dewey Griggs was stunned at Aaron's prowess at the plate, telling his superiors, "[Aaron] is one of the finest hitters God ever put on this earth." The Braves outbid the Giants in signing Aaron, paying the Clowns $7,500 for his contract and Aaron $300 a month to play in Eau Claire, Wisconsin, at Class-C.

In Class-C in 1952 and Class-A in 1953, Aaron destroyed just about every pitcher he faced and was being promoted all the way to Triple-A for the 1954 season. Manager Charlie Grimm had read all the organizational reports on Aaron—he'd led the Class-A South Atlantic League in '53 with a .352 average and 125 RBIs—but like any good baseball man, Grimm knew how deceiving stats could be. "I couldn't believe anyone could be as good as they said Aaron was," Grimm later said, but the stats and Thomson's injury helped him decide that it was time to peek at the prospect's bat speed.

The day after Thomson's accident, Grimm started Aaron in left field in an exhibition game against the Reds, and the rookie hit a single, a triple, and a huge home run to left-center. Aaron's homer started as a low line drive—so innocent-looking off the bat the Reds' shortstop actually leaped to attempt a catch. Seconds later, the ball flew over the wall, indisputable proof of Aaron's wrist strength.

It wasn't long before everyone in camp knew who Aaron was, not just Grimm and his coaches, but the veterans as well. "I didn't remember Aaron at first," Eddie Mathews said, "and there was no reason I should have. Regulars don't pay much attention to rookies, and he wasn't even on our roster. I'd heard there was a kid second baseman that was supposedly a cinch to make it big, but you hear that stuff all the time. It was the Bobby Thomson crackup that made me aware of Aaron."

Ernie Johnson (center) gets cooled off by Joe Adcock (left) and Danny O'Connell (right) after a 1954 victory over the Dodgers. In the 9-3 win, Johnson hurled eight innings of two-bit shutout ball in relief of starter Bob Buhl, while Adcock and O'Connell each homered.

True to his retiring nature, Aaron said as little as possible to teammates, hoping to remain invisible. He said, "I didn't even introduce myself [to Mathews]"—not out of disrespect, but from shyness. Nevertheless, Aaron kept quietly hitting his line drives day after day in the Florida exhibition season, letting his bat act as his spokesman. By the time Opening Day arrived in 1954, Aaron was the Braves' starting left fielder. Aaron debuted quietly—going 0-for-5 in a 9-8 season-opening loss to the Cincinnati Reds. But ten days later, he began his assault on the all-time home-run record, connecting off the Cardinals' Vic Raschi for the first of his 755 career homers. Even then, as a rookie, Aaron impressed the former Yankee: "He had such great wrists and it was hard to fool him."

Aaron's presence certainly helped Mathews and Joe Adcock become even more dangerous. In fact, these men were three of the most impressive home-run threats in the league. But they still were no match for the Giants, who led the Braves by as many as 15 games on July 22. Then Milwaukee caught fire, winning 20 of 22 and blazing to within 3½ games of first place.

By Labor Day, the Braves were in a real hunt, only four games out. Aaron had five straight hits as the Braves were sweeping a doubleheader from the Reds, but the last one, a triple, cost dearly. Sliding into third base, Aaron broke his ankle, and in a perfect irony, it was Bobby Thomson who replaced him as a pinch-runner as he was taken off the field to a waiting ambulance.

Aaron's year ended in pain, but was a statistical success: He had hit .280 with 13 home runs. Not bad for a shy rookie. Aaron even earned himself a nickname—Hank, coined by the Braves' publicity man, Donald Davidson, who decided Hank Aaron sounded friendlier, livelier than Henry Aaron. But around the National League, they had a different name for him: The Dodgers started calling him Bad Henry, because he was poison to pitchers. "We'd go over the scouting reports," Dodgers' coach and, later, San Diego Padres manager Preston Gomez once said, "and no one wanted to pitch to him." So Bad Henry was born, and with him, three decades of home-run history would follow.

THE SHOT HEARD 'ROUND THE WORLD

"Everybody wanted them to win."

—Cardinals outfielder Hank Sauer on the Braves,
after St. Louis kept them from claiming the pennant in 1956

The history books record the numbers

without pity, but anyone who lived through the Braves' 1956 season had to die with them a little. They finished in second place with 92 wins—only one game behind the Dodgers. "We just couldn't do it," Manager Fred Haney sadly remembered. "It's almost as if we weren't supposed to do it." That was the year Hank Aaron proved he was not only a home-run threat, but a batting champion, too. He took the crown with a .328 average, along with 26 homers and 92 RBIs. Joe Adcock hit .291 with 38 homers and 103 RBIs, and Eddie Mathews batted .272 with 37 homers and 95 RBIs. The three of them—Aaron, Adcock, and Mathews—comprised one of the most fearsome middle-of-the-lineup alignments in all of baseball, let alone the National League.

Bill Bruton scores behind Dodgers catcher Roy Campanella.

The Braves had solid pitching, too, as Warren Spahn at age thirty-five continued to excel. He won 20 games for the seventh time in his career, and had 20 complete games to go with a 2.79 ERA. Lew Burdette, the once-anonymous pitcher acquired from the Yankees in exchange for Johnny Sain, captured the ERA title at 2.71, and won 19 games. The Braves rotation was rounded out by Bob Buhl, who was 18-8.

But as powerful as the team appeared on paper, the Braves played awful baseball in June, falling to fifth place after having lost nine of thirteen games. What wounded manager Charlie Grimm most deeply was a series with the lackluster Pirates, in which the Braves lost three of four to a team that had generally served as a magic elixir to most National League teams looking for a win.

The Braves went on to lose two of three to the Dodgers (including a shutout loss to the thirty-nine-year-old Sal Maglie, who, a year before with the Giants, had been pounded for four runs by the Braves before he could get his first out), two of three to the last-place Phillies, and then two more to the Dodgers in Ebbets Field, and it became apparent Grimm was

about to lose his job. He had served as manager for nearly four full seasons before 1956, overseeing the Braves' resurgence after the relocation to Milwaukee. Under Grimm, the Braves were respected in the league, even feared occasionally. But now they were slipping away fast, and there was too much talent on the roster for that. With a 24-22 record, the Braves needed a new manager, and on June 16 they got one.

Grimm met the press after an especially frustrating 3-2 loss to the Dodgers in which the Braves allowed two unearned runs and an eighth-inning home run to Duke Snider. "I've decided to let someone else take a crack at the job," Grimm diplomatically told reporters.

His replacement was Fred Haney. Originally hired as a coach under Grimm, Haney had managed the Pirates as they finished last for three straight seasons, 1953–55, before getting fired. No one had expected a managerial change so soon, when the Braves were still surprisingly close to first place, but the team was undergoing a face-lift before the 1956 season was even halfway through. With the Braves only four games out, Grimm observed prophetically, "Anyone who can win ten or eleven in a row can win this thing"—and the Braves went on to do exactly that, winning their first eleven games under Haney.

This was the same manager who was unable to resurrect the last-place Pirates in three straight seasons, whose managerial career was considered over. After leaving Pittsburgh, Haney had been philosophical about his journey down the ladder of success.

"I'm not bitter about the Pirates, but I thought it was hardly fair to fire me," he said. "[The firing] was the only thing I went along with. I followed orders and I was let go. I often thought of quitting. It was surprising and abrupt to me when I was fired, but I had to take it."

Somehow, Haney's presence—or Grimm's absence—inspired the performance of Joe Adcock, one of the great unrealized talents of the 1950s. During the Braves' return to the pennant race in 1956, Adcock hit three home runs in a game against the Dodgers, leading the way to a three-game sweep at Ebbets Field. The Braves blew by the Pirates in four straight games, then took four more from the Giants.

Although the Braves cooled off after that, the catalyst Haney provided set the stage for a furious pennant race. Milwaukee entered September in first place, 2½ games ahead of the Dodgers and 3½ in front of third-place Cincinnati. In a Labor Day doubleheader against the Reds, Lew Burdette beat Cincinnati 4-2, but the Braves would not win again for five more games—a losing streak that would ultimately cost them first place. They were back on top on September 25, though, when Warren Spahn won No. 20 against the Reds. Meanwhile, the Dodgers' Sal Maglie threw a no-hitter at the Phillies, and Brooklyn trailed the Braves by a mere half-game.

The next day the Phillies beat the Dodgers, giving Milwaukee a one-game lead. With three games to go, all the Braves had to do was win two of three, and they would clinch a tie for the pennant, and very possibly make it to the World Series in only their second season in Milwaukee. With their fearsome lineup of pitchers, the Braves had every reason to believe they would fare well against the Cardinals.

Fred Haney (second from right) replaced Charley Grimm as Milwaukee Braves manager forty-seven games into the 1956 season. The Braves promptly reeled in eleven straight wins to begin a four-year run of unparalleled success under Haney.

ON THE ROAD TO THE WORLD SERIES

Bob Buhl, however, was ambushed for three runs in the first inning and the Braves ended up with a 5-4 loss. Still, they remained a half-game in first place when the Dodgers were rained out against the Pirates.

More than ever, the Braves were leaning on Spahn. Although, as much as everyone might have privately rooted for him, there were reasons to wonder about his durability. He was, after all, thirty-five, and had been struggling with a 10-9 record as late as August 6. Early on the day of September 29, news arrived in St. Louis that the Dodgers had swept the lowly Pirates and moved into first place by a half-game. It was the quintessential must-win situation for the Braves, but Spahn said he was used to that. Over and over during the summer, he had talked about his Army experiences, and how they had prepared him for the comparatively soft emotional burdens of baseball. Somehow the wizard in Spahn took over, and he won ten of his next eleven decisions, picking up career win No. 200. The baseball community watched, fascinated, as the soft-spoken pitcher led the rebirth of this franchise, practically dead in its last days in Boston, now a legitimate pennant contender in 1956.

If momentum meant anything going into Game No. 153, the Braves were in terrific shape. That's because they were facing Herm Wehmeier, who, with a 12-11 record and 3.72 ERA that year, was no match for Spahn. Wehmeier allowed Billy Bruton a home run in the first inning and Spahn took a no-hitter in the fifth. The only base runner the Cardinals produced was Bobby Del Greco, who barely squeezed out a full-count walk from Spahn. The Cardinals finally tied the score at 1-1 in the sixth, however, when Don Blasingame lined a one-out double to right-center, then scored when Alvin Dark, Spahn's old teammate from the 1948 World Series, singled Blasingame home.

The game remained tied all the way into the ninth inning, when Eddie Mathews hit what appeared to everyone in the park—fans, reporters, players from both teams—a home run. To the untrained eye, the blast had

On June 17, 1956, Milwaukee first baseman Joe Adcock hit one of the longest home runs in the history of Brooklyn's Ebbets Field. Facing the Dodgers' Ed Roebuck, Adcock drove one onto the roof, just to the left of the left-field light tower. No one had ever hit the roof before Adcock.

ON THE ROAD TO THE WORLD SERIES

enough muscle to clear the wall in center, 420 feet away. But center fielder Del Greco, in full sprint now, thought otherwise. He caught the ball at the wall—robbing Mathews and the Braves of a game-winning run, then, incredibly, did it again in the same inning. With two out and Joe Adcock on first base, Jack Dittmer hit a Wehmeier fastball almost as well as Mathews had. At the very least, the ball was heading up the gap, and with two out and Adcock running on impact, a double would have been enough to give the Braves a 2-1 lead. But Del Greco's legs were a blur, and seemingly out of nowhere, he caught the ball at the base of the wall in right-center. The Braves and their fans slumped in disbelief, wondering how much longer they would have to rely on Spahn to save them.

The ninth inning became the tenth, then the eleventh. The Cardinals' lineup had frightened no one in 1956, but by now, the Braves were aware that any mistake could end their season and hand the pennant to the Dodgers. Manager Fred Haney was faced with a critical choice in the twelfth inning after Dittmer led off with a walk. He was replaced for a pinch-runner, who was then bunted to second.

In most instances, the decision would have been automatic despite Spahn's credentials. Employ a pinch-hitter, try to get that run in, then trust in your bullpen to hold the lead. But in the long history of the game, there have been a select few pitchers whose bat was almost as potent a weapon as their arm. Warren Spahn was one of these pitchers: A lifetime .194 hitter, Spahn still holds the National League record for career home runs by a pitcher with thirty-five. He was often used as a pinch-hitter himself. Haney allowed his pitcher to bat. But Spahn flied to center, and when Johnny Logan followed with another fly ball to Del Greco, the inning was over.

The Cardinals gained momentum after they survived the rally in the top of the twelfth and ambushed Spahn in the bottom of the inning. Stan Musial had been 0-for-4 until the twelfth, but he led off with a double to right-center. After an intentional walk that put runners on first and second, Spahn got what looked like a sure double-play ball from Rip Repulski, who hit a sharp one-bouncer right at Eddie Mathews.

It should have been easy enough: Mathews to Jack Dittmer to Joe Adcock, 5-4-3 in the

After a brushback pitch from the Dodgers' Don Drysdale, Johnny Logan (23) charged the mound, igniting a brawl in a 1957 game. Dodgers manager Walter Alston (24) and Pee Wee Reese (top, center) attempt to restore order as Eddie Mathews dives into the melee.

scorebook, and the Braves would be two-thirds of the way closer. After that, all Spahn needed was one more out, and the Braves would have had one more inning, one more chance to stay alive in the great pennant race. But somehow, Repulski's ball struck Mathews on the knee, and as he helplessly watched it roll into foul territory down the left-field line, Musial scored the game-winning run.

As might be expected, the Braves took the loss hard. Tears flowed freely down Spahn's cheeks as he headed back to the dugout, and, in a rare display of anger, he flung his glove at a photographer trying to record his grief. Even though the Braves won the next day, thanks to Burdette, so did the Dodgers, and they went to the World Series—one game ahead of the Braves. The Cardinals were well aware of the role they had played in ruining the Braves' dream, and sensed the disappoint-

ment—not just in Milwaukee, but around the baseball community. Said St. Louis out-fielder Hank Sauer, "The whole country is going to be sore at us for spoiling it for the Braves. Everybody wanted them to win."

Maybe it was because the country had grown tired of October's interborough rivalry in New York. Year after year, it was the Dodgers vs. the Yankees, Brooklynites vs. Bronxites. Sauer was right, the rest of the country wanted a piece of autumn, too, and the Braves were everyone's champions. If you hated New York, then you loved Milwaukee. One year later, however, that New York and Milwaukee showdown would finally material-ize on October's stage.

The Cardinals' Bobby Del Greco scores behind Braves catcher Del Crandall in the 1956 season-ending series. Del Greco was the defensive star of the series, making one spectacular catch after another, ending Milwaukee's pennant dreams.

ON THE ROAD TO THE WORLD SERIES

new york, new york...

11

"Someone always came through to keep us up there. I was convinced this was a ball club that wasn't going to be beaten by anyone or anything."

—Braves manager Fred Haney, 1957

As close as the Braves got to first

place in 1956, they made several changes for the 1957 campaign. Second baseman Jack Dittmer was traded to the Detroit Tigers in February, and two weeks before Opening Day they traded outfielder Jim Pendleton to the Pirates for infielder Dick Cole. Among the veterans who were released were Chet Nichols and Lou Sleater, and the minor-league acquisitions included Carl Sawatski from Toronto and pitcher Juan Pizarro from Wichita. But the most significant decision was when Bobby Thomson, who had arrived in Milwaukee with such great expectations, was dealt away to the Giants for second baseman Red Schoendienst. Schoendienst was an integral part of the Braves' success. Like most years, though, the most vital elements were

Milwaukee celebrates the 1957 World Series Championship.

pitching and long-ball offense. Especially pitching. There were no secrets about the Braves' Big Three—Spahn, Burdette, and Buhl were all capable of winning must-games. Spahn again reached 20 wins, leading the National League with a 21-11 record. He also topped the National League with 18 complete games, and won nine straight in a 33-day span from August 6 through September 7.

Right-hander Lew Burdette was almost as effective, posting a 17-9 record with a 3.72 ERA. The year before Burdette had led the National League with a 2.71 ERA en route to a 19-10 record. And all Bob Buhl did was add another 18 wins in the Braves' breakthrough summer.

Even though the National League was convinced that Lew Burdette was throwing a spitter, no one was able to prove it, so he kept winning games all summer as the Braves chugged along toward their first pennant since 1948. Perhaps the most startling performance that summer came from Hank Aaron, who had won the batting title with a .328 average the year before. He slugged 26 home runs in 1956, a healthy number considering his average, but it was not until 1957 that Aaron exploded upon National League pitchers as a home-run threat. He won his first home-run crown, slugging 44, leading the league with a career-high 132 RBIs and still batting .322.

No one could pin Aaron's style down, and no scouting report could be devised to defeat him, or even contain him. Dodgers catcher Roy Campanella called Aaron "the most unpredictable hitter in the league." Phillies manager Mayo Smith said, "There's no book on Aaron. You have to pitch him like you do Yogi Berra—right down the middle with everything you've got, then close your eyes."

Aaron's manager, Fred Haney, went even further in his praise. "Hank is more like Rogers Hornsby than anyone I ever saw, and Rogers Hornsby was the greatest right-handed hitter I ever saw. It's incredible the way [Aaron] can go to right with all that power. And he's more than just a natural hitter. He has the temperament and the disposition to go with it."

By midsummer, Aaron had finally reached the highest echelon among hitters. The respect he now commanded was easy to gauge by noting how close opposing pitchers were throwing at his head—Aaron was getting knocked down more frequently, especially as the pennant race tightened.

The Braves had built a ten-game winning streak in mid-August, good enough to stretch the lead to 8½ games by Labor Day. But they proceeded to lose 8-of-11, and the club reached a crisis point on September 15 after a 3-2 loss to the Phillies, thanks to a 10th-inning squeeze bunt. Not only did it slice the Braves' lead to 2½ games, but the defeat was charged to Warren Spahn, who somehow had lost two straight games during the Braves' most critical hour.

After that game, the Braves kept the clubhouse closed for an hour. Who knew what was racing through their heads as the pennant evaporated before them. Manager Haney had done his best, though. When he finally opened the doors, allowing reporters to enter the room, he said to his Braves, "Here are your pallbearers, gentlemen. Don't you want to meet your pallbearers?"

But the Braves were too far ahead to fail as they had in 1956, and as Haney said, after the season ended: "Someone always came through to keep us up there. I was convinced this was a club that wasn't going to be beaten by anyone or anything." Following the September 15 fiasco against the Phillies, the Braves proceeded to win six straight, taking them into the final week of the season. With six games left, they had a five-game lead over the Cardinals, who were arriving in Milwaukee for a three-game set. It did not take much to figure out the Cardinals had to win all three.

In the first game of the series, Lew Burdette worked his usual sorcery on the Cardinals, but they were able to match him with reliever Billy Muffet, and managed to take the Braves into the eleventh inning with the score tied at 2-2. It was Henry Aaron versus Muffet leading off the eleventh inning. Muffet, a twenty-seven-year-old fresh from the Cardinals' minor league affiliate in Houston, had no real game-plan to deal with Aaron, other than to throw a corner-strike, then hope and pray the inevitable line drive Aaron would hit would land in someone's glove. There was no way to overmatch Aaron, certainly not for a rookie. On his very first pitch, Muffet tried a slow curve, thinking that Aaron would be guessing on a fastball and therefore would be out in front of the pitch. But if Aaron was fooled, he recovered so fast it was impossible to tell, and he hit a massive fly ball to left-center, defeating center fielder Wally Moon in a matter of seconds. Moon went to the wall, leapt, and watched helplessly as the ball cleared over his head for a home run.

Aaron would later call this pennant-winning hit "the most important home run I ever hit. My first thought was Bobby Thomson's homer. That had always been my idea of the most important homer. Now I got one for myself." He was mobbed at home plate, lost in a crush of delirious teammates, as the Braves concluded their nine-year marathon. They had their first pennant since 1948 and the first ever in Milwaukee.

The next goal, naturally, was the Yankees, who had just captured their eighth American League pennant in nine years. To everyone except their diehard fans, the Yankees were a faceless machine, so bloodless in their winning ways that New York's National League fans especially loathed them. As disappointed as Brooklyn Dodger followers might have been in 1957—third place, eleven games out—they were openly rooting for the Braves to wound the Yankee monolith. And as the New York Giants posted a 69-85 record, good for sixth place and a 26-game deficit, their fans temporarily switched alle-

giances to the Braves as well. Suddenly, everyone was a Braves fan.

Surely, the Yankees were impressed when they saw the heavy artillery the Braves were carrying into the World Series. Not only was Aaron the National League's MVP, but alongside him was Eddie Mathews, who had crashed 32 homers, and outfielder Wes Covington, who hit 21 home runs in only 96 games. And like Covington—a late-season call-up because of injuries—outfielder Bob "Hurricane" Hazle was a pennant-race savior. He replaced Billy Bruton, hitting .403 in 134 at-bats. Hazle, who would only total 261 at-bats in his three-year career, was so hot in the summer of '57 that Aaron said of him, "He makes me feel like I'm always in a slump."

Yet the Braves knew the odds were against them, regardless of how much momentum they had gathered in the last two seasons. In terms of postseason experience, the Yankees had an awesome collection of veterans. Mickey Mantle did not quite match his 1956 Triple Crown numbers, but he was coming off a powerful season nonetheless, batting .365 with 34 home runs and 94 RBIs. Behind Mantle, the Yankees' chief run-producers were Yogi Berra, who had hit 24 home runs and driven in 82 runs, and Moose Skowron, who had added 17 homers and 88 RBIs with a .304 average. Furthermore, the Yankee pitching staff was led by Tom Sturdivant, who was 16-6 with a 2.54 ERA. With all this talent, the Yankees won 98 games and finished eight games ahead of the White Sox, and, as always, were driven by Casey Stengel's dugout wisdom.

New York Yankees manager Casey Stengel (left) and Milwaukee Braves skipper Fred Haney (right) flank television executive Jim Hagerty before the start of the 1957 World Series.

So it seemed like business as usual when the Yankees took Game One of the Series, a 3-1 win behind Whitey Ford's five-hitter. He outpitched Warren Spahn in front of nearly 70,000 fans in the Bronx, rendering the Braves so helpless that it was impossible to imagine the Series going further than maybe five games.

That's when Lew Burdette took the mound in his first appearance against the Yankees, who would quickly discover what the National League had known for years: His fastball could cast a strange spell over hitters. A certain irony lay in Burdette's start because he was once a Yankee himself, traded in 1951 for Johnny Sain. Sain's skills had long since diminished, and as Burdette emerged as a force in the National League, it was he who enjoyed a private last laugh on the Yankees. And Stengel. Burdette did not mind telling reporters at the World Series how Stengel never once addressed him by his name. "It was always, 'Hey, you, get in there and warm up,'" Burdette said. "Casey didn't really know I was around. I think I threw two pitches in my whole time in Yankee Stadium. Most of the time I threw batting practice and was in the bullpen."

Stengel, of course, never apologized for the way he treated Burdette. Actually, the pitcher was right: Casey hardly remembered him, and besides, he wasn't good with names anyway. Even with the players he liked, Stengel could be amazingly cold. Yankee observers noted how casually Casey cut his emotional ties with Billy Martin earlier in the 1957 season, when an after-hours brawl at the Copacabana ended his Yankee tenure. As much as Stengel loved Martin—he called his second baseman "the best little player I ever had"—Stengel did not offer much of an argument when general manager George Weiss decided the incident at the Copa was Martin's fault, and that he had to go.

Maybe Burdette could not get Stengel to apologize, but there was a better alternative: He could beat the American League champions in the Series and make Stengel recognize and respect him—if not as a Yankee, then as

a Brave. And he proceeded to do just that, outpitching Bobby Shantz in Game Two, 4-2, and tying the Series at one game apiece.

Splitting two games at Yankee Stadium was all the Braves were really hoping for because Games Three, Four, and Five were scheduled for County Stadium in Milwaukee. Even though their ballpark seated only half as many as a sold-out Yankee Stadium (although they still drew 2.2 million), no one had to tell the Braves how comfortable Milwaukee fans would make them. For the Braves, home was home, and there they always played well.

For the Yankees, though, Milwaukee was a foreign country—inhabited by midwesterners who didn't know or understand baseball. From the Yankees' imperious perspective, the Braves and their fans had no right to be on equal footing with them, the American League's tough guys. Nor did they bother to hide their disdain for their small-town counterparts. This arrogance manifested itself

before Game Three when the Yankees, traveling to Milwaukee by train, stopped on the way in a little town near Racine called Sturtivant. The locals were waiting, as was the mayor, who was ready to make a few remarks. To complete the festivities, a marching band was on hand, too. All the Yankees were expected to do was show up and prove to the townspeople that New Yorkers weren't all so big, bad and ugly. Unfortunately, the Yankees did nothing to soften their arrogant image. They pushed through the town without even stopping to say hello.

When the Yankees finally arrived in Milwaukee, their manners had not improved. Not surprisingly, Milwaukee had turned into the country's largest outdoor festival, waiting for the Series to resume on its turf. The *Milwaukee Journal* ran an enormous page-one headline that promised "Today We Make History." This, on the same day Americans learned the Russians had launched Sputnik

and beaten the United States in the race to orbit the earth. There were more official activities planned, but the Yankees were interested only in getting to their hotel. Once the train had eased into the station, they hurried to a waiting bus, shooed away the local reporters who asked to ride along, and headed for their hotel, all the while ignoring the city's welcome parties. When the Milwaukee press corps persisted, one Yankee official is said to have shouted, "Come on, stop acting bush. Get off the bus." "Bush," of course, is short for bush-leaguer—meaning second-class, amateurish, unworthy, unimportant—the worst possible slur that could have been hurled by a member of the baseball community. The newsmen proceeded to write their next-day stories around the bus incident, making sure Milwaukeeans understood how they had been insulted, and the *Journal* responded with another overheated headline: "Bushville!"

When the Yankees were introduced for

Milwaukee's County Stadium.

Game Three, they were the targets of terrible verbal abuse. Somehow, the "bush" comment had been attributed to Stengel, even though he had managed the minor league Milwaukee Brewers to a championship in 1944 and would not seem to be prejudiced against mid-westerners. Yet the County Stadium crowd was ready to blame Casey, booing him mercilessly from the moment he stepped on the field. To his credit, Stengel hardly seemed offended by the reception. As he put it, "I been booed before. I been booed all over the country. I been booed for years." When the decibel level seemed to reach its peak, Stengel gallantly blew a kiss to the masses.

Given all the Yankee-bashing going on in the Stadium, Milwaukee fans never thought they would end up cheering for a Yankee, but Game Three proved them wrong. They fell in love with a rookie shortstop named Tony Kubek, who they accepted as one of their own since Kubek was Milwaukee-born and his father had played for the Milwaukee Brewers at old Borchert Field. Kubek, full of adrenaline, out-hit the Braves' entire lineup—he totaled three hits and four RBIs, including two home runs. The Braves scored off pitcher Bob Turley in the second inning, forcing Stengel to go to his bullpen. But Don Larsen, making his first World Series appearance since pitching a perfect game in the '56 Series, scattered five hits in 7⅓ innings for the win. The Yankees crushed the Braves, 12-3, and looked forward to out-pitching Warren Spahn again in Game Four.

Instead, the Braves ambushed the Yankees up until the ninth inning. Spahn had a 4-1

Game One of the 1957 World Series was decided in the sixth inning when Yogi Berra scored on Jerry Coleman's squeeze bunt (right). Braves catcher is Del Crandall. New York's 3-1 victory put them a game up on Milwaukee.

lead and was within one out of evening the Series at 2-2 when he suddenly unraveled. Yogi Berra and Gil McDougald each stroked eleventh-hour hits, and with a 3-2 count, Elston Howard crashed a three-run home run to tie the game at 4-4.

Although the Braves survived this inning, they were all but dead in the tenth when Yankee outfielder Hank Bauer tripled Kubek home. The Yankees, who had been only one strike away from a 4-1 ninth-inning loss, were now only three outs away from a 5-4 victory. But then came the famous Nippy Jones shoe-polish incident.

In that era, players' spikes were groomed with polish and a soft cloth—the shoe leather actually shined—leaving a residue that would smear onto anyone or anything with which it came in contact. That's exactly what happened to Yankee reliever Tommy Byrne's first pitch to Nippy Jones in the tenth inning. The curveball broke sharply down, striking Jones on the foot. However, umpire Augie Donatelli said the pitch bounced in the dirt first, and merely called it a ball. Jones calmly produced the ball and showed Donatelli the shoe-polish scuff mark, evidence enough to convince Donatelli he was wrong, thereby awarding Jones first base. That reversal set the stage for the Braves' game-winning rally, as Johnny Logan doubled to tie the score at 5-5, and Eddie Mathews smashed a two-run home run, giving the Braves a stunning 7-5, come-from-behind victory for Game Four.

In Game Five, the Yankees learned once more how impossible Burdette's sinker could be when he threw a seven-hit shutout for a 1-0 win, out-dueling Whitey Ford. The two-hour game left Milwaukee only nine innings away from a world championship. But back at home in New York, the Yankees claimed Game Six, 3-2, on Hank Bauer's seventh-inning home run. After six weeks of spring training, 154 regular season games, and six games in the World Series, the Braves' season was still up in the air.

It has been said that Game Seven of the World Series is baseball's gift to America—no other sport can match it for sustained excitement.

Wes Covington saves the day in Game Five of the 1957 World Series. This catch against the wall in the fourth inning robbed Yankee Gil McDougald of a home run and preserved Milwaukee's 1-0 win, giving Milwaukee a 3-2 lead over New York in the series. Covington's prolific power was a key element for the pennant–winning Braves in both 1957 and 1958. He hit 21 home runs in 96 games in 1957, and 24 homers in only 90 games in 1958.

119

A Spitter?

"No man can make a ball sink like that." —Jackie Robinson

It was Lew Burdette who attracted the greatest controversy in 1957, one that would last all season, right into the World Series. The question raged throughout the National League: Did Burdette throw a spitter or not?

The pitch had been declared illegal since 1920, so Burdette would only smile and call himself a sinkerball specialist. That's what every pitcher says when he's stretching the rules. It is true that some are born with a natural ability to make a fastball dance, but there's no doubt that a little foreign substance—vaseline or saliva, for instance—can make a fastball behave so unpredictably it becomes almost impossible to hit.

Of course, the hardest part of dealing with a spitball pitcher is catching him in the act. If he is skilled enough, a pitcher can commit a baseball crime in full view of the opposing team and umpires without ever being detected. That's because there are too many places to hide a sliver of vaseline. For all the years the National League suspected Burdette was cheating, he was never caught.

Instead, Burdette was content to call his alleged spitter "my psychological pitch." As he put it, "I wouldn't know how to throw a spitter even if I wanted to. But if the hitters have that in their minds that I'm throwing one, then all it does is give them something else to think about."

And National League hitters did exactly that. In fact, by 1956, Burdette had irritated Jackie Robinson so thoroughly, the Dodger infielder was practically calling him a cheater. "If it's a

sinker, it's the best in the business," Robinson said. Manager Walter Alston eventually instructed his Dodgers to step out of the batter's box and let the ball dry any time they suspected Burdette was cheating.

Cardinals pitching coach Bill Posedel recalled one incident in spring training when Burdette was openly doctoring the ball. "Burdette threw a dandy of a spitter to [first baseman Joe] Cunningham for strike three in the fourth inning, and when Wilmer Mizell went to the mound to start the fifth, he stood out there and laughed," Posedel said. "Know why? The ball was still wet."

Reds' manager Birdie Tebbetts wanted the league to take action against Burdette, a request that was formally made by general manager Gabe Paul. Burdette responded by saying, "Tebbetts owes my wife and family an apology." National

Lew Burdette, pitching hero of the 1957 World Series.

League president Warren Giles did get involved in the controversy, but failed to take any action against Burdette. In a letter to Paul, Giles wrote, "Nothing in the rules prohibits a pitcher from moistening his fingers if he doesn't apply moisture to the ball. We have watched Burdette warm up and we are satisfied up to now, he has not violated rule 8.02."

Burdette finally offered an explanation. "I'm nervous on the mound. I touch my cap, I tug at my pants, I pull my sleeve loose, I wipe the sweat off my eyebrows," Burdette said without conviction. "The sweat comes off my forehead into these bushy things and then drips into my eyes. I got a right to see, don't I? I would've taken off my pants if Birdie wanted me to. He just wanted to get my goat."

NEW YORK, NEW YORK...

Milwaukee couldn't get enough of their Braves in 1957. This parade down Wisconsin Avenue, before the World Series, celebrated the Braves' National League pennant and attracted more than 150,000 fans.

Regardless of what year, what era, every pitch is enormous, every at-bat becomes a miniature apocalypse. And in 1957, the setting was perfect for such a climactic, sudden-death ending, due to the pitching matchup. The Yankees' Don Larsen, who only a year and two days earlier had thrown a perfect game against the Dodgers, was going against Lew Burdette, who had already beaten the Yankees twice in one week. Spahn had been the regularly scheduled starter for Game Seven, but he was overcome with a virus and manager Fred Haney realized there was only one possible alternative: Burdette. Never mind that

Burdette was throwing on just two days' rest. In October, adrenaline beats muscle fatigue every time. Burdette said years later, "When Fred told me he needed me to pitch, there wasn't any way I was going to say no." Despite any fatigue, Burdette was still too much for the Yankees. In front of 61,000 hostile fans in the Bronx, he out-pitched Larsen—who lasted only 2⅓ innings—for a 5-0 victory, forcing the Yankees to endure the embarrassment of being dethroned by one of their former teammates in front of their hometown fans.

Stengel praised the Braves' pitcher after the final game, telling reporters: "Burdette was the big man of the Series. He took care of us all the way. He was just as good in the third game as he was in the second and as he was in the first. He made us hit the ball on the ground in nearly every tight spot. He was great." This was no understatement. In all of 1957, only two American League pitchers managed to shut out the Yankees, and Burdette did it twice in a row. Not that he was a consistent shutout pitcher himself—though he shut out the Reds months earlier on Opening Day, he didn't hurl another shutout until Game Five against the Yankees. Was this revenge, then? Even in victory, Burdette wouldn't gloat over the Yankees.

He explained afterward, "You know why I can't go along with that revenge stuff? Because I'm the kind of guy who likes to win so much there's no difference what . . . letters they have on their uniforms. I threw sliders to the right-handed hitters and the screwball

to lefties and sinkers to all of them, especially in the late innings. Not too many curves in any of the games."

Of course, the residents of Milwaukee were more than happy to rub it in for him. The most publicized photo in the *Milwaukee Journal*, taken during the post-Series celebration, showed a woman gleefully hoisting a banner that read: "Bushville wins!" In an enormous victory parade downtown, another sneering banner led the way: "Rest in peace, Yankees." That became the motto of the day. The Yankees should not have been embarrassed losing to such a powerful team as the Braves, but their own arrogance made it tough for them to swallow defeat. For the first time in many years, the Yankees had to mouth the words of their cross-town rivals, the Dodgers: "Wait 'til next year."

Milwaukee stages another parade celebrating the Braves' World Series title. Pitching heroes Lew Burdette (left) and Warren Spahn (right) accounted for the four World Series wins: Burdette winning three, Spahn winning one.

NEW YORK, NEW YORK . . .

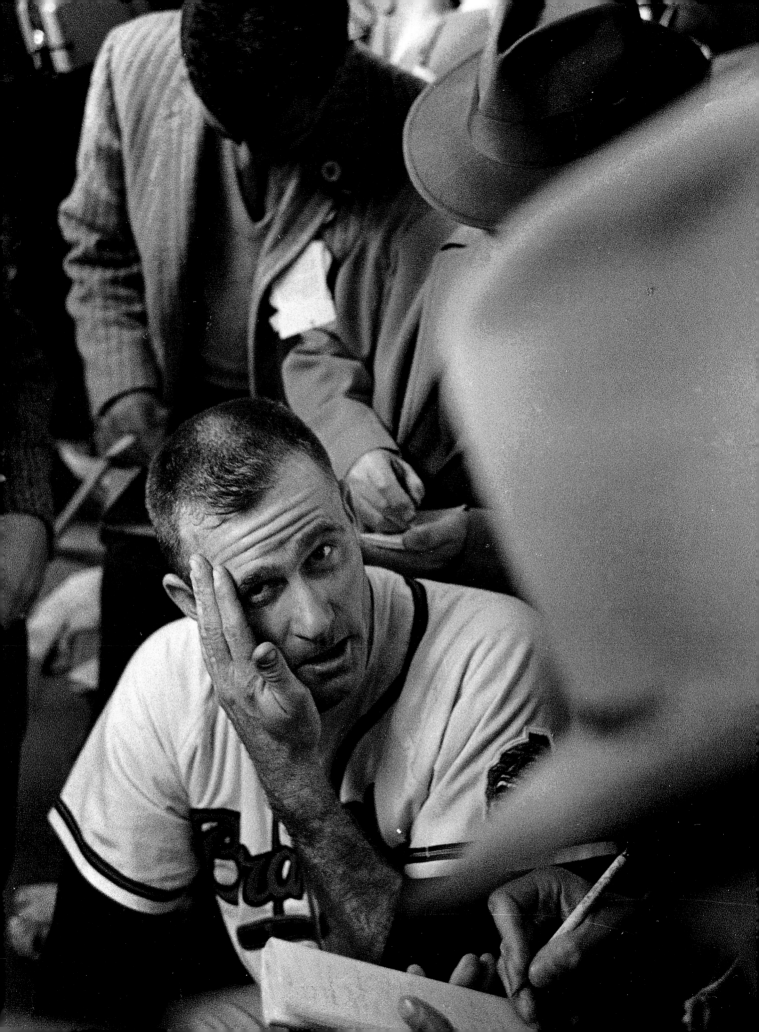

1958: october's déjà vu

12

"I didn't realize it at the time, but after we won the seventh game of the World Series in 1957, everything started to go downhill."

—Henry Aaron, 1958

During the next season, baseball fans

experienced a shocking realignment as the Dodgers and Giants both abandoned New York for California. With the promise of money, new stadiums, and not having to compete for the same pool of fans, Brooklyn owner Walter O'Malley took his team to Los Angeles, while Horace Stoneham pulled the Giants away from the Polo Grounds in favor of San Francisco. Suddenly, ardent New York fans were without a National League team and would have to wait five years for baseball to create the New York Mets. The Yankees were now the city's sole baseball occupants, but New Yorkers did not embrace them—in fact, Dodgers and Giants fans were so fiercely opposed to the corporation in the Bronx, Yankee attendance actually

Lew Burdette could not repeat his 1957 magic in 1958.

dropped in 1958. Perhaps there was lingering disappointment at the way the Yankees had lost to the Braves right there in the Bronx. For the second time in three years the Yankees had lost the Series in Game Seven, and maybe they looked too vulnerable to fans who had come to expect a world championship every year. But in 1958, winning 92 games and outdistancing the second-place White Sox by 10 games, the Yankees came back strong. It was never a race: on August 1, the Yankees were 16½ games in front, as every other team in the league was under .500. Mickey Mantle was even more of a threat than in 1957, leading the American League with 42 home runs while batting .304.

The Braves seemed just as poised for the rematch in 1958, as they too won 92 games, taking the pennant by eight games over the Pirates. They had five players who hit 18 or more home runs, and Aaron and Mathews combined for 61. As usual, the pitching staff provided the Braves' added muscle: Spahn won 22 games, Burdette added another 20, and everyone else on the staff was above .500. Throughout the summer, the two teams considered their respective schedules as a warm-up for October.

As if either club needed any additional motivation, the Yankees never forgot or forgave Burdette for an off-season magazine story in which he was quoted as saying he and Spahn expected to "share another four wins over the Yankees [in the '58 World Series] assuming they make the Series again." That was bold rhetoric, even if the Braves had earned the right to boast a little. No one had ever taken on the Yankees on the record, not even the hated Dodgers. Then again, the Braves had not forgotten the Yankees' slur hurled their way last autumn—bush.

An outsider could assume the Braves were at their peak with so much pitching, hitting, and a strong local following. But there were organizational cracks: somehow, the Braves were losing their fans. Although the decrease was slight, it was unmistakable. After pulling in a record 2.2 million in 1957, attendance dropped to 1.97 the following year. That pattern ran contrary to conventional baseball wisdom, which says a team is most popular the year after it wins a championship.

Manager Haney was also in trouble. Fans grumbled about his conservative strategy, and on July 5, while the Braves were in the midst of a five-game losing streak, Haney was hung in effigy from a construction crane at a demolition site in downtown Milwaukee. Never mind that the Braves were in first place at the time: the city was getting accustomed to winning, and now demanded perfection. And dissatisfaction wasn't limited to the fans. While the Braves lost three of four to the Dodgers in July, shortstop Johnny Logan said, "We're a tiresome team." Whether he meant tired or tiresome, his point was made.

But this much can be said about the '58 Braves: They prospered in spite of numerous injuries. Bob Buhl developed shoulder trouble in May; Red Schoendienst broke a finger in July; and his replacement, Mel Roach, tore up his knee sliding in August. Wes Covington struggled on two arthritic knees, and Billy Bruton recovered slowly from his 1957 injuries and didn't return to the lineup until late May. Rarely did Haney have all his regulars available, although the Braves managed to withstand the pennant-race heat generated by the Dodgers. In fact, the entire National League took part in one of the fiercest dogfights since the turn of the century. By the All-Star break the last place team had never been more than 9½ games away from the leaders.

But the Braves persevered, and the pitching staff practically owned August. Warren Spahn won four games, Carlton Willey won five, and Lew Burdette won seven, capturing the National League's Player of the Month award. In the best illustration of pressure pitching, the Braves went into Philadelphia in the middle of the month and proceeded to smother the Phillies. Willey threw a shutout in the first game, 1-0; Spahn took the second game, 2-1; and Juan Pizarro and Burdette took both ends of a doubleheader, 5-1 and 4-1, as the Braves left town with a four-game sweep. By the time September arrived, the Braves had vanquished everyone in the race.

Now they looked to October, and another chance to embarrass the Yankees. Spahn took the opener, 4-3 in ten innings, outdueling Whitey Ford, and Burdette was given the breathing room of a 15-hit attack in Game Two against Bob Turley and four other Yankees pitchers. Having beaten the Yankees in both games at County Stadium, the Braves only needed two more victories to complete a back-to-back series domination of baseball's most dominating team.

The Yankees recovered in Game Three, thanks to Don Larsen, who beat Milwaukee, 4-0, with help from Hank Bauer, who drove in all four runs. Despite such a well-played game, Game Four saw the Yankees unravel, as Spahn once again became untouchable and the Braves shocked Whitey Ford by beating him, 3-0. What was unforgivable to the Yankees were the defensive lapses suffered by left fielder Norm Siebern.

Fighting a fierce sun, Siebern misplayed simple pop-ups in both the sixth and seventh innings. The frustration was so evident among

the Yankees, even the usually mild-mannered Ford stood on the mound with hands on hips, staring out to left field. It was Spahn's soft, sinking flare to shallow left that broke the Yankees, as Siebern got a late jump on the ball and allowed it to fall in front of him. That allowed catcher Del Crandall to score the third and most important run. Siebern later said, "I might have caught it, but I didn't start quick enough."

Stengel accepted responsibility for Siebern's failures, yet privately seethed, especially when he saw the outfielder joking around the batting cage the next day. "A man drops two or three fly balls in the sun, you'd think he'd get a glove and go out there and practice a little," the Yankee manager told reporters. Siebern never played another inning the rest of the Series, and a year later was traded away.

With Burdette on the mound for Game Five, the Braves were within nine innings of taking their second straight Series. Even though Burdette's magic finally ran out, as the Yankees pounded him for six runs in 5⅓

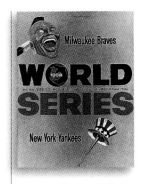

1958 official World Series program.

In Game Seven of the 1958 World Series, Del Crandall crosses the plate after his sixth-inning home run off of Bob Turley, tying the game at 2-2. Johnny Logan (23) waits to greet him. The Yankees broke the tie with four runs in the eighth inning (the key blow—a three-run homer by Bill Skowron), to win the series, 4 games to 3.

innings during a 7-0 flogging, the Braves were still confident as the Series returned to Milwaukee for Games Six and Seven. Yet something had changed for the Braves, which Aaron would observe at the Series' conclusion. No matter that Whitey Ford, pitching on just two days' rest, was knocked out in the second inning—the Braves lost again, this time 4-3 in ten innings.

The stakes were practically equal going into the final game of the 1958 season. Once again it was Burdette, the Yankee-slayer, against Don Larsen, October's perfectionist. It had been two years since Larsen's history-making performance in Game Five against the Dodgers, but hardly anyone invoked that image anymore. The Yankees would have been content with a solid seven innings—or at least avoiding a repeat of the 1957 Game Seven, when the Braves had routed Larsen out in the third.

The rout began early for the Braves in Game Two of the 1958 World Series. Here, Wes Covington scores one of seven first-inning Milwaukee runs as Yogi Berra bare-hands a high throw from Yankee left fielder Elston Howard. The Braves went on to win the game, 13-5, to take a 2-0 lead over New York.

For seven innings, the Yankees and Braves staged tremendous theater, tied 2-2, each side waiting for the other to blink. Ironically, Larsen failed again, knocked out in the third inning, but the Braves were unable to lay a finger on reliever Bob Turley. For 6⅔ innings, he accomplished what the Yankees had hoped for from Larsen—plenty of ground balls, fast outs, and non-threatening innings. So when the Yankees struck with two out in the top of the eighth, the Braves faced ruin. Yogi Berra doubled, Elston Howard singled, and Moose Skowron waited perfectly on Burdette's usually-unhittable change-up and hit a three-run home run. The Yankees were now ahead, 6-2.

Down by four runs with six outs to go, the Braves were psychologically crushed. So were the fans at County Stadium, who watched in resignation as the season came to a sad end. When a drunken fan dressed in a brown suit charged onto the field in the ninth inning, executing a perfect hook slide into second base, the fans, sensing defeat, managed a rueful laugh. But other than waiting for the man to be caught by police and arrested, all that was left for the crowd was the long, slow march to the parking lot. The possibility of stomping on the Yankees' chests one more time now only a fantasy. As Spahn said after the Series, "We scored seventeen runs in the first two games, and twenty-five for the [entire] Series. That's it in a nutshell."

But even more disturbing than the loss was the greater malaise that was overcoming the Braves. Maybe it was the mid-season injuries, or the three straight Series losses, or even the break in the attendance gain. Something was wrong. Aaron said it best: "I didn't realize it at the time, but after we won the seventh game of the World Series in 1957, everything started to go downhill." His point was only too clearly confirmed at the gate. The 1958 season saw the beginning of an attendance decline that quickly gathered momentum, ultimately forcing the Braves to leave Milwaukee by 1966. Perhaps the novelty of a new team had worn off since 1953. Or maybe Milwaukee's residents decided they liked football better. Or television. By 1965 the Braves barely drew a half-million, meaning three of every four fans who followed in the late '50s had fled.

Bob Buhl (left) and Lew Burdette on the cover of the Street and Smith Baseball Yearbook, *1958.*

the start of the crash

13

"Fred Haney didn't manage the club. He sat in one corner of the dugout, gulping down pills and saying to Crandall, 'What should we do, Del?'"
—Braves pitcher Joey Jay

Someone loses, someone gets blamed.

It has been that way since the beginning of baseball, and almost every manager who has engineered a winning season eventually has to answer for the inevitable crash. The Yankees fired Casey Stengel after he lost a seven-game World Series to the Pirates in 1960. The same happened to Fred Haney after the Braves blew the 3-1 Series lead to the Yankees in 1958. Never mind that the American League champions had better pitching and a more dangerous lineup. No one could forgive the Braves—or more precisely, Haney—for failing to capitalize on such an open chance to dominate the American League. The rumblings that were heard in the middle of the 1959 season were louder by the off-season, practically a symphony of protest. The

A discarded program is all that remains of the Milwaukee Braves after their final home game at County Stadium.

Spahn's 300th

The end of the 1950s and early 1960s was a time when attendance was in serious decline, as were the Braves themselves. After finishing second in 1960, and bound for fourth place, the attendance draw was a still respectable but somewhat disturbing 1.1 million. Yet there were 48,642 on hand August 11, 1961—the date that will be remembered forever by Milwaukee loyalists—when the largest crowd in two years came to see Warren Spahn write history. He was after win No. 300, becoming part of a club that included Grover Cleveland Alexander, Christy Mathewson, and Lefty Grove. No one could accuse Spahn of stumbling into win No. 300, as he was in the middle of his customary summer hot streak. Spahn had been only 8-11 at the All–Star break and 9-12 as late as July 30, but he did not lose again until September 15. And on August 11, the Cubs were no match for him.

In all, Spahn allowed Chicago only six singles and one run, although rookie Jack Curtis was just as effective as Spahn. Clearly, Spahn was going to need a little help—and got it from journeyman outfielder Gino Cimoli. Cimoli had been acquired from the Pirates two months earlier in exchange for the popular Johnny Logan, and although he had batted .293 with the Dodgers two years earlier as a regular, no one expected much power from him. But in the bottom of the eighth, Cimoli slugged what he called, "the biggest shot of my career" off Curtis—a long home run to right-center that gave Spahn a 2-1 lead, and three outs later, his 300th career win. The last out in the ninth was Jim McAnany's soft fly ball to right, which nestled into Aaron's glove. Spahn walked off the mound, and before he was mobbed by teammates, sought out Aaron to embrace him. Aaron gave Spahn the ball from the historic out, ending what Spahn would call, "the greatest game I ever pitched."

"Maybe winning my 300th game wasn't in my mind at first, I really don't know. But now I know it's something special," Spahn said breathlessly in the postgame interview. "Before I got close, I wasn't too excited about it, because I figured winning 300 was bound to come eventually. But a few hours before the game, the pressure began to build. About 6 P.M. I wished the game would start right then and there. I've never done anything so tough in my life."

Spahn was only being modest. Nearly a year later, on September 16, 1960, he threw the first no-hitter of his career, a fifteen-strikeout performance in a 4-0 win over the Phillies. The last out of the no-hitter—which happened to be Spahn's twentieth win of the season—came about when

Warren Spahn.

Philadelphia's Bobby Malkmus hit a sharp grounder off Spahn's glove, which then ricocheted to shortstop Johnny Logan, who threw to Joe Adcock just in time.

It took Spahn 267 career wins before he threw that first no-hitter, but he promptly hurled another one on April 28, 1961, five days after his fortieth birthday. In that game, Spahn beat the Giants, 1-0, with nine strikeouts, the first time in San Francisco's history they had been no-hit victims.

only way Haney could have survived in Milwaukee past 1959 was to win—not just another National League pennant, but the World Series, too, preferably against the Yankees. Haney accomplished neither goal.

The 1959 Braves played well, although not as well as in 1957 or 1958. But they finished in a tie for first place with the suddenly reborn Los Angeles Dodgers. The Braves lost a best-of-three playoff series, 2-0, and that was the end of their short-term dynasty. Critics have said since that with the talent available between 1956 and 1959, Haney should have won four world championships. Instead, he claimed only one World Series, two pennants, and a slew of second-guessers in the clubhouse, press box, and grandstands. Haney's detractors said he was too reliant on Spahn and Burdette, costing the Braves' younger pitchers a chance to develop their skills. Moreover, Haney was admonished for being too conservative, not daring enough in his strategy. It was no coincidence that, under Haney, the Braves finished last, or at least near the bottom, of the National League in steals. Haney abhorred the hit-and-run, although it could be argued that with a lineup like his, who needed to manufacture runs? Get a few men on base, and let Mathews, Aaron, and Covington hit the ball five hundred feet.

After the '59 season, the criticism had become so intense that Haney had no choice but to resign. In fact, general manager John Quinn was moved to defend his fallen manager. "I don't go for that rot that says Fred was too conservative," Quinn said. "First off, no major league team hires a manager who is not sound fundamentally. By that I mean he knows his players, what they can do, and fits his strategy to the pattern. We wouldn't have hired Fred if he wasn't the best man for the job. I still maintain he is the best man for the job. It's easy to second guess but in my mind he got everything he could out of the club. He went as far as he could with the players he had."

The popular Red Schoendienst, who missed most of the season with tuberculosis, also tried to deflect the heat directed at

Haney, saying, "It just wasn't meant to be for us [in 1959]." But it was clear that Haney was not missed. Outfielder Johnny Logan said the Braves "should have won the [1959 race] by ten games." Pitcher Joey Jay was even fiercer in his attack against his former boss. "Fred Haney didn't manage the club," Jay said. "He sat in one corner of the dugout, gulping down pills and saying to [Del] Crandall, 'What should we do, Del?'" (Of course, Jay might have had his own agenda in embarrassing Haney: the manager had banished the pitcher to the bullpen in July, claiming he was lazy.)

Through it all, however, there had been several constants that kept the Braves competitive. There were Aaron's home runs, of course, and Mathews' ever-dangerous swing, and Spahn's ongoing triumph over age. Every year, it seemed, he got stronger, and his screwball seemed more and more unhittable. Spahn picked up his 300th win in 1961, at the age of forty. But by then, the Braves were in the midst of another disappointing season, and not even their ageless wonder could save them.

The romance, which burned so hotly in the 1950s, was bound to flame out sooner or later. For all the passion that Milwaukee exhibited towards the Braves a dozen years earlier, the city had abandoned them by 1965. Maybe it was the mediocre baseball to which the fans had been subjected: from 1961 through 1965, the Braves failed to finished higher than fourth. Or perhaps it was seeing time finally catch up to Warren Spahn, as he finished the '64 season as a mop-up man in

Del Crandall (center) was Milwaukee's number-one catcher from 1953 through 1963. An excellent handler of pitchers, Crandall was also a .254 lifetime hitter and averaged fifteen home runs a year while with Milwaukee. Flanking Crandall are rookie hopefuls Paul Burris (left) and Walter Linden (right).

Warren Spahn picture magazine, 1964.

THE START OF THE CRASH

the bullpen, posting a 5.29 ERA. Or it could have been the final severing of the fans' ties with Spahn, as his contract was sold to the New York Mets after the 1964 season. Whatever the reason, the Braves were ready for a new home in 1965, and only a court order forced them to remain in Milwaukee one more year.

Actually, rumors of the Braves' exodus started as early as 1963, when attendance had fallen below 800,000, less than a third of its peak figures. This decline obviously disturbed the new group of Chicago-based owners who had purchased the Braves that year, but for the moment, Chairman of the Board William Bartholomay denied any impending move. "We didn't buy the Milwaukee franchise to move it to Atlanta. How do these things get started?" he asked. Still, the whispers were so persistent and eventually grew so loud that at the end of the 1963 season Braves president John McHale issued a statement saying, "The Braves will be in Milwaukee today, tomorrow, next year, and as long as we are welcome."

The key word was "welcome," and by 1964 the Braves were all but certain to leave

Milwaukee Braves President John McHale, 1963.

Braves slugger Eddie Mathews receives his final Milwaukee ovation when the Braves play their last game at County Stadium, September 22, 1965.

Milwaukee, no matter what the club's elders were saying to the public. There were lawsuits threatened, congressional action promised, and insults issued from both sides. The animosity grew so intense, Milwaukee County Chairman Eugene Grobschmidt accused the Braves of playing poorly to make the city look bad. Although the Braves were struggling at the All-Star break—38-40, in seventh place, 10½ games out—it was an outrageous charge, and McHale threatened to sue Grobschmidt for slander. The fans were disgusted by the entire affair, and even though the Braves rallied to finish the season just five games behind the first-place Cardinals, only 36,000 Milwaukeeans attended the final six home games.

After the 1964 season, pitcher Bobby Hoeft actually sided with Milwaukee's city officials, saying Braves manager Bobby Bragan tried to lose games, using one hundred ten different starting lineups. "We should've won the pennant, but management didn't want to win," said Hoeft, who reasoned that a championship would have made it impossible to justify leaving for Atlanta. True or not, the Braves were poised to announce the move for the 1965 season when Milwaukee County filed suit to keep them, accusing the Braves of antitrust violations. The Braves counter-sued, claiming Milwaukee County was "harassing" them into scheduling baseball games for 1966. As a compromise, the Braves offered the County a $500,000 cash settlement if they could leave Milwaukee at once, but the deal was refused 24-0 by the county board. The Braves were stuck in Milwaukee one more year, and the war raged on: Board Chairman Grobschmidt again accused the Braves of deliberately sabotaging their season, and board members introduced a resolution calling for an investigation of the management's "apparent ineptitude" and possible contract violations in sales of its tickets.

As a way to further insult Milwaukee, the Braves played three exhibition games in

Atlanta on the final weekend before Opening Day, 1965. They drew 106,000 in three games, and in June, used Atlanta on consecutive Mondays as the site of charity games against the White Sox and Twins. On June 21, Braves management delighted in telling the world that their five exhibition games in Atlanta drew more fans than their first twenty-eight games in Milwaukee.

The 1965 Braves finished 10 games over .500, but 11 games behind the Dodgers. The entire franchise, management and players, were looking for an end to the exhausting legal battle, and it finally came on September 22, 1965. That was the last home game the Braves played that season, ironically against the Dodgers. There were 12,577 present, and a bugler in the stands chose to play "Taps" during Braves' rallies, not "Charge." Although the Braves took a 4-1 lead against Sandy Koufax, they eventually lost, 7-6 in 11 innings. Afterward, Braves slugger Eddie Mathews said, "This may be the end of the thirteen best years of my life."

The Milwaukee era officially ended on April 12, 1966, Opening Day, when the Braves welcomed the Pittsburgh Pirates into their new home, Fulton County Stadium in Atlanta. The Braves had decided that winter to move and simply let Milwaukee's lawsuit run its course. So determined was Braves management to remain in Atlanta that on April 13, owner William Bartholomay said, "There is as much chance of the Braves playing in Milwaukee this summer as there is of the New York Yankees." Later that day, Circuit Judge Elmer Roller ruled against the National League, claiming the Braves had violated Wisconsin's anti-trust laws; the National League had to find Milwaukee a new baseball team by 1967 or else return the Braves to Milwaukee within one month.

The National League appealed in state supreme court and won. Wisconsin asked that the U.S. Supreme Court hear the case, but by a 4-3 decision, the high court decided to take no action. Atlanta finally had its Braves.

atlanta

1966

Atlanta-Fulton County Stadium, Atlanta.

someone else's miracle

14

"The Mets . . . they don't do anything wrong."

—Braves first baseman Orlando Cepeda,
after the 1969 National League Championship Series

Nineteen sixty-nine was the year
baseball expanded from twenty to twenty-four teams, and for the first time
in its history, divisions were created within each league. Canada officially
became part of America's pastime, attracting a National League franchise in
Montreal, and the San Diego Padres became Southern California's newest
team in the National League. In the American League, franchises were
added in Kansas City and Seattle. Instead of a single pennant winner, there
would be an Eastern and Western Division champion. These division champions would play each other in a best-of-five series to determine who would
go to the World Series. Purists howled, complaining that a team no longer
needed to have the best record in its league to become its champion. While

Braves catcher Joe Torre tags out the Mets' Ed Kranepool in 1968.

this point couldn't be refuted, the fact remained that there were now too many baseball franchises; the single pennant system was no longer practical. The times demanded a change.

On July 20, 1969, Neil Armstrong emerged from Apollo 11 to walk on the moon. That same summer over 400,000 people would gather at a music festival in Woodstock, New York. In Southeast Asia the war in Vietnam was escalating, while the antiwar movement in the United States was gaining momentum. On October 14, nearly 500,000 Americans descended on Washington, calling for a moratorium on U.S. involvement.

In baseball, the New York Mets, an expansion team so awful they were lovable in 1962, had ascended to the throne. Under the cool, quiet leadership of former Brooklyn Dodger first baseman Gil Hodges, they had won one hundred games, catching and passing the heavily favored Cubs in the East. It was such an unlikely feat, the team was nicknamed the Miracle Mets. "Bring on the Braves," pitcher Tom Seaver shouted as he raised a bottle of champagne to his lips, when the Mets clinched the first Eastern Division crown in National League history.

The Braves' appearance in postseason play seemed almost as implausible as the Mets'. The Braves, who had been owned and operated by the Atlanta-LaSalle Corporation since leaving Milwaukee, had finished fifth, seventh, and fifth in the two years since their defection to Atlanta. In 1968, they had epitomized mediocrity with an 81-81 record, 16 games behind the pennant-winning Cardinals. Even Henry Aaron slumped, as his home-run production fell from 39 in 1967 to 29 in '68. Attendance reflected the downward spiral, as the Braves drew only 1.1 million—nearly 25 percent fewer fans than in their first year in Atlanta.

But 1969 brought renewed baseball enthusiasm to the town. The creation of the new divisions doubled each team's chances of playing in the postseason, and although it wasn't exactly like chasing a pennant, the Braves found themselves in their first race in five years. Henry Aaron clubbed 44 home runs with 97 RBIs and Phil Niekro was a 23-game winner. Right-hander Ron Reed, who three years earlier decided to switch sports careers and leave the NBA, won 9 of 11 down the stretch. And knuckleballing reliever Hoyt Wilhelm, acquired from the California Angels on waivers, picked up four saves and two wins in the final month.

On August 19, the Braves were beat by the Cubs' Ken Holtzman, who pitched a no-hitter. They dropped to fifth place, three games behind the leaders. The Braves quickly regained the lost ground, and by September were in so tight a race with San Francisco and Cincinnati that in one twenty-four-hour period, the Braves held first place in the morning, the Reds claimed it in the afternoon, and the Giants passed the other two in the evening. The Braves won 27 of their last 38 games, including ten in a row, and clinched the division on September 30 with a 3-2 win over the Reds.

That summer, Aaron tied Ted Williams for sixth on the all-time home-run list, blasting No. 521 on June 21 against the Cubs. In his next at-bat, Cubs right-hander Dick Selma twice knocked Aaron down with successive fastballs, and although Aaron took a few menacing steps toward the mound, a fight was averted. After the game, however, Aaron was justly harsh in his criticism of Chicago manager Leo Durocher. "He ordered Selma to throw at my legs," he remarked, "They're about all I have now. I didn't wait this long to get hit and get hurt."

Aaron survived the season without any other beanings, and the National League's first-ever Western Division champions were crowned. Third baseman Clete Boyer, who had spent eight years with the Yankees and played in five World Series, was in the Braves' clubhouse the day they clinched the Western Division crown. "This is the greatest thrill I've ever had in baseball," he told reporters. "When I was with the Yankees it was great, but they had such a dynasty with so many publicized stars that everyone got lost in the shuffle. They just expected us to win. Here they didn't."

Aaron was caught up in the moment, too, as he was asked to compare the 1969 Braves to the National League champions of 1957 and 1958. Aaron looked around, studied the young faces—catcher Bob Didier, pitchers Pat Jarvis and Ron Reed, slugger Rico Carty, and second baseman Felix Millan—and said, "This is definitely a different team than in '57 or '58. Back then, we might've been deeper in pitching, because we had Spahn and

Burdette. Each of them always won twenty, and Bob Buhl would win seventeen. But this team . . . there's still a lot of greatness ahead of these guys."

So the 1969 National League pennant showdown was set: a miracle team from the East against a miracle team from the West. Game One of the matchup—emphatically called "the Championship Series" by each league and not "the playoffs" to avoid any similarity with football's postseason—was played at Atlanta-Fulton County Stadium and opened in front of 50,122 fans. Robert Merrill, who frequently sang the national anthem at Yankee Stadium as well as New York's Metropolitan Opera, did so for the Braves at the request of Braves' board chairman William Bartholomay. The Mets seemed to have fate as their ally, but who could dismiss any team that had Henry Aaron? "At some point in this series," Seaver predicted before Game One of the playoffs, "I'm going to make a mistake to Aaron, and he's going to hit the ball over the fence. That's all there is to it." "Bad" Henry's 44 home runs in 1969 brought him to 554 for his career, and he was

Opening night ticket, April 12, 1966.

The legendary Leroy "Satchel" Paige was signed by the Braves in August, 1968. The signing was a benevolent gesture by team president Bill Bartholomay, allowing the sixty-two-year-old Paige the 158 days of service he needed to qualify for a major league pension.

SOMEONE ELSE'S MIRACLE

on course to challenge Babe Ruth's 714. But the Mets were the Cinderella team, and as the Braves' Phil Niekro strode to the mound for the first pitch, Mets slugger Ed Kranepool smiled and said, "Seven hundred losses later [since 1962], here we are."

The Braves didn't need much time to learn firsthand about the momentum the Mets had generated in the second half of the season. New York right fielder Art Shamsky opened the second inning with a long single to right off Niekro, after which second baseman Ken Boswell walked on four pitches and catcher Jerry Grote singled home the first run. Niekro appeared to wriggle free of any further trouble, however, striking out shortstop Buddy Harrelson with a mean knuckleball. The ball broke so sharply that even catcher Bob Didier's oversized glove—the one he used exclusively when Niekro pitched—could not handle the knuckler's last-second dance. The ball went whistling past Didier all the way to the backstop, allowing Boswell to score and

putting the Braves in a 2-0 disadvantage.

But the Braves served notice on the Mets that they, too, could score runs in a hurry—even against Seaver, who had led the National League with 25 wins and kept opposing hitters to a mere .207 average. In the bottom of the second, the Braves' Rico Carty led off with a double and later scored on first baseman Orlando Cepeda's sacrifice fly, narrowing the Mets' lead to 2-1, and an inning later, Atlanta second baseman Felix Millan, left fielder Tony Gonzalez, and Aaron each hit successive doubles off Seaver, as the Braves took a 3-2 lead. The game was tied in the seventh when, just as Seaver had predicted, Aaron was waiting to crush him. It was a curveball that Seaver offered Aaron in the bottom of the seventh, left invitingly over the middle of the plate, around belt level, just where Aaron liked it. Later, Aaron tried to be diplomatic about the ease with which he handled Seaver, saying, "I just happened to guess curveball and he threw it. If it'd been a fastball, I would've struck out." But in fact, this was just one more example of the futility in trying to out-think Aaron, or trying to over-power him, or trying to finesse him with cor-ner-strikes. "No matter what you tried," Mets left-hander Jerry Koosman later said, "sooner or later Henry Aaron would hit it out of the park on you."

Seaver's curveball met just that fate as it sailed over the left field fence, appropriately past the Braves' mascot Chief Noc-a-Homa's wigwam. That meant the Braves had a 5-4 lead and needed six more outs to take Game One from New York. But what Braves man-ager Luman Harris would call "the turning point" arrived in the eighth inning. The Mets tied the score against Niekro when third base-man Wayne Garrett doubled past third and scored on Cleon Jones' looping single to left. Art Shamsky, the Mets' right fielder, then sin-gled to right.

That put runners on first and second, and with the score tied at 5-5, everyone in Atlanta Stadium knew the Mets would be bunting the two runners over. Ken Boswell was at the plate, looking for a way to solve the flutter of Niekro's knuckleball in order to create the perfect bunt ten feet in front of home plate. Bunting is said to be one of baseball's lost arts, requiring subtle bat skills and extreme con-centration. Even in ideal conditions—say, a middle-of-the-plate, 85-mph fastball—bunting is hard work, so trying to perform against an 80-mph no-spin, all-dance knuck-ler is almost impossible. Boswell missed com-pletely on his first attempt, and the Braves were shocked to see the Mets make a mental mistake on the bases. For there, stranded some fifteen feet off second base, was Cleon Jones, who had expected Boswell to bunt and froze when he didn't.

"I was cheating a little bit, taking a bigger lead than I should have," Jones explained later. "So when Boswell couldn't get the bunt down, I'm standing there, wanting [Braves catcher] Didier to throw to second, knowing if he does, I can make it to third. If Didier had run at me, I would've been dead." Jones stole third on Didier's throw to shortstop Gil

The Quiet Man in the Dugout

The home runs were supplied courtesy of Henry Aaron, and the knuckleballs were delivered by Phil Niekro, but the brains behind the 1969 Braves belonged to manager Luman Harris. A quiet, dignified man, Harris had managed in relatively obscurity before leading the Braves to their division championship.

He had brief managerial experience with Baltimore in 1961 and with Houston in 1964, but it wasn't until 1965 that Harris had his first full year as a manager. His Houston club finished in ninth place with 97 losses. Following that disappointing season, Harris then managed in the Braves' farm system, winning an International League champi-onship at Richmond in 1967 before being promoted to the Braves in 1968. That year, Atlanta finished fifth with an 81-81 record, and the next season, Harris and the Braves earned their first Western Division crown. He remained with the Braves through the 1972 season, posting a career 466-488 record as manager.

Luman Harris.

Harris also pitched for the Philadelphia A's in the 1940s, although without much support. He lost 13 straight games in 1943, finishing with 21 losses, the most in the American League that year. But Harris used his years with manager Connie Mack wisely. Once he became a manager, Braves public relations man Donald Davidson wrote in 1972, "[Harris] treated his players as individ-uals, just like Mr. Mack, and they respected him for it."

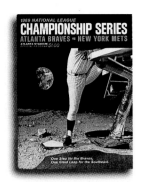

Garrido, and the Mets now had runners on first and third against Niekro. The Mets' Ed Kranepool then hit a routine grounder to first baseman Orlando Cepeda, who looked up and was shocked to see Jones breaking for the plate. The Braves had drawn their infield in, and there was no reason to assume the Mets would attempt to score on any ground ball. But there was Jones again, daring the Braves to make the routine play. Jones was the first to admit, "He had me dead at the plate." In fact, the Mets' left fielder went as far as to say, "I wasn't even running hard, because I figured I could at least get in a rundown and let the other runners advance."

For reasons that he could never understand, Cepeda's throw was high and wild and allowed Jones to score the gift run. An avalanche of bad luck buried the Braves as the Mets added three more runs and took Game One, 9-5.

In the Braves' clubhouse after the game, there were guilty faces everywhere. "This is all my fault," Niekro said. "I'm the one who couldn't keep them off the bases. It was my job to hold the lead and I didn't." But the five runs were all unearned, and for that, Cepeda said, "I'm the one to blame. I tried to take my time on the throw to the plate, but I hurried. It seems things go that way when we play the Mets. They don't do anything wrong."

It hardly mattered to the Mets that Seaver had been pounded, allowing five runs in seven innings. The Mets' No. 2 starter Jerry Koosman didn't fare much better in the next game, opposing Ron Reed. Henry Aaron hit another home run—this time a three-run blast in Atlanta's five-run rally in the fifth inning. Unfortunately for the Braves, the Mets devastated Reed, the dependable right-hander who had won eighteen games during the regular season. After Niekro had been manhandled, Braves manager Luman Harris predicted, "We're going to get a big game from Ron, and we'll get right back in this series." So it came as an awful shock to Harris and his Braves when Reed lasted only 1⅔ innings, allowing four runs and five hits. The Braves sensed there would be immediate trouble after Mets center fielder Tommie Agee led off the game with a single, stole second, and scored on first baseman Ed Kranepool's single to right. Reed never made it past the second inning, after Agee hit a two-run home run.

With the score 3-0 in the Mets' favor, Reed was finished. Harris called on his bullpen for

Phil Niekro (left) and catcher Bob Didier on the way to the 1969 Western Division Championship. Niekro went 23-13 with a sparkling 2.57 ERA. Didier was known for his ability to catch the knuckleball, handling not only Niekro, but reliever Hoyt Wilhelm, who was acquired by the Braves for the 1969 stretch drive.

help, figuring that sooner or later his batters would get to Koosman. But every Braves' reliever met with an outcome similar to Reed's, as Paul Doyle, Jim Britton, and Cecil Upshaw were all so ineffective that the Mets had an 8-0 lead by the fourth inning, rendering the Braves' subsequent rallies ineffective. Even though Aaron beat Koosman—this blast hit the flag pole in center field, almost 450 feet away—the effect was purely cosmetic. The Braves lost Game Two of the National League Championship Series, 11-6, and, returning to New York for the third game, were on the verge of elimination.

"No one here is giving up," Manager Harris bravely said, although he admitted he was disheartened at the way his Braves had combined to score eleven runs against Tom Seaver and Jerry Koosman and had nothing to show for it. "If anyone had told me before the series we'd have that kind of success against two pitchers of that quality—and be down 2-0—I'd wouldn't have believed them," Harris said. "Obviously, we're in a tough spot now." So the Braves turned their eyes to right-hander Pat Jarvis, their third and final hope to keep alive the 1969 season. Jarvis had a mediocre season, having won thirteen games and posting a 4.44 ERA. Yet there was nothing timid about Jarvis, a man known for his tenacity, who was called "Bulldog" by his teammates.

Worse for the Braves was that Game Three was to be played at Shea Stadium in New York, where 53,195 fans fully expected to see the Mets advance to the World Series. In fact, it seemed almost impossible to imagine the Braves emerging from New York with three straight wins against a team so pumped with energy and fan support. But there was Jarvis before the game, bravely telling the press, "Phil [Niekro] tried knuckleballs, and Ron [Reed] throws really hard, and we lost our first two games. I'm somewhere in between those two [philosophies] so maybe that's the answer."

But it wasn't. Even though the Mets did not score in the first inning, they hit the ball hard and nearly killed Jarvis in the process. Tommie Agee led off with a double and third

On July 3, 1966, Tony Cloninger set a major league record for hitting by a pitcher. Cloninger belted two grand-slam home runs and drove in nine as the Braves pummeled the San Francisco Giants, 17-3.

baseman Wayne Garret lined a 1-2 pitch back through the middle. It should have been a run-scoring single, except that the ball was headed directly for Jarvis' head. In self defense, practically a reflex, Jarvis caught the ball in front of his face, wheeled and fired to second base in time to double up Agee. The Braves emerged unscathed, but now they knew the Mets would be as fierce in Game Three as they were in Games One and Two.

Still, the Braves managed to throw a scare of their own into the Mets in the third inning, when Tony Gonzalez singled to right off Mets right-hander Gary Gentry, followed by Henry Aaron's double to right. Gentry, a rookie, had just allowed Rico Carty a long foul ball, and even though the count was in Gentry's favor at 1-2, the Braves were on the verge of breaking open the game: They had a 2-0 lead, runners on second and third, and a hitter whose .342 average that season spoke for itself. All these factors contributed to Mets manager Gil Hodges' decision to break with conventional wisdom and replace Gentry in the middle of the at-bat with Carty. Hodges needed a strikeout so he strode slowly to the mound, took the ball from Gentry, and summoned a quiet, shy Texan named Nolan Ryan.

Ryan would eventually become baseball's all-time strikeout champion, thanks to a fastball that blazed at 94-mph even after he reached his fortieth birthday. But in 1969 Ryan was only twenty-two, and though he had that fastball, he had yet to acquire the poise that would make him unhittable in later

SOMEONE ELSE'S MIRACLE

Rico Carty: A Pitcher's Poison

One of the finest pure hitters in Braves history was Rico Carty, whose contribution to the 1969 season was impressive enough with a .342 average, but even more astounding considering Carty spent all of 1968 battling tuberculosis.

Carty was admitted to a sanitorium to combat the disease and spent nearly five months there before recovering. His illness interrupted what had been a successful tenure with the Braves, as he had batted .330 in 1964, .310 in 1965, and .326 in 1966. Following his recuperation, Carty went on to lead the National League in batting in 1970 and posted a .366 average, the highest major league mark since Ted Williams hit .388 in 1957. Carty also set an Atlanta record in 1970 with a 31-game hitting streak.

But bad luck struck Carty again that off-season, as he suffered a broken knee in a winter-ball collision. Already a poor runner, the injury robbed Carty of much of his mobility, and he was traded to the Texas Rangers, where he served as a designated hitter. Carty played for Texas, Cleveland, and the Chicago Cubs, and finished his career with the Toronto Blue Jays in 1979 as a .299 lifetime hitter.

Rico Carty.

years. In fact, the Ryan the Braves faced in Game Three offered no sorcery at all: He threw the ball as hard as he could and simply dared hitters to beat him. Certainly it was a matchup of pitching power against pure hitting skill when Carty faced Ryan. The moment the ball left Ryan's fingertips, the rotation on the seams told Carty a fastball was indeed coming; the only question was whether Carty could catch up to it.

Judging by the way Carty swung, the ball would have traveled five hundred feet—if he had connected. But like so many of Ryan's victims, Carty thought he had timed the pitch only to have it disappear at the last second, an acceleration that took place a few feet before it reached catcher Jerry Grote's glove. The crowd at Shea went wild, sensing the Braves' moment was coming to an end. But there was still work for Ryan to do after he had struck out Carty: He walked Orlando Cepeda to load the bases, and then had to face Clete Boyer, the tough old Yankee who had been traded to the Braves. Boyer earned his reputation with the Yankees as one of the American League's finest defensive third basemen, but could surprise with his hitting power. Boyer's main weapon against Ryan was his postseason experience and nerves that wouldn't wilt. Still, bravery was no match for a 94-mph fastball, as Boyer struck out just like Carty. All Ryan needed was one out, and he got it when Didier flied out to left field.

The Mets ended the inning still trailing 2-1, but ahead psychologically. Braves manager Harris conceded that being able to convert even one run from a bases-loaded situation would have been "our last chance at winning this game." The Mets then went to work on Jarvis, as Agee hit his first pitch in the third inning out of the park, narrowing Atlanta's lead to 2-1. In the fourth inning, Jarvis allowed Art Shamsky a single to right and yet another home run to second baseman Ken Boswell, giving the Mets a 3-2 lead. The Braves' hopes were raised briefly in the fifth inning when Orlando Cepeda hit a two-run home run to center off Ryan—proving that when someone does connect properly with a

fastball that quickly, it is bound to travel far. The Braves were now ahead 4-3.

But their luck ran out in the fifth when Ryan unexpectedly led off with a single to right. This was the same pitcher who had managed just three hits all season, but he now stood on first base as the opening salvo in what proved to be the game's decisive rally. After Tommie Agee lined out to Rico Carty in left field, third baseman Wayne Garrett hit a two-run home run just inside the right-field foul pole, giving the Mets a 5-4 lead. Garrett had a personal grudge against the Braves: He felt his two brothers, who were in Atlanta's farm system, were being overlooked. But the Braves had even bigger problems than Garrett's desire for revenge, as Ryan continued to dominate over the final four innings. Except for Cepeda's two-run home run, Atlanta's dangerous batting order went down meekly inning after inning, and the closer the Mets got to the World Series, the more delirious and rowdy the crowd at Shea Stadium became. As the Braves were batting in the ninth, down 7-4, the crowd was thundering "Let's go, Mets."

The final moments moved in slow motion for the Braves. They were a fine team and had had a fine season, but none of that could stand up to the Mets. For the first out, Ryan got Bob Aspromonte on a liner to Agee. Then Braves second baseman Felix Millan grounded out to shortstop Buddy Harrelson. And the Braves' 1969 season came to an official end when Tony Gonzalez bounced out to Garrett at third. From their dugout along the third-base line, the Braves watched numbly as the Mets celebrated, Tom Seaver leading the charge to the mound. Within moments there was a pile of Mets atop Seaver, delirious in their celebration along with the thousands of fans who poured past the police onto the field. The Mets were on the way to the World Series, where the heavily favored American League champions, the Baltimore Orioles, would soon meet the same end as the Braves.

Maybe the Braves knew, finally, there was no stopping the Mets in 1969, because they accepted their defeat without bitterness. Manager Harris said matter of factly, "The Mets beat the hell out of us. I can't believe the way they hit in this series, all of them. I told my guys they have nothing to be ashamed of, losing to the Mets."

oh, henry!

15

"I'm not angry. If I was angry I would've never accomplished what I did. I just don't think people appreciate the skill with which I played baseball."

—Henry Aaron, 1974

By 1970, America was finally coming

to understand what the National League had known for years: Henry Aaron was beyond the measure of any average baseball player. Maybe it was the 44 home runs he hit in 1969, or the fact that the Braves had almost won the pennant. Competing against the Mets in October, Hank Aaron was noticed by the public, and with America watching hit three home runs in the National League Championship Series. Home runs. The ghost of Babe Ruth began to follow Aaron wherever he went. After sixteen seasons with the Braves, Aaron had 554 career home runs. While it was true Ruth's record remained a stationary target for Aaron, time wasn't his ally. Aaron was thirty-six in 1970. "[Nineteen seventy] and 1971 are going to be critical years

Hank Aaron, April 8, 1974.

for me if I'm going to catch Ruth," he correctly observed. Because there would be a natural decline in physical skills as he neared forty, Aaron knew he would have to hit the bulk of the 160 home runs he needed to catch Ruth by 1972, and then would see if there was enough bat speed left for the all-time home-run record to finally fall.

Aaron did clear one major obstacle in 1970, and that was reaching the 3,000-hit mark. Whatever was said about Aaron's assault on Ruth—already the Babe's loyalists were pointing out how many more at-bats Aaron would need to reach 714—no one could deny that Ruth had never reached 3,000 hits, finishing his career with 2,873. Nor did Ted Williams, Rogers Hornsby, Lou Gehrig, Joe DiMaggio, Mel Ott, or Mickey Mantle. But Aaron created a little history by breaking the 3,000 mark on May 17, 1970, against the Reds—hitting a ground ball up the middle off Wayne Simpson that was fielded by shortstop Woody Woodward, who made no throw. "Catching Ruth would be a thrill," Aaron said afterward, "but reaching 3,000 hits was more important because it shows consistency. People keep

wanting to know if I'll be around long enough to break Ruth's record. I don't know, but I do know I won't hang around just for the sake of hanging around, picking up twelve homers a year."

Aaron felt he would have to hit close to 50 homers in 1971 and 1972 to be able to reach 714 homers. Aaron had never reached 50 in a single season up to that point, although he hit at least 40 six times going into the 1970 season. Consistency was the word. As former teammate Joe Torre put it, "Henry belongs in a higher league."

Aaron had an approach to hitting home runs. It had plenty to do with strong wrists and a fast bat and a good attitude. But Aaron also had an ability to second-guess a pitcher during an at-bat so effectively that by the time the ball left the pitcher's hand, Aaron had guessed what the pitch would be and had begun to swing accordingly. "I keep a mental book on what pitchers throw me. When I'm hitting well, I can tell what a pitch will be when it's halfway to the plate. I suppose it's the brain up there ticking," he remarked.

"Guessing what the pitcher is throwing is

Hank Aaron scoring one of his 2,174 career runs. He tied Babe Ruth for second on the all-time list behind Ty Cobb, who scored 2,245.

about 80 percent of hitting. The other 20 percent is execution," Aaron continued. "All good hitters guess a lot; you're a dumb hitter if you don't guess some." Aaron also had a set of rules that shaped his personal life. "I'm not a teetotaler," as he put it. "I'll take an occasional drink, and I do smoke. But I take care of myself. Anything that interferes with my hitting I don't do."

With his professional and personal guidelines firmly set, Aaron seemed to have his world in order. He hit 38 homers in 1970, and came close to the 50 homers he predicted he would need when he smashed a career high of 47 in 1971. By then Aaron had 639, was on the verge of catching the aging Willie Mays, and was within two to three years of reaching Ruth. As difficult as it would be for Aaron to approach that 715th home run, eclipsing the legendary Mays wouldn't be a comfortable task, either. That's because Aaron and Mays were never particularly close, and their relationship became even more strained when Mays said in 1971 that if Aaron wanted to become the game's all-time home run champion, "He's got to catch me first." Aaron later admitted that Mays' challenge "only fired me up even more."

Mays had entered the 1972 season needing only 68 more home runs to catch Ruth, but he was aging quickly. He hit only eight home runs that year, and by the end of the summer it was clear that Aaron would be the only one within reach of the record. Mays was thirty-nine and well aware he was slipping. In the middle of what seemed to be an interminable slump, a moist-eyed Mays asked reporters, "Do I really look that bad at the plate?" Suddenly, Mays started blaming the unforgiving winds at Candlestick Park and the two years of military service (1952–53) which he believed "cost me about 50 or 60 home runs." Mays' decline seemed complete in 1972, when the Giants sold his contract to the Mets. New Yorkers welcomed Willie back to his old home turf, and Mays hit six more home runs in 1973, his last season. His career home runs would stand at 660.

With Mays out of Aaron's way, only the

Henry "Hank" Aaron

Henry Aaron grew up in Mobile, Alabama, one of eight children. A quiet child who liked to be by himself, Henry exhibited a strong and immediate interest in baseball, one that eclipsed school, girls, and even socializing with his friends. Aaron played baseball almost every day from the time he was four years old until he left home in 1951, a seventeen-year-old on his way to play for the Indianapolis Clowns of the Negro American League. At 5-11 and 175 pounds, Aaron lacked the size expected of powerful batters, but even then he hit with tremendous strength. After only a few months into his first season, Aaron's .476 average attracted the attention of major league scouts and ultimately it was the Braves who outbid everyone else.

Henry Aaron, Jacksonville Braves, 1953.

ghost of Babe Ruth remained. Aaron needed another 76 home runs to set the record and set his goal for the 1973 season at 35 home runs. In any other year that would have seemed like a reasonable target, even with Aaron pushing forty. But the closer he got to Ruth, the uglier the chase became. There was an entire generation of baseball fans who detested the idea that someone might surpass the great Babe, who, in the eyes of many, was the game's greatest player. As dignified and composed as Aaron tried to be in his march toward the home-run record, he attracted the ire of both racists and Ruth-worshippers, who made him the target of abuse.

There were hecklers from the stands, of course, and in a way, Aaron could handle them. At least they were on the other side of a railing. But after the game and away from the stadium, he could be approached by any-one and everyone. No matter where he went, hotels, airports, restaurants, Aaron felt the need to be on the defensive. His caution grew to such extremes that he would not drink from a cup of water he had left at a table, for fear that someone might have poisoned it in his absence. What really appalled Aaron was the hate mail: Some letters were actually threats on his life, but most were racially charged insults, all demeaning his run on the home-run crown.

"You have to be black in America to know how sick some people are. In fact, there isn't a black person in America who hasn't been dis-criminated against because of the color of their skin," Aaron said. "Any black person who has reached a certain level of success and doesn't acknowledge he's been a victim of dis-crimination or segregation, then I would put that person in the category of an Uncle Tom. My mail was about 75-25 against me, most of it racial. They call me 'nigger' and every other bad word you can imagine. If I was white, America would be proud of me."

A lesser man might have been intimidated, but the hatred directed at Aaron only fueled his drive. "The more they push me, the more I want the record," he said. "Some people seem to sense that I'm getting into an area

where no black man has a right to be. But I can't do anything about the mail." Aaron chose his words carefully when it came to Ruth, and his conciliatory message struck a cord with more sensible fans. In fact, Aaron stemmed the tide of hate mail in 1973 by simply saying, "I have no intention of making people forget about Babe Ruth. I just want them to remember Hank Aaron, too." Still, the attack on Aaron's privacy in 1973 almost forced him into a complete public retreat. "I couldn't go anywhere at all," he said. "My life was like one big fishbowl." The well-inten-tioned fans were just as needy as the crazies were vicious. Eating in a restaurant became an impossibility, and Aaron had to ask teammate Paul Casanova to bring his meals to his room during Braves road trips. The Braves were so concerned for Aaron's personal security that they eventually hired a bodyguard to protect him and requested each National League team to assign two police cars to escort the Braves' bus to and from the team's hotel.

The irony is that throughout his entire career, Aaron had actually sought greater pub-lic recognition. He had been eclipsed in the '50s by teammates Warren Spahn and Lew Burdette, and on a national level by Willie Mays, Mickey Mantle, and the Brooklyn Dodgers' Duke Snider. Even after Aaron emerged as a home-run hitter, Roger Maris captured the spotlight by breaking Ruth's sin-gle-season record of 60, hitting 61 in 1961. In the '70s, as he passed 600 mark, the spotlight finally belonged to Aaron, and he found it uncomfortable. "I wouldn't wish those two or three years [1972–74] on anyone. There's things I'll never forget, and I don't want to forget them."

Public sentiment toward Aaron might have been a little more generous if the Braves were involved in a pennant race, and if his home runs counted for more than just an assault on Ruth's record. But the Braves were only 70-84 in 1972, finishing 25 games behind the Cincinnati Reds, who were now so dominant they had been dubbed "the Big Red Machine." Manager Luman Harris was replaced after the All-Star break by former slugger Eddie

Another national magazine cover for Hank Aaron.

Mathews. But the Braves didn't respond well to the Hall of Famer, either, as they finished the '72 season with a 23-27 record and went 76-85 in 1973—a fifth-place finish—22½ games behind the big, bad Reds.

There was only one baseball attraction in Atlanta in the early '70s, and his name was Henry Aaron. The closer he got to Ruth, the more he was compared to him. Leo Durocher was a Yankee teammate of Ruth's for several years in the late 1920s before he began his long and successful managerial career. "When Babe hit them," he said, "you had to have a good seat to get a ball. He hit them so far you knew right away they'd be gone. Babe Ruth was a fantastic hitter, and so is Henry Aaron. In my opinion, Aaron is the greatest right-handed hitter since Rogers Hornsby, and nobody in my book will ever be better than Hornsby."

The testimonials were echoed by the Cubs' Ernie Banks, who marveled at Aaron's composure at the plate. "What does [Aaron] think about when the count is 3-1?" Banks asked. "Does he feel he has to carry the team? Does he realize that most normal people tense up with two strikes? I was impressed with him the first time I saw him, and ever since then I've been more and more impressed as the years go by."

Through it all, Aaron kept hitting home runs. He blasted No. 699 on July 20, 1973, off of Philadelphia right-hander Wayne Twitchell, and suddenly the question wasn't whether Aaron would pass Ruth, but when: Would it happen in 1973 or would Aaron and the rest of the baseball community have to wait an entire off-season and begin the vigil all over again 1974? The national media was now covering the story, not just baseball writers. *Time* and *Newsweek* both followed Aaron daily in the summer of '73. On any given afternoon, there were twenty reporters hanging around the Braves' clubhouse, all waiting for Aaron to say something outrageous, which he wouldn't, or for fellow Braves to say something new, which they couldn't. The media discovered that away from the stadium, when he wasn't unleashing that powerful swing, Aaron was a reserved man. He dressed

Johnson and Johnson and Johnson and . . .

As Henry Aaron captivated America with his assault on Babe Ruth's home run record in 1973, the Braves' Davey Johnson was also rewriting history. He hit 43 homers, one more than second baseman Rogers Hornsby of the Cardinals hit in 1922—since one of Johnson's homers came as a pinch hitter, he is credited with tying Hornsby's record for second baseman.

Johnson had never hit more than 18 home runs in his eight-year career with the Baltimore Orioles, but took advantage of Atlanta-Fulton County Stadium's shorter left-field porch. Johnson denied that a smaller stadium made any difference. "I hit eighteen of my home runs on the road," he said, "and the rest were real home runs. None of them were cheap."

Johnson, Aaron, and Darrell Evans formed a record-breaking trio that year—all three Braves hit forty or more home runs that year, the first time any three players from one team had accomplished that in a single season.

(Left to right) Darrell Evans, Hank Aaron, Dave Johnson.

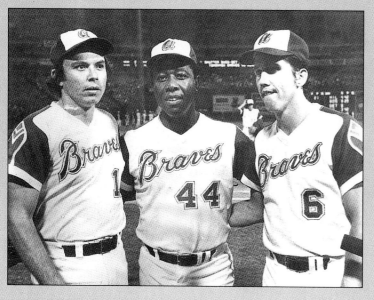

conservatively, rarely ate out, and was content to simply watch TV at home. Aaron and his wife, Barbara, had divorced in 1970, and because he did not see his four children as often, Aaron poured himself into baseball. There was no nightlife for him, just baseball and sleep and more home runs.

But the homers didn't come so quickly. Aaron noted that the closer he got to No. 700, the more carefully he was being pitched to. "I'm just not getting very much to hit," Aaron would complain. Few pitchers wanted to be one of his final victims, and certainly no hurler looked forward to the day when Aaron had 714 home runs and needed only one more homer to break Ruth's record. So the fastballs that came at him rarely crossed the heart of the plate and more frequently passed down by his knees. Occasionally mistakes were made, but the thirty-nine-year-old Aaron discovered that pitches he once hit out of the park were sometimes being fouled off. No matter. Aaron was bound to beat Ruth sooner or later, and the nation held its breath, waiting.

Oddly, though, Aaron's home runs were not enough to bring Atlanta fans to the ballpark. The gate-draw was unexpectedly low—in all, the Braves drew an even 800,000, fewer than any year in Milwaukee except 1962, 1963, and 1967, when it became increasingly evident the Braves would be leaving that town.

Still, the mood was festive on July 21, 1973, when Aaron hit No. 700 off the Phillies' Ken Brett. An eighteen-year-old fan, Robert Winborne, retrieved the ball and returned it to Aaron, who gave him $700 in silver dollars. Buoyed by reaching such a milestone, Aaron emphatically said, "I think I can do it this year. Hitting fourteen more home runs isn't going to be impossible." The confidence may have been inspired by Aaron's fiancée, Billye Williams; just days earlier Aaron had announced they would marry. The future Mrs. Aaron was the widow of a Morehouse College professor, was active in civil rights, and hosted an early-morning TV show, "Today in Atlanta." As the pressure grew on Henry, it no doubt appealed to him that

Williams was no baseball fanatic. "I had never seen Henry play," she admitted. "I had heard of him, but I was only dimly aware of his existence." Williams had met Aaron on "Today" only after he had twice canceled his scheduled guest appearance.

The countdown began in earnest after No. 700, although hitting those last fourteen homers wouldn't be easy. He wished he could predict the date when Ruth's record would fall, but better than anyone he understood that hitting a ball 400 feet requires a precise set of circumstances—the perfect pitch at the right speed crossing the strike zone at the right spot and being met by the right swing. That's why Aaron scoffed at the idea that the Babe had predicted his famous home run in the 1932 World Series against the Cubs. "I mean no disrespect to Babe Ruth and what he did," Aaron said, "but I played the game. There ain't no way somebody can tell me Babe Ruth or anybody can stand up and point their finger and say, 'I'm going to hit a home run.' I may have been born at night, but it wasn't last night."

Following home run No. 700, Aaron suffered through a nine-day drought in which he didn't hit a single home run. There were another sixteen days between 701 and 702, but he regained his stroke later in August and finished the month with 706. That left him with all of September to hit nine home runs, but Aaron's own stats indicated that it would be a struggle. In his entire career, Aaron had only twice hit nine in the final month. He started hot, though, hitting two home runs on September 3 against the San Diego Padres. On September 8, he hit No. 709 off Cincinnati's Jack Billingham, and No. 710 came two days later against the Giants. Seven days later Aaron hit No. 711 against the Padres' Gary Ross, and five days after that, on September 22, Aaron slugged No. 712 against the Astros' Dave Roberts. The Braves had six games remaining.

Six games. Two home runs. Teammates, opponents, the press, fans, and almost everyone else in the country was asking the same question: Can he do it? He tried his best to accommodate the press during this wild crush of attention, kidding, "I can handle you guys.

I'm no Roger Maris." Aaron was referring to the Yankee slugger who was so overwhelmed by the countdown to Babe Ruth's single-season record in 1961 that he withdrew completely. By September of that year, Maris' hair began falling out in clumps, and he was never truly comfortable until the Yankees traded him to the St. Louis Cardinals in 1967. But Aaron wasn't going anywhere, no matter how long it took him to catch Ruth.

Aaron hit No. 713 off of Houston's Jerry Reuss on September 29, leaving him with just one game in the 1973 season to tie Ruth. That last game provided Aaron with what he called "the kind of test I've waiting for all these years." On September 30, nearly 41,000 fans arrived on a rainy afternoon at Fulton County Stadium to see if Henry Aaron would make history. He would be facing Roberts again, who he had victimized a week earlier in Houston for No. 712. The Astros' lefty made no secret of his desire to stay out of the path of Aaron's destruction. "I don't want to be the one giving up the 714th or 715th home runs," Roberts said. "If he comes up in a situation with a chance to beat me, I'm going to pitch around him." The Astros, however, were able to find some humor in the moment, taping a note to Roberts' locker that said, "Thanks for Nos. 568, 599, 618, 655, 712, 714, and 715. Hank." They urged Roberts to take his chances with fate, and if he surrendered the record-tying home run . . . so what? "They told me, 'You'll be famous, you'll make the banquet tour all winter,' " Roberts said. "You can get fat serving up a fat pitch."

Whether he'd been psyched out or not, the very first pitch Roberts delivered to Aaron was a fastball, straight down the middle of the plate. Aaron would later shake his head at the "reverse psychology" Roberts had used on him. More likely, it was sheer nerves on both men's parts. Aaron pulled the ball slowly down the third base line, legging out an infield hit. In the third inning, Aaron lined a soft single to center, raising his average to .300, and in the sixth, bounced his third single of the game off Roberts. With the Astros leading 5-1, Aaron would have just one more

Hank Aaron pennant.

OH, HENRY!

Hank Aaron touches home after hitting career home run No. 700 off the Phillies' Ken Brett on July 21, 1973.

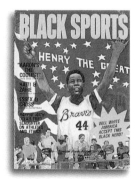

Hank Aaron dominates the cover of Black Sports magazine, June 1974.

chance at Ruth, and he came to bat in the eighth inning against the hard-throwing Don Wilson. There was enough heat on the fastball—and just enough hesitation on Aaron's part—for the pitcher to defeat the hitter in that moment. Aaron popped out to third, breaking his bat in the process. The crowd watched in silence for a moment, then showered Aaron in applause. Braves fans had seen a stellar performance from their home-run hitter in the summer of '73, and even though Aaron came up one short, there would be all of 1974 to celebrate when he finally did surpass Ruth. As Aaron said, "All I've got to do this winter is stay alive." He made sure, though, to thank the fans for their support, because so many had been won over to Aaron's side in recent months. In fact, Aaron issued them a personal apology for any disappointment 713 home runs might have caused. "I'm sorry I couldn't hit one for them, sitting in the rain like that. I was going for the home run. I wasn't trying to hit singles. And that applause, I guess, was the biggest moment I've had in baseball."

Aaron spent a quiet winter in 1974—quiet when compared to all the media attention he had attracted during the final weeks of the 1973 season. The press retreated, content to resume the Aaron-watch the following April. In the meantime, Aaron married Billye Williams and signed a long-term endorsement deal with Magnavox Corporation, which meant he could concentrate on breaking Ruth's record without worrying about money or planning a wedding. All that remained was trying to choreograph a record-breaking moment and becoming the all-time home-run champion.

The Braves were set to open the '74 season away from home, in Cincinnati, and as much as Aaron wanted to be done with the chase, he also wanted to break Ruth's record in front of his fans in Atlanta. In fact, Aaron made public his wish to play only the second game of the series against the Reds and sit out the other two. That position drew an immediate response from Commissioner Bowie Kuhn, who was uncomfortable with the idea of a player arranging his own entry point into the history books. Kuhn spoke at length with

Braves board chairman Bill Bartholomay and directed the team to use Aaron "in the same pattern of 1973, when he started approximately two of every three games."

Kuhn's edict met with swift and harsh criticism from Aaron, who reasserted his loyalty to his hometown. "I live in Atlanta, and that's where I want to hit the home run that ties the record and the home run that breaks the record," Aaron said. "I feel I owe it to the fans." Maybe it was his anger at Kuhn that resulted in Aaron hitting his 714th home run so quickly—the very first at-bat, in the first very swing he took in 1974. His victim was Jack Billingham, a Reds' right-hander who was known for his nasty curveball. This time, however, Billingham tried to beat Aaron with a sinking 3-1 fastball which the pitcher later ruefully called "a mistake." The ball went sailing over the wall in left-center, and as Aaron took a slow tour of the bases, the Braves waited for him, mobbing their teammate at home. With one flick of the wrists, Hank Aaron and Babe Ruth were in a dead heat.

Billingham stood on the mound, waiting impatiently for the celebration to end. He later admitted there was no pleasure in being on the wrong side of Aaron's passage into the history books, and went as far as to say, "I don't think Aaron can hit a home run off me if I get my sinker where I want it. The pitch just tailed back in over the plate."

Aaron had three more at-bats that day, but there wouldn't be any further assaults on the record. He grounded out in the third inning, walked on four pitches in the fifth inning, lined out to center in the seventh with the Braves leading, 6-2, and then came out of the game. Aaron was scheduled to sit out the next two days, as manager Eddie Mathews said, "Right or wrong, this is my decision." Kuhn, however, would have none it: He ordered Mathews to insert Aaron into the lineup for the Sunday game, the final one of the series. Mathews asked Kuhn what the penalty would be for defying the order, and although the commissioner never gave him a straight answer, Mathews decided not to fight any longer. In a terse statement issued before the Sunday game,

The Roadrunner

The offensive game plan was simple enough in 1974: Henry Aaron hit the ball into the seats, and Ralph Garr hit the ball into the gaps. Garr, a former football star at Grambling, had surprised the Braves and the Mets when, on May 17, 1971, in Atlanta, he became the fourth major leaguer to hit two home runs in extra innings. He was the National League's batting champion in 1974, batting .353, also leading the league with 214 hits and 17 triples. Although the left-handed-hitting Garr slumped to .278 the following year, he still led the National League with 11 triples. The next season Garr was traded to Chicago White Sox and hit over .300 in both 1976 and 1977.

Garr—a notorious "bad ball" hitter, who swung at virtually anything—holds numerous club records, including highest career average (.317), most triples (40), and most hits in one season (219) in 1971.

Ralph Garr.

Mathews acknowledged that "the commissioner has unlimited powers to issue very serious penalties on individuals or the ball club itself. For the first time I realize these penalties are not only fines but also suspension and other threats to the franchise itself. Because of this order and the threatened penalties, I intend to start Hank Aaron [on Sunday]."

Of course, Kuhn didn't make many friends with his threats, and there were questions from the press as to how far a commissioner could go in dictating a batting order: If Kuhn could force Mathews to start Aaron, then why stop there? Why not demand that Aaron pitch, too? The debate was rendered moot, however, when Aaron was held hitless on Sunday by the Reds' Clay Kirby, striking out on three straight pitches in his first two times up. As usual, Mathews removed Aaron after the seventh inning, making everyone happy—Kuhn, who saw his edict obeyed; Mathews, who avoided punishment for his team; and Aaron, who could now concentrate on the record in front a friendly public in Atlanta Stadium.

"He knows what I can throw. He hit two home runs off me last year," Dodgers pitcher Al Downing said before the historic game on April 8, 1974, in Atlanta. "But I'm not going to change my pattern. I can't go against what I've been successful with."

Downing, who would surrender the 715th home run to Hank Aaron, had pitched for the great Yankee teams of the early '60s and was finishing his career with their rivals by the time April 8, 1974, rolled around. He had a fine fastball and with it had led the American League in strikeouts in 1963. Although Downing didn't throw as hard as he had a decade earlier, he was still effective enough to go 9-9 in 1973, and with an impressive 124 strikeouts in 193 innings. He felt the weight of the moment as the country tuned in on their televisions and radios to witness Aaron's attempt to top Babe Ruth.

In his first at-bat, Aaron never even lifted the bat off his shoulder. Downing had been too careful with his fastballs, throwing two of them down and away, getting a corner strike, then missing two more times and issuing Aaron a walk. The next time up, Aaron again looked at a sinker in the dirt. Home-plate umpire Satch Davidson threw the ball out of the game and gave Downing a slick, brand-new ball, and as the pitcher paused to rub it up, Aaron waited in the batter's box.

All around the ballpark, fans were poised—not only to see the 715th home run, but perhaps to catch it. Everyone had heard about Robert Winborne, the fan who had received $700 for returning Aaron's 700th home run ball, and Sal Durante, the kid from the Bronx who had caught Roger Maris' 61st home run in 1961 and earned $5,000 in exchange. So what would Aaron's record-breaker bring in? (Entertainer Sammy Davis, Jr., offered Aaron $25,000 for the ball.) Even the Braves' mascot, Chief Noc-a-Homa, caught the home-run fever, bringing a lacrosse stick to the ballpark in the hopes that he could reach over the left-field railing. But the Chippewa Indian, whose real name was Levi Walker, knew he wouldn't have much of a chance since every Braves relief pitcher was pacing in the enclosed area that lay beyond the left-field fence but short of the left-field wall. Technically this was the Braves' bullpen, but on this night it was where Aaron's 715th home run was likely to land, some 375–400 feet from home plate.

At exactly 9:07 P.M. Downing offered another fastball. He would explain later that its intended trajectory was toward the outside corner, with enough "ride" on it so that it would carry away from the strike zone. With any luck, Aaron would chase it and swing and miss, or else he would pop the ball up harmlessly. In theory, it could have worked, but Downing's pitch did not do what he wanted. The ball remained over the middle of the strike zone, giving Aaron every opportunity to crush it. He swung, made contact, and the ball began a huge, long arc toward left-center. Leaning into catcher Joe Ferguson's ear, umpire Davidson said, "Fergie, I think this might be it."

Outfielders Jimmy Wynn and Bill Buckner converged at the wall and possibly could have

Were you there? Decal "certificate" to commemorate Hank Aaron's 715th home run.

"People will be calling to see if I've jumped out the window yet, but I'm not going to wake up in the middle of the night and begin banging on the walls. This thing is over. It's history."
—Dodgers pitcher Al Downing, after surrendering Henry Aaron's 715th home run, April 8, 1974.

OH, HENRY!

Even news magazines recognized the enormity of Hank Aaron's personal race to pass Babe Ruth.

scaled it and robbed Aaron with a last-second leap. But he had hit the pitch too hard, and there was too much muscle behind the blast. Wynn and Buckner could only watch, and, as Buckner admitted, "We kind of wanted Aaron to get it over with so he could go back to being a human being." Aaron watched the ball for only a fraction of a second, and, as was his trademark, gently tossed his bat along the first base line as he began running toward first base. It wasn't until Aaron saw first base coach Jim Busby jumping wildly that Aaron knew he was baseball's all-time home-run champion.

As Aaron circled the bases, he was joined by two fans who had jumped the stands, and was offered a handshake by Davey Lopes and Bill Russell, the Dodgers' second baseman and shortstop, when he jogged by. When the ball did land—in the bullpen as the Braves' relievers had expected—it fell directly into the glove of teammate Tom House. He was standing approximately 350 feet from home plate with his glove raised, and seeing the home run come his way, House said, "blew my mind. The ball was rising on a line. If I'd frozen like a dummy the ball would've hit me in the forehead. The only problem, though, was a guy above me who had a fishnet on a pole; [but] he couldn't get it operating in time." Jamie Easterly also attempted to catch the ball but ran smack into a cannon parked behind the fence.

House ran in from the bullpen and returned the ball to Aaron right after he crossed home plate. All the Braves' relievers had agreed to do this, but House got kidded by his friends who knew he was pursuing a master's degree in marketing and had blown a chance to market the greatest souvenir in baseball history. After the game, the home-run king took a call from President Nixon, raised a glass of champagne in the middle of the clubhouse, and told reporters a weight as heavy as "a stove" had been lifted from his back.

"To be honest, all I wanted to do was touch the bases," Aaron said quietly. "Other than that, I don't really remember the noise, or the two kids on the field. My teammates at the plate, I do remember seeing them. I remember my mother out there, and her hugging me.

That's what I remember more than anything when I think back on it. I don't know where she came from, but she was there. I feel I can relax now. I feel my teammates can relax."

For his part, Downing said he didn't have much rhythm in his delivery, and because of that the fastball didn't have its usual life. But there were no real regrets from Downing, who stood by his conviction that a fastball was "the best possible pitch in that situation if it'd done what it was supposed to. Since my ball usually sinks, there was every reason to believe [Aaron] would bang it on the ground. It's over. It's history. The next time I face him I'll get him out." Even twenty years later, long since retired, Downing has not rethought his strategy. "It was just one home run, one out of 715," he said. "And hitting 715 home runs isn't just a great achievement, it's completely out of the stratosphere."

After hitting those 715 home runs, there seemed to be little else for Aaron to accomplish. He hit 18 home runs overall in 1974, ending the season with a fine .268 average, and was traded to the Milwaukee Brewers in 1975. Aaron would go on to hit another 22 home runs in two seasons in front of his former fans, although he admitted that the 1975 and 1976 seasons were "real letdowns for me." By then it was clear to Aaron that his body was betraying him. As he put it, "Mother Nature just took over."

Still, the fans in the American League wanted a piece of Aaron's legacy, no matter that it was fading. And that bothered Aaron, who felt he had given so much to the game, cleared so many obstacles, and performed with grace under pressure. After all that, Aaron learned that the public's appetite for home runs—for his greatness—would not accept the natural surcharge time extracts from the body. "I went through the same thing in Milwaukee that I went through in Atlanta," Aaron said. "I mean, I'd go to Detroit, go 4-for-4, and they just didn't understand how I could get four hits and not hit a home run."

Aaron played in his final major league game on October 3, 1976, in front of only 6,858 fans. Despite going out as a .229 hitter, the career statistics were amazing: He now stands just behind Pete Rose (4,256) and Ty Cobb (4,191) with 3,771 hits, and was the all-time leader in RBIs (2,297), extra base hits (1,477), and total bases (6,856). His statistics also included a .305 career average, 3,298 games played, two batting titles, and not a single season in which he struck out more than 97 times. And Aaron was the home-run king. "I have no regrets," he said. "I've done just about everything I could, finishing with 755 homers and leading the National League in ten or fifteen other categories. I've been playing on borrowed time the last two years. It's been embarrassing for the kind of career I had to finish my last season with a .229 average. The things I wanted to do, I couldn't. I attempted one stolen base in the last two years. That was Opening Day [1975]. I decided the legs were gone."

There was, however, one last piece of unfinished business: By Aaron's last game, he had totaled 2,174 runs—tied for second on the all-time list with Babe Ruth. Only Ty Cobb had scored more with 2,246, and this game could have provided Aaron another chance to eclipse the Babe. But Brewers' manager Alex Grammas unwittingly deprived Aaron of that opportunity, removing him from the game for a pinch-runner after a base hit in the seventh inning. Aaron exhibited no public disappointment over Grammas' move, but later admitted, "I would have loved to have had another run. What went through my head was that I needed one more run to pass Ruth, but I don't want to get into that controversy. My career is done with, over with. Let it go at that." Grammas sorrowfully said, " I didn't know [about the record]. I just wanted him to go out with a base hit."

Today, Henry Aaron is employed by the Braves as a full-time consultant, and wherever he goes, he carries history with him. That, and a lingering bad memory about the way some fans treated him on the way to the top. "It's funny how Babe Ruth's 714 home runs was the most impressive, unbreakable record in sports until a black man broke it," Aaron said. "Then it shifted. Now it's [Joe] DiMaggio's hitting streak."

On the Other Side of the Record

Al Downing, who surrendered the historic 715th home run to Hank Aaron, pitched for the great Yankee teams in the early '60s, and was finishing his career with the Dodgers by the time April 8, 1974, rolled around. Downing had a fine fastball, and with it led the American League in strikeouts in 1963. But he hurt his arm in 1968 and spent three years bouncing from the Yankees to the A's to the Brewers and finally the Dodgers, where, in 1971, he finally won 20 games. He was still effective enough to go 9-9 in 1973, and with an impressive 124 strikeouts in 155 innings. He felt the weight of the moment on April 8, 1974, as the country tuned in to witness Aaron beat him and Babe Ruth with the same swing.

"He knows what I can throw. He hit two home runs off me last year," Downing said before the game. "But I'm not going to change my pattern. I can't go against what I've been successful with." Downing lost the battle, of course, but it was hardly a blemish on his career. He remained with the Dodgers until the 1977 season, finally retiring with 123 career wins, 1,639 strikeouts, and at least one home run he'll never forget.

Hank Aaron, Al Downing.

ted's excellent adventure

16

*"I bought the Braves because I'm tired of seeing
them kicked around. I'm the little guy's hero."*

—Ted Turner, 1976

In 1975 there was a small UHF station

in Atlanta, WTCG, whose reception was so poor the signal would sometimes
disappear in the city's outlying areas. WTCG, the fourth station in a market
of four, had no original programming that could compete with the other
stations in town. It ran old movies, "Leave It to Beaver," "I Love Lucy," and
other reruns, but nothing that the station's owner, Ted Turner, could really
count on to draw the viewers he wanted. So Turner decided to take a chance
on the mediocre Braves, offering the club $3 million to broadcast sixty games
a year for five seasons.　Although the Braves organization worried that
the broadcast schedule might result in overexposure in the local market, and
adversely effect gate receipts—would people really be interested in coming to

Bill Bartholomay (left) and Ted Turner.

Bill Lucas

Even though Ted Turner never pretended to be a baseball expert, one of his wisest personnel decisions came in the 1977 season, when he chose Bill Lucas to be the Braves' general manager. Lucas had previously run the Braves' farm system and was credited with cultivating the talents of such prospects as Dale Murphy and Brett Butler. But until 1977, Lucas had one hurdle in his way: he was black, and there were no black general managers in baseball. Turner pushed right past that taboo, saying, "I don't care what color he is, Bill Lucas is the best man to help me run the Braves."

That decision was applauded throughout the major league community, and helped the Braves win the hearts of Atlanta. Club executives still recall with a smile the time Lucas crashed the 1972 All-Star Game party, which was being held in Atlanta. For years baseball's off-field festivities were restricted to stag-only. Lucas was on his way to the party and saw the wife of Braves public relations man Bob Hope being turned away at the door. Lucas took her arm and said, "Let's go have a drink." When Susan Hope explained she wasn't allowed in, Lucas said, "Look, my people weren't allowed to enter nice places for years, either. Come on, someone's got to be the first woman to integrate baseball." And the two walked in.

In just three seasons, Lucas established himself as one of the most well-respected and well-liked general managers in baseball. But he died suddenly in 1979 of an aneurysm, at the age of forty-three. Lucas never got to see the dividend of his hard work in the '70s, as the Braves finally won the Western Division in 1982, but as Ted Turner said at Lucas' funeral, "Now Bill is the general manager of a team that has Babe Ruth, Ty Cobb, and Lou Gehrig."

Bill Lucas.

Atlanta-Fulton County Stadium after seeing how the team played sixty times a year?—the cash infusion helped keep them in Atlanta. For in 1975, rumors were everywhere that the franchise was ready to move again, this time to Denver, or perhaps Toronto. After all, Henry Aaron's pursuit of Babe Ruth's home-run record was over, and Aaron himself was gone. The Braves had won only 67 games in '75, finishing 40½ games out of first place, and not surprisingly drew a mere 534,000 fans. But there was Turner, a local entrepreneur who also owned a billboard company, suddenly marketing this baseball team that no one was interested in. The Braves were his passion, and he was not about to let them die. Of course, not everyone in the Braves' organization was initially thrilled by the association with Turner. "It didn't seem right for a big-league team to be on a Mickey Mouse station with a reputation for showing only cartoons, grade-D movies, and 1950s reruns," the team's public relations director, Bob Hope, said. "We weren't even sure people could get WTCG on their TV sets."

But the idea of multi-market TV stations was beginning to grow in the '70s, and Turner resold the rights to broadcast the Braves to twenty-four other stations across six southern states, creating a regional network for Braves baseball. Turner's expansion didn't stop there, though. He was also deeply committed to the idea of cable. When Donald Andersson, a vice-president of research for the National Cable Television Association, a powerful industry lobby, mentioned to Turner that cable would be driven by movies and sports, Turner was prompted to blurt out, "Would it help if I bought the Braves?"

The resulting sale was almost effortless, and on January 6, 1976, Ted Turner became the Braves' new owner, paying $11 million to the Chicago-based Atlanta-LaSalle Corporation, which had controlled the Braves ever since they moved from Milwaukee in 1966. The National League's owners and Baseball Commissioner Bowie Kuhn had to approve the sale, which they did, although no one was really sure what to expect from this outsider. Turner knew virtually nothing about baseball management and personally shot a commercial to pitch season tickets. In the ad Turner, holding a bat and wearing a Braves cap, talked about baseball's family virtues and then said, "Call me when you need anything from the Braves. If you can't reach me, call my pal Bob Hope at the stadium."

Turner's first task was to make the Braves if not successful, then at least interesting, and he didn't mind personally taking up the cause. He introduced himself to a sold-out crowd on Opening Day at Atlanta-Fulton County Stadium in 1976, then won the crowd's hearts in the first inning. When the Braves' Ken Henderson hit a long home run to right, Turner jumped out of his field-level box to shake Henderson's hand as he reached home plate. The Braves themselves smiled in amusement, thankful that someone cared that much, even if Turner was a bit unorthodox in expressing his affection.

"There's never been an owner like him. I think he'd like to put on a uniform and play in the game," Phil Niekro said. That zealous attitude would eventually cause Turner problems, and he inadvertently created some enemies in baseball, especially among the old-guard baseball purists. Bob Howsam, the Cincinnati Reds' chairman, said Turner would be arrested on the spot if he ever attempted to run on the field in Riverfront Stadium, and Commissioner Bowie Kuhn would soon become an enemy of Turner's as well.

Among his many provocative ideas, Turner briefly considered changing the team's name to the Eagles, in honor of the yacht with which he would eventually win the America's Cup. The story was leaked to the media, and the national response was swift and angry: how dare Tuner consider tampering with the Braves' tradition? Turner quickly backed off, but realized at the same time that as a baseball owner he had a national audience. The major leagues mattered, so Turner made up his mind to do anything and everything to enhance the strength of his franchise. That meant he needed to draw more fans to the ballpark. Turner told Bob Hope, "I want this team to be like McDonald's. I want an atmosphere that will make kids want to come to the ballpark." Hope rattled off the traditional promotional events the Braves had planned—Fan Appreciation Day, Old Timers Day, Bat Day—and Turner dismissed them all with a wave. "That's not good enough," he said.

What Turner demanded was creativity. He decided the Braves' front office work day would begin at 8:30 A.M. instead of 9 A.M. so, "We'll have a thirty-minute head start on the rest of the other teams." Hope was not really sure that anyone would get a jump on anyone else in the major leagues by showing up a half-hour early, but Turner's call for more imaginative promotions hit home. On the first Sunday of the 1976 season, Hope introduced one of the world's largest Easter egg hunts—on the stadium field—and that was only the beginning. Hope decided to serve watermelon to the fans after one game on July 6, but to make it a truly special event, he called for a frog-jumping contest as well. Trouble was, the Braves weren't sure they could provide enough frogs—so Hope urged fans, on radio and TV and in the newspapers, to "bring your own frog." The contest was a huge success. Fans brought frogs by the dozens to the park in picnic coolers. Following the game, fans and frogs alike swarmed the infield for the contest. The post-game antics attracted national attention.

Hope thought it was important for fans to share the experience of walking on the field, so entire towns routinely appeared at home plate for one ceremony or another. Mayors showed up, cheerleaders, high school athletes, Boy Scouts, national anthem singers—anyone and everyone. And the Braves had a liberal policy about the anthem: If you wanted to sing, you could, no questions asked.

In the summer of '76, while the Olympics were being held in Montreal, the team held their own Braves Olympics. Before a game with the Phillies, the team provided basketballs, footballs, barrels, and hula hoops for a series of contests between the players. One contest called for the throwing a basketball from home plate into a barrel placed on second base, and throwing a football into a peach basket. Under Turner's new promotions policy, nothing was too outrageous. Still, only two courageous souls were willing to enter the Great Baseball Nose Push—which required contestants to get on all fours and push the ball down the base lines to home plate with their noses. The first one to cross the plate would win. The Phillies' Tug McGraw, an independent thinker, gladly volunteered—his eager opponent was Ted Turner himself. The crowd went wild watching this unpretentious executive with his face in the dirt, so intent on bringing the Braves a victory, any victory, that when he did cross home plate ahead of McGraw, his face was covered in blood. Turner held the ball over his head in triumph, and he still keeps the ball in his office as a memento.

One of the other innovative promotions the Braves unveiled in the late '70s included an ostrich race, in which Turner took on *Atlanta Journal* sportswriter Frank Hyland; Braves' sportscasters Skip Caray, Ernie Johnson, and Pete Van Wieren; and a local disc jockey, Skinny Bobby Harper. Public relations man Hope wanted to authenticate the race, in which the ostriches would pull the jockeys in carts as in harness-racing, so he called the racetrack at Churchill Downs looking for bright silk shirts for the contestants. Hyland was given a shirt with the nickname "Poison Pen" on the back; Johnson was simply "Big E." Turner was "Teddy Ballgame," although Turner preferred to be called simply "Ted" and used a razor to remove "Ballgame" from his shirt.

The race, which took place before the Braves played the Dodgers, was conducted in heats, and in the first one Skinny Bobby Harper's ostrich ran right up to the Dodgers dugout. In the second heat, Turner's ostrich went berserk, running directly into the outfield rather than along the first base line and

around the outfield warning track as planned. It then made a direct path toward the Dodgers' dugout, scattering terrified players. Sportswriter Hyland's ostrich, on the other hand, behaved wonderfully.

Later there would be the Cash Scramble, in which $25,000 in single dollar bills was littered all over the field and five or six people were allowed ninety seconds to collect as much money as possible. The idea was attractive to fans but the Braves knew it was a safe and surprisingly cheap give-away, since it was only possible for any one person to collect $300 or $400 in that time. As Hope said, "We could have had a $100,000 or a $1 million Cash Scramble and it wouldn't have cost us any more money." Even so, the Braves ensured the moment would be as dramatic as possible, bringing in the National Guard to deliver the money from a Brinks armored truck and patrol the field. Little did anyone in the stands know, it was just play money, redeemable for the real thing after the game. There was also the Wishbone Salad Dressing Night, in which fans were allowed to scramble through an enormous salad bowl at home plate in hopes of finding the key to a brand-new automobile.

One unusual idea was Wedlock Night, when the Braves invited Atlanta couples to get married at Atlanta-Fulton County Stadium. Thirty-four couples responded, and with their groomsmen, bridesmaids, and attendants on hand, hundreds of people filled the field. Headlock Night was Ted Turner's idea, a promotion that grew out of a promise he had made to his friend, Jim Barnett, who owned Georgia Championship Wrestling. The promise was to hold a wrestling event at a Braves game. Since the only date available was the same as Wedlock Night, July 11, 1976, Turner and Hope decided to have both promotions on the same day. So, on Wedlock and Headlock Night, after the weddings and after the Braves played the Mets, everyone gathered around a wrestling ring set up on the field and got their fill of body slams and choke holds.

At one point that summer, the Braves invited the famous high-wire walker Karl Wallenda to perform at the stadium between games of a doubleheader, a stunt consistent with every other promotion the Braves had pulled that year. But on the day the elderly performer was scheduled to walk without a safety net along a 300-foot wire strung atop the stadium, which spanned the distance between first and third base, the winds were howling. "Cancel the walk," Turner instructed Hope. "Tell him it's too risky." Wallenda, of course, wouldn't back down from any wind, and with the Braves, the crowd—not to mention Turner and Hope—watching and gasping, Wallenda completed his walk above their heads. It took him twelve minutes, and every few steps he appeared almost to lose his balance. That was more for show, of course, and in the end everyone was satisfied.

Turner's goal in 1976 was to have a promotion for every single game played at Atlanta-Fulton County Stadium, which pushed Hope and his staff to their limits. There were the usual events for these home games, like Photo Day and Ladies Day, which were built into the schedules of more traditional franchises, but Turner made it clear he wanted to do more and different promotions. That meant Bathtub Races had to be run, wet T-shirt contests had to be held . . . the list of events was almost endless on Hope's watch. Perhaps the strangest attraction Hope thought of was combining the Mattress Stacking contest with 25-cent beer night.

Seventy-year-old Karl Wallenda nearing the end of his dramatic high-wire walk across the stadium. Several years later, Wallenda died when he fell attempting a similar stunt between two high-rise buildings in San Juan, Puerto Rico.

TED'S EXCELLENT ADVENTURE

Atlanta Braves logo decal from the '70s.

That attracted college fraternities and sororities from across the Southeast, all of whom were hoping to earn an entry into the *Guinness Book of World Records*. The idea was to stack as many people as possible on top of a single mattress in one minute, and one fraternity, Sigma Chi of Emory University, somehow attracted Turner to its ranks. There he was, the owner of the Braves, on the bottom of a pile of college kids, his facing turning red, then blue, as the stack of bodies grew higher and higher. Turner's team didn't win, but he decided never to try that trick again. "I've got to stop," he said. "I'll kill myself and I've never been to a World Series."

These wonderful and crazy promotions had a tremendous effect on the Braves' attendance figures. The team drew more than 800,000 fans in 1976, an increase of more than 50 percent from 1975. The contests were new and funny, and for the time being, Atlanta residents enjoyed them. But sooner or later the burden of drawing people to the stadium would fall on the Braves players, not the Braves publicity office. Turner was well aware of the need to improve his team, and for that reason made public his wish to sign outfielder Gary Matthews. Matthews, a member of the San Francisco Giants, was a twenty-six-year-old who hit .279 with 20 home runs in 1976. Matthews figured to command a large salary from potential suitors, but Turner had made up his mind: whatever it cost, whatever it took, Matthews would be playing for the Braves in 1977. As an outsider to the baseball hierarchy, however, Turner learned the hard way that being blunt can be expensive.

Turner had already been fined $10,000 in the summer of '76 for talking to Matthews while he was still a member of the Giants—

Donald Davidson began his association with the Braves as a batboy in Boston in the 1930s, but is best remembered as the team's traveling secretary in the '60s and '70s.

a clear violation of baseball's tampering rules, which state no team can negotiate with another team's players. That fall, during a World Series party thrown for the major league's executives, Turner approached Giants owner Bob Lurie and asked point-blank, "Where's my $10,000?" Lurie responded with a thinly-veiled warning to Turner, cautioning him that "[Pursuing Matthews] may cost you more than that. You're aware you can't make him an offer until November 4 [two weeks after the conclusion of the World Series]."

If Turner couldn't begin negotiating with Matthews, he certainly could throw a party for him. That's exactly what the Braves did, inviting the outfielder to Atlanta, making sure every important person in town was there, and allowing Matthews the chance to enjoy a little southern hospitality. Turner went as far as to construct a billboard at the airport which read: Welcome to Atlanta, Gary Matthews! Turner reasoned there was nothing in baseball's tampering rules that prohibited offering a player a tour of a city, but Turner apparently went too far when he promised Lurie, "When the time comes, I'm going to offer [Matthews] more money than the Giants will take in next year."

Unfortunately for Turner, several reporters witnessed this exchange and it appeared in the papers the next day. That served to further infuriated Commissioner Kuhn, who by now was growing tired of Turner and his wild ways. (Previously, Turner had irritated the baseball establishment by signing the first free agent ever, pitcher Andy Messersmith, the opening game of the 1976 season. A judge had declared Messersmith a free agent, but that didn't mean the owners would court him. In fact, it's possible Messersmith would have been blackballed as punishment for beating baseball through the courts, but Turner boldly and without hesitation broke ranks.) So when Matthews finally did sign with the Braves, Kuhn announced Turner would be punished, the terms of which would be announced at baseball winter meetings held that December.

Ted Turner gets his man, Gary Matthews, in a controversial 1977 signing. Matthews spent four years with the Braves, his best season occurring in 1979 when he hit .304 with 27 homers and 90 RBIs.

Turner seemed unperturbed. "Kuhn can give Matthews back to the Giants," he said, "but he won't do that because he'd be punishing Matthews. He could fine me, but that won't do him any good. I'd just pay and be perfectly happy. Or he could suspend me, kick me out for a whole season, get me out of the way. He's been wanting to get rid of me. This is his chance."

The Braves' owner was right: In a three-page notice of suspension from the Commissioner, Turner was fined $35,000 and prohibited for one year from "exercising any powers, duties or authority in connection with the management of the Atlanta club, visit or be physically be present in the Atlanta clubhouse or offices." This edict was to take effect on June 1, 1977, and Turner accepted the terms without a fight. (But he didn't disappear. Later that off-season he quietly closed a deal which would give him 95 percent controlling interest in the Atlanta Hawks basketball team—all for just $400,000 and a $1 million note.)

In 1977, Turner proved just how much he truly sought the spotlight—or at least, how far he was willing to go to take the heat off his beloved Braves. Despite signing Matthews and Jeff Burroughs, a former American League Most Valuable Player who had been obtained from the Texas Rangers during the off-season, the Braves were still playing terribly. On May 10, 1977, the Braves lost their sixteenth straight game, and the next morning Turner told Hope there would be a new manager: Robert Edward Turner III, himself. This was not a publicity

Braves players provide
an arch for couples who
are about to exchange
wedding vows at home
plate prior to an Atlanta
game. Professional
wrestling followed the
game on "Headlock and
Wedlock" night.

stunt, but by no means was he firing his real manager, Dave Bristol, either. Turner simply wanted to change the luck of a team that needed any break it could get. As for Bristol, Turner told him he could go home for a day or two, rest up, and be ready when the Braves were returned to him as winners.

The team was in Pittsburgh, finishing up a brutal road trip, when Turner arrived. He made it to the ballpark early, put on a uniform, and just to get into the proper mindset ran wind sprints in the outfield. Turner was in love with the idea of piloting the team, although he was the first to admit he had no real knowledge of the game. For that reason, Turner surrounded himself with the Braves' brain trust, as third base coach Vern Benson dictated the in-game strategy, and pitching coach Johnny Sain decided how best to use the Braves' bullpen. Chris Cannizzaro, who was the bullpen coach, was brought into the dugout to keep Turner appraised of the inning-by-inning situation.

The Braves lost the game, 2-1, although Turner was responsible for an unorthodox personnel decision late in the game with runners on first and second and the Pirates leading 2-0. Turner inserted Darrel Chaney as a pinch-hitter, despite the fact that Chaney had only four plate appearances as a pinch-hitter

the year before. Yet Turner's hunch paid a dividend, as Chaney hit a ground-rule double into the left-field corner, cutting the Pirates' lead to 2-1. Had the ball not bounced over the wall, one more run would have been scored and the Braves would have tied the game. Turner in fact might have left the dugout with the best winning percentage in the history of baseball, because the very next day, National League president Chub Feeney prohibited Turner from managing again, citing Rule 20, Section A, which says no player or manager could own stock in the club.

The Braves didn't perform any better in 1977 than in 1976—they lost 101 games and finished 37 games behind the first-place Dodgers. But attendance rose again, and on the way was a new manager, Bobby Cox, and with him a hint of better times to come. As for Ted Turner, his involvement with the Braves began to diminish as his superstation, now called WTBS, grew along with his idea for a twenty-four-hour cable news network, which by 1980 became a reality. CNN's debut marked the official end of Ted Turner's day-to-day interest in the Braves, but his legacy was now unmistakable. And in case anyone wasn't sure, Turner would tell them. He said, "If it wasn't for WTCG, we wouldn't have had a basketball team here in Atlanta. We might not even have had a baseball team. When I do something, I try to do it the best way I know how. I think my life has been a reflection of that."

Braves broadcasters
Pete Van Wieren (left)
and Ernie Johnson
(right) don their racing
silks before climbing
into sulkies for pregame
ostrich racing.

Back to Bouton

The '70s were a time for gimmicks in Atlanta, and one of the more interesting involved not an ostrich or a wet T-shirt, but a pitcher. A real one. A former New York Yankee, at that.

Jim Bouton had shocked the baseball world by writing *Ball Four* in 1970, a diary of a season with the Seattle Pilots. Although he had made some enemies within the Yankee empire, Bouton's real legacy was that of a hard-throwing right-hander who won 21 games in 1963 and two games in the 1964 World Series. But Bouton had hurt his arm in 1967 and not long after drifted out of baseball.

In 1977 Bouton, then thirty-eight, encountered Ted Turner in New York. Bouton had already been offered a chance to return to baseball by the White Sox and had gone 6-11 that summer in Chicago's minor league system, but he wanted back in the majors and wouldn't relent. He had learned to throw a knuckleball and asked Turner for a chance with the Braves.

Jim Bouton.

"I said, 'Ted, you're thirty-nine and you're not washed up. I know I'm not, either,'" Bouton recalled. Turner laughed and granted the former Yankee his wish. Bouton went to the minor leagues, ignoring all the curious stares and hostile remarks that often came from his own Double-A teammates. Bouton's turning point came in an exhibition game the Savannah team played against the major league Braves, in which Bouton not only pitched, but struck out seven batters in seven innings. Duly impressed, the Braves summoned Bouton to the big leagues in September 1978.

What was there to lose? The Braves themselves were awful, and Bouton was just another attraction at Atlanta-Fulton County Stadium's freak show. But he proved his detractors wrong. In his first start against the Dodgers, Bouton pitched three hitless innings. He smiled as he heard the Dodgers yelling from the dugout, "You've got nothing" or "You don't belong here" or "We're hitting against Bozo the clown." In his next start, Bouton beat the San Francisco Giants, 4-1. He then left in the eighth inning against the Astros, tied, 2-2, and afterward allowed only five hits in eight innings against the Reds in a 2-1 loss.

In all, Bouton was 1-3 in 1978, a thirty-nine-year-old kid who'd satisfied a dream. "And for that, I have only Ted Turner to thank," he said.

17

"We're becoming America's Team."
—Ted Turner, 1981

The Braves lost a total of 187 games

in 1978 and 1979, and while it may have looked to an outsider as if there was no reason to believe the team's decade-long slump would ease in the '80s, there were internal changes that hinted at better times ahead. First there was a new manager—a rookie, but one who had already earned the respect of his peers. Bobby Cox was hired away from the Yankees in 1978 and asked to overhaul the National League's worst franchise. At thirty-seven, Cox was still young enough to be in touch with the players he was now managing, but old enough to command their respect as well. A former third baseman, Cox had played for the Yankees. His future had seemed especially bright in New York when he beat out Mike Ferraro for the

Glenn Hubbard turns the doubleplay, eluding the Dodgers' Mike Scioscia.

third base job in 1968 and was named to the Topps Rookie All-Star team before losing his job to Bobby Murcer in 1969. After bad knees forced his retirement in 1971, Cox began a successful managerial career with the New York Yankees, where from 1971 to 1976 his farm teams never finished below .500. The baseball community took notice of Cox, a knowledgeable, easygoing man, and after one year as the Yankees' third base coach in 1977, Ted Turner asked him to deliver the Braves from themselves.

The Braves finished in last place in each of Cox's first two seasons as manager, but there were some reasons to believe the team's slide would reverse itself. For starters, there was the always reliable Phil Niekro, who had won forty games in 1978 and 1979, and there was Dale Murphy, a first baseman with a devastating home-run swing, and Bob Horner, who joined the Braves in 1978 direct from the campus of Arizona State University, where he had been one of the nation's top collegiate ballplayers. Relief pitcher Gene Garber was also added to the team in 1978, acquired from the Phillies. Garber and starting pitcher Larry McWilliams were responsible for stopping Pete Rose's hitting streak at 44 games—the last serious assault on Joe

DiMaggio's 56-game record, which was the most by any National League player in the twentieth century.

Although the sudden death of general manager Bill Lucas proved a serious setback for the team in 1979, the Braves continued to make progress in 1980. Cox pushed for the acquisition of Chris Chambliss of the New York Yankees, the first baseman who had broken the hearts of the Kansas City Royals in the fifth and deciding game of the 1976 American League Championship Series when he hit a ninth-inning home run that sent the Yankees to the World Series, where they lost to the Reds. Chambliss was now a member of the Braves, a seasoned veteran who would provide quiet leadership to the team.

As testimony to Cox's managerial skills and the number of quality players added to the team roster, the Braves improved to 81-80 in 1980—the first time they finished above .500 since 1974—and drew more than one million fans in the process. A year later, a players' strike disrupted the team's momentum, but by 1982, the National League West stumbled on a new powerhouse, the Atlanta Braves. For those who hadn't been watching closely, the Braves' rebirth was a complete surprise. Even though Atlanta boasted a lineup that included Dale Murphy, the National League's Most Valuable Player, in center field; Bob Horner at third base; and pitching ace Phil Niekro; no one was sure what to expect of the rest of the crew. But shortstop Rafael Ramirez, catcher Bruce Benedict, right fielder Claudell Washington, and second baseman Glenn Hubbard were about to have their best years.

The Braves' community credited Cox with assembling this team and wished that he were around to enjoy the fruits of his labors. But Cox had been fired at the end of the 1981 season and was replaced by Joe Torre, who himself had been fired that same season by the New York Mets. Torre had played for the Braves from 1960 to 1968 before being traded to the St. Louis Cardinals. A career .297 hitter, Torre was best remembered by Atlanta fans for batting .315 in 1966 and driving in 101 runs on the way to hitting a career-high

Bobby Cox during his first term as Braves manager (1978–81). After four years in Toronto, Cox returned to the Braves as general manager in 1986, and resumed his managerial career after Russ Nixon was fired in 1990.

Braves manager Bobby Cox (second from right) argues his case with umpire Gerry Crawford, while Braves infielders Pepe Fries and Glenn Hubbard try their luck with crew chief John Kibler.

36 home runs. Torre was now back, but that didn't mean Cox was forgotten. In fact, Ted Turner felt so guilty about replacing him that he had invited Cox to the press conference announcing his dismissal.

There were some in the Braves' organization who felt that, having worked so hard to create a sound foundation, Cox should have been allowed to stay. And if a change had to be made, Turner's baseball experts said, they preferred Triple-A manager Eddie Haas, a lifelong baseball man with impeccable credentials. But Turner overruled them, claiming he wanted someone with major-league managing experience. What Ted Turner didn't say was that TV played a role in this decision, too. TBS was now showing 130 Braves games a year all over the country, and suddenly, the Braves had fans everywhere who were showing up at Braves road games with signs and banners professing their affection for "America's Team." *Sports Illustrated* even ran a piece on this new phenomenon: total strangers falling in love with the Braves through the TV set.

According to some observers, it was network television executives who pressured Ted Turner into hiring Torre. If the Braves were going to be a high-profile team that played in markets all over the country, then they needed a media-polished manager like Torre, who had just spent five years in the toughest media market of all, New York City. Torre was intelligent, well-spoken, and gave a terrific interview. Cox was more reserved than Torre, and although his knowledge of the game was beyond reproach, that quality in itself wasn't enough to appease Turner's TV experts. As for Haas, well, he might have known his baseball, but no one outside of Atlanta's front office had ever heard of him. So Turner worked hard to promote his manager, telling reporters at a press conference, "We wanted someone who wasn't old, and Joe's not old. And he doesn't have a drinking problem like some of the candidates have. Drinking problems are easy to get in baseball. I've traveled a lot with the team, and those hotels in Cincinnati and Pittsburgh make it a long life."

what should have been the game-winning hit. Linares, who spoke only a little English, smiled afterwards and said in his gravelly voice, "I dive for ball. I look to left, no ball. I look to right, no ball. I look in glove, ball. I say, 'Rufi, you one lucky guy.' " The next inning, the Braves won the game.

The Braves saved their best theater, however, for the twelfth win, which set a major league record for the longest winning streak at the start of the season, as well as for their thirteenth, which extended that record. In win No. 12, the Reds took an early lead against Tommy Boggs, as he walked four in 1⅔ innings. Rookie Steve Bedrosian arrived to calm the Reds, though, throwing 4⅓ shutout innings. Meanwhile, the Braves exploded for four runs in the third inning, including solo home runs from Chris Chambliss and Rafael Ramirez, and Claudell Washington's two-run triple. With a crowd of 37,268 roaring on every pitch, Gene Garber worked the final three innings, allowing only one hit, as the Braves held on for a 4-2 victory. When left fielder Dale Murphy caught Dan Driessen's fly ball for the final out, hundreds of fans spilled onto the field to celebrate the victory and the Braves' entry into the

Joe Torre sat next to Ted Turner at the podium, smiling at his boss' blunt words. Torre made sure to say the Braves weren't in any rebuilding process, instead proclaiming them to be "on the verge of winning." How right Torre was, and how politically astute he was in not treading on the lingering loyalty many Braves fans felt towards Cox. More than once during the 1982 season, Torre told reporters, "This is Bobby Cox's team." Despite a spring-training injury to Phil Niekro, the Braves won their first thirteen games, and if there were any doubts about how serious the Braves were about taking the West, those doubts had vanished by mid-April. The pitching staff included respected players like Rick Mahler and Rick Camp, and in center field there was a tough, fast kid named Brett Butler, whom Cox had spotted in the minor leagues. A year earlier Cox had predicted, "This Brett Butler is going to be our lead-off hitter very soon."

Everyone was a hero in those thirteen games. One day in Cincinnati, as the Braves were locked in an extra-inning duel, a line drive was hit to the gap in left-center, prompting a full-out dive from Rufino Linares. The Braves outfielder—known for his bat, not his glove—stretched and somehow caught the ball, robbing the Reds of

record books. "We wanted the record because it was an immediate goal that would help us get the respect we desire," said Chambliss.

"Considering no one else in baseball history has done it," Joe Torre added, "considering that baseball has been around more than one hundred years, it's incredible."

Win No. 13 was more than drama, it was almost eery. The Braves seemed ready to fold at the hands Cincinnati right-hander Mario Soto, who was cruising along with a 3-1 lead, having struck out seven in the first 6⅓ innings. But in the bottom of the ninth, the Braves, now trailing 3-2, had runners on first and second. Brett Butler hit a ground ball toward short, and, with Dave Concepcion waiting, a 6-4-3 game-ending, streak-ending doubleplay seemed a certainty. But the ball never reached Concepcion: it struck rookie catcher Matt Sinatro as he was trying to advance from second to third. Sinatro was called out, for out No. 2, but more importantly, the doubleplay was foiled. With runners on first and second and two out, Reds reliever Jim Kern threw a wild pitch, advancing the runners, and Biff Pocoroba was then intentionally walked to load the bases.

With Claudell Washington due up next, the Reds brought in left-hander Joe Price, who promptly surrendered a two-run single to Washington, ending the dramatic, 4-3 come-from-behind victory—No. 13, which was later matched by the 1987 Milwaukee Brewers for the longest unbeaten streak at the start of a major league season.

This kind fate lasted through much of the summer, and by July 29 the Braves had a stunning nine-game lead in the division. Then disaster struck: They lost nineteen of twenty-one games, and everyone was looking for a scapegoat. Some fans even went as far as to wonder if Chief Noc-a-Homa had cast a spell on the Braves after his teepee was taken down and his plot used for extra seating.

The Braves and Dodgers traded places several times in the final six weeks of the season, neither team putting together a long-enough winning streak to clinch the division. Actually, the race was bitterly fought into the final seven games, which found the Braves on a West Coast trip. They started in San Francisco against a hard-charging Giants team that had stormed back from a 13½ game July deficit to a 84-71 dead-heat with the Braves, one game behind the Dodgers. The Braves turned to forty-three-year old Phil Niekro, who served up his first shutout of the

A RETURN TO RESPECTABILITY—BRIEFLY

season, a 7-0 two-hitter that lifted the Braves back into a first place tie with the Dodgers. (The Dodgers had dropped a 6-1 decision to the Reds.) A relaxed Braves team was testimony to Niekro, who observed after the game, "We've been through the sunny days, and we've been through the thunderstorms. There's not a lot that's going to rattle this team right now, not with what we've been through this season."

The next night, the Braves struck for five runs in the third to take a 6-1 lead, but a struggling Rick Mahler gave way to Pascual Perez in the bottom of the third, after the Giants cut Atlanta's lead to 6-3. Perez stopped the Giants thereafter, allowing only three hits over 6.2 innings. The Braves completed a two-game sweep of San Francisco with an 8-3 victory, and also took sole possession of first place after the Dodgers' seventh straight loss, a 4-3 setback in ten innings. The Braves promptly extended their lead to two games with four remaining by beating the Dodgers, 4-3, in twelve innings, in a contest highlighted by great pitching and defense on both

sides. Gene Garber pitched out of a bases loaded, one-out situation in the bottom of the ninth to send the game into extra innings, when run-scoring singles by Terry Harper and Jerry Royster proved too much for Los Angeles to overcome.

Royster served as a catalyst for the Braves in the second half, hitting .326 after July 28 while rotating between left field, shortstop, and second base, before replacing the injured Horner at third over the season's final two weeks (Horner suffered a hyperextended left elbow on September 18 in a game against the Reds.). From August 4 on, Royster compiled hitting streaks of 17, 12, and 8 games, the latter streak making up the last 8 games of the regular season.

The Dodgers roughed up Rick Camp early the next night and came away with a 10-3 win, cutting the Braves lead back to one game. But in game No.160, Phil Niekro again stepped to the forefront in the first game of the season-ending, three-game series in San Diego, delivering his second straight shutout in a 4-0 triumph over the Padres, and aiding his own cause with his first homer since 1976. The two-run blow came in the eighth inning with Niekro holding on to a 1-0 lead, and even Padres fans were moved to cheer Niekro as he rounded the bases. The homer capped a pretty fair road trip for the Braves' elder statesman. Niekro had risen to the occasion in his final two starts of the campaign with eighteen shutout innings, while allowing only five hits.

Los Angeles remained a game behind by beating the Giants, 4-0, but saw the Braves clinch a tie for the Western Division title the following night with their 4-2 win over the Padres. The Dodgers eliminated the Giants from the race that night in a 15-2 rout, sending the season into its final day with the Braves maintaining their one-game lead. Then, after Atlanta lost the season finale, 5-1, a one-game playoff in Los Angeles loomed on the horizon if the Dodgers completed a three-game sweep of the Giants.

The Braves' mood was grim in the moments leading up to their defeat. With one out in the ninth inning Jerry Royster flied out to center field and trotted back to a silent dugout. At that moment, manager Torre sidled up to him and said, "Don't worry about a thing. Joe Morgan just hit a home run. We're going to win the pennant." Torre couldn't have uttered better news: Someone

had called the Braves dugout to relay the important development from San Francisco, where Giants second baseman Joe Morgan had just slammed a three-run homer off Dodgers reliever Terry Forster. Instead of wallowing in any post-game depression after losing to the Padres, the Braves sprinted to the clubhouse to watch the final inning of the Giants' game with the Dodgers. If the Dodgers won, the West would end in a tie, necessitating a one-game playoff to determine who would face the St. Louis Cardinals for the right to go to the World Series.

Morgan's eighth-inning home run had put the Giants ahead, 5-3, and although the Giants had no interest in whether the Braves won the West, they took great pleasure in spoiling the race for their hated rivals, the Dodgers. For nearly a half-hour, the Braves were huddled around their clubhouse TV set, hoping the Giants' antipathy towards the Dodgers would translate into a division crown. The Dodgers rallied but fell short, and after L.A.'s last out, the Braves exploded in a celebration. Bob Horner raised a glass of champagne and shouted, "A toast to the San Francisco Giants!" Phil Niekro wept openly, telling reporters, "I've always wanted to pitch in a World Series. Hopefully this is the year it will happen."

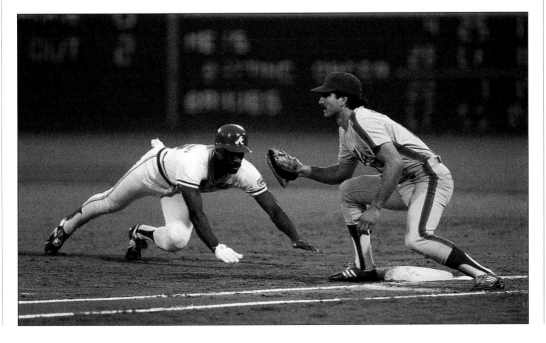

Claudell Washington, signed by the Braves as a free agent in 1981, helped them to a division title in 1982 (.266, 16 HR, 80 RBIs, and 33 SB).

Bruce Benedict holds on to the ball after tagging out the Dodgers' John Shelby. Benedict was one of Atlanta's most popular players during his twelve-year stay (1978–89). His best season came in 1983 when he hit .298. Benedict rejoined the Braves organization in 1993 as a minor league manager.

"The past seven years have been tough," Jerry Royster added, "but this puts it all in perspective. We've been through 100-loss seasons, seventeen-game losing streaks, one bad thing after another . . . now we get this. Everything Ted Turner has been involved in has been a success, except us. I'm just glad we're a success now." Across the room in the manager's office, Torre slumped deep in his chair and said, "Thank God for Joe Morgan."

Of course, Turner wasn't about to miss out on the festivities. He had accompanied the team to the West Coast and was right in the middle of a champagne shower, working a cigar in his mouth, reflecting on his team's long, painful road to prosperity. "This makes everything I went through—everything we went through—worth it," Turner said. "Two years ago I was having lunch with the owner of the [NFL] Falcons, and he asked me, 'How does it feel to be the owner of a team that loses one hundred games a year?' I told him, 'You're looking at it wrong. We're not a team that loses one hundred games, but wins sixty games a year.' And I said, 'Your team doesn't win sixty games in ten years.'"

For the first time in thirteen years, the Braves could make plans for the Championship Series—only this time they weren't facing a miracle team from New York but a dangerous, well-managed group from St. Louis. The Cardinals had won 92 games in 1982, finishing three games ahead of the Phillies. Their offense was led by outfielder Lonnie Smith, who batted .307 with 68 stolen bases, and the pitching staff was anchored by Joaquin Andujar, who had posted the second-best ERA in the National League, 2.47. The Cardinals played outstanding defense, liked to steal bases, use the hit-and-run play, and otherwise do anything and everything to manufacture offense without home runs. They were the product of their manager, Whitey Herzog, who was considered the finest strategist of his day.

The Cardinals were heavily favored in the National League Championship Series, primarily because the Braves' pitching was decimated. Aside from Phil Niekro, who had won seventeen games that season, the Braves had no dominant pitchers. Between right-handers Pascual Perez, Rick Camp, and Rick Mahler, not one of them was above .500 that year, and there were no left-handers on the staff at all. In essence, Joe Torre had to start Niekro and—like the Braves teams of the '50s who relied on Warren Spahn and Johnny Sain—pray for rain.

The weather gods actually heard Torre's prayers, but the timing couldn't have been worse for the Braves. In Game One of the best-of-five series, Atlanta was leading 1-0 in the fifth inning, with Niekro's knuckleball doing a wonderful job of frustrating the Cardinals. In fact, he had allowed them only four hits, and needed just another ⅔ of an inning for the game to be considered official. But then came the rain—a steady and sometimes heavy drizzle that lasted eighty-eight minutes. The Braves watched in agony, hoping for any kind of letup. Not only were they missing a chance to beat the Cardinals, but if the game was canceled, they would lose Niekro for at least two days while he rested his arm. The umpires were faced with an equally troubling problem. They could have allowed for another two outs, and after five innings yielded to the rain. At least after five full innings, the result would have been considered official. But having a rain-shortened game in the playoffs would have compromised the post-season's integrity, and for that reason the umpires stopped play just as the Braves were approaching what technically would have been a Game One win.

Torre tried hard to mask his disappointment, but accepted his team's fate gracefully. "I have no bitterness or animosity whatsoever," he said. "I understand it's a playoff game and they don't want a game won by just playing five innings. On the other hand, it wasn't raining very hard when they called the game. You never see time called with so little rain." Umpire crew chief Billy Williams disagreed: "It was more than a drizzle. It wasn't a downpour, but definitely more than a drizzle."

The Braves were obviously demoralized by the interruption. The next night, when Game One was played again, they were crushed in the sixth inning. While the Braves were struggling with St. Louis right-hander Bob Forsch,

"Perimeter" Perez

By August 19, 1982, the Braves had blown their 10½-game lead over the Dodgers in the National League West, losing 19 of their last 21 games, and they had fallen 4 games behind Los Angeles. As they prepared for that night's game with Montreal, a serious problem developed. Pitcher Pascual Perez, the game's starter, was nowhere to be found. Phil Niekro was hurriedly summoned to pitch and he began warming up. Fearing that Perez may have been involved in an accident, the Braves notified the Atlanta police. When the game began, Perez was still a no-show.

As it turned out, he was simply and literally lost. Perez was new to Atlanta and had taken possession of an apartment in the suburbs that very day. He left for the stadium at about 4:30 P.M. and got onto I-285, the "Perimeter," a sixty-mile interstate that encircles the city. Thinking that the stadium was just off the Perimeter, Perez searched in vain, and after about an hour (and one complete loop around the city) he found himself right back where he started.

Pascual Perez.

Convinced that he had simply missed the stadium, Perez set off again—with the same results. He finally pulled off the highway into a service station. An attendant, recognizing Perez, rushed up to him and said, "Hey, man, they're looking for you." Now pointed in the right direction, Perez headed south and soon arrived at the stadium at 7:50—ten minutes after the game had started.

Pascual's misadventure seemed to loosen up his teammates. The Braves rallied for a come-from-behind 5-4 victory over the Expos, and went on to win thirteen of their next fifteen games, thereby moving back into first place.

the Cardinals staged a five-run rally in the sixth against Pascual Perez. In that inning, St. Louis set playoff records for most batters sent to the plate (11), most hits (six), most runs (five) and tied for most consecutive hits (five). The uprising started innocently enough, after Lonnie Smith's two-out grounder was fielded cleanly by Chris Chambliss at first base. Chambliss was too far off the bag to make the play himself, so he flipped to Perez, who was covering. It's a play practiced and completed hundreds of times a year, as routine as catching a fly ball. But on this night, Perez simply dropped the ball, mishandling what should have been the third out. "I don't have any excuses" he later said. After that, the Cardinals pounded him, sending line drive after line drive through the infield. When it was over, the Braves were 7-0 losers, down 1-0 in the Series. Torre could only state the obvious when he said, "We didn't play well. I would not say we were embarrassed, but we certainly didn't play well enough to win."

The Braves insisted they weren't panicking, but Torre decided to start Phil Niekro in Game Two after just one day of rest. Even though a knuckleball places less stress on the arm than a 90-mph fastball, allowing Niekro so little time to recover from his aborted Game One start was a risk. Then again, the Braves were only two losses away from elimination, and Torre knew he would have to gamble. Niekro, calm as ever, smiled and told reporters, "You know, I'm going to feel okay." He was right, but he lasted only until the seventh inning, and was removed for a pinch-hitter. In hindsight the Braves wished he had stayed a little longer, because Niekro had been pitching brilliantly, protecting a 3-2 lead, when Torre decided to turn the game over to his bullpen.

Gene Garber stood on the mound, took a deep breath, and started on a path to finish the game. There was every reason for the Braves to feel safe, since Garber had registered thirty saves during the regular season, the leader among the Braves' relievers and second in the entire National League. But disaster struck again as Garber allowed the tying run in the eighth and allowed the Cardinals to

After using nine different shortstops in their first 15 years in Atlanta, the Braves installed Rafael Ramirez in the position in 1981. Ramirez stayed there for the next six seasons, his best year coming in 1983, when he hit .297.

win it in the ninth, when Ken Oberkfell's line drive went screaming over Brett Butler's head with a runner on second. Of course, the second-guessers were ready to devour Torre for abandoning Niekro with a lead, but the manager defended his decision by saying, "I got what I wanted out of Phil. I got to the seventh with a lead and a chance to score some more runs. I wasn't looking for a complete game."

Niekro was left in a difficult spot, obviously disagreeing with Torre but not wanting to challenge his manager in public. "I thought I had good knuckleball; I thought it was moving quite a bit," Niekro said diplomatically. "I felt like I could've gone two or three more innings. I wasn't surprised, though, because Joe has [taken me out] a number of times during the season."

The Braves' season was down to its last nine innings, and the only real hope they had in Game Three was that the 52,000 fans who showed up at Atlanta-Fulton County Stadium would inspire a turnaround. Rick Camp started for Atlanta, and after his first inning, the Braves' hearts went off in a sprint. He limited the Cardinals to three ground balls. "I had a terrific sinker," he later said. But then came the second inning, and somehow Camp was a different pitcher. "I had nothing on the ball at that point," he said, explaining why he didn't retire a single batter in the inning. Camp allowed a single to Keith Hernandez, a walk to Darrell Porter, an RBI single to George Hendrick, and a two-run single to Willie McGee. By the time Perez arrived, the Cardinals were ahead 4-0, and the Braves' two-run rally in the seventh inning was meaningless. They were powerless against Joaquin Andujar and reliever Bruce Sutter, just as they had been invisible during the entire series. The muscle of the Braves' batting order—Dale Murphy, Bob Horner, and Chris Chambliss—combined for only four hits in 32 at-bats, all of which made Atlanta's 6-2 loss in Game Three understandable, almost predictable.

Catcher Bruce Benedict spoke for an entire clubhouse when he said, "I'm numb. Maybe this will hit in a couple of weeks, but right

First baseman Chris Chambliss was acquired by the Braves in a 1979 trade with Toronto. Chambliss played a key role in the winning of the West Division in 1982, hitting .270 with 20 home runs and 86 RBIs.

now, I'm numb." Still, there was another perspective on this surprising season, and the more the Braves thought about it, the better they felt about their accomplishment of the past summer: They had surged from fifth place in the second half of the strike-shortened season in 1981 all the way to Western Division champions in 1982. "It was still a good season, no matter what," Jerry Royster flatly said. A few lockers down, Gene Garber agreed. "We had a goal to get to the World Series, and in that respect I'm disappointed, but we overcame a lot to win the West, even though a lot of people doubted us. We won seven of our last ten in a pennant stretch."

"We didn't go into the tank when we could have and that showed me a lot," Phil Niekro echoed. "There's a lot of young talent here."

What the Braves thought, what they actually expected, was a long, glorious run through the '80s, with plenty more division titles just like the one in 1982. If only they had known what was in store for the rest of the decade, they wouldn't have treated their brief and forgettable appearance in the 1982 National League Championship Series so lightly.

A RETURN TO RESPECTABILITY—BRIEFLY

18

"I just want to be left alone."
—Bob Horner, 1983

Slowly but surely, the Braves faded

in the West. In 1983 they squandered an 6½-game lead with 45 games left in the season and they finished in second place, three games behind the Dodgers. The next year the Braves placed second again—this time 12 games behind the reborn San Diego Padres. By 1984, the Braves were languishing, posting an 80-82 record. Attendance, which had peaked in 1983 at 2.1 million, dropped off by 20 percent the following year. Television ratings remained high as more and more American homes began to receive the TBS station through cable, but that only meant added pressure to win games. Advertisers now were paying a national rate for commercials during a Braves telecast. Maintaining a respectable rating

Bob Horner, one of the most productive home-run hitters in baseball history.

meant dollars, and nothing could generate those dollars more easily than winning.

The growing impatience with the team's slide was one reason Phil Niekro was released after the 1983 season—a decision that left raw feelings on both sides. For three decades Niekro had frustrated National League hitters with his knuckleball and earned the affection of his teammates and fans with his easy smile. Even Ted Turner wasn't immune to Niekro's charm. On September 30, 1978, prior to a game with the Houston Astros, Turner approached Niekro in the clubhouse and handed him a letter that promised a $100,000 bonus, a gift that would entitle Niekro to $10,000 a year for the first ten years following his retirement. Five years later, Turner was ready to start paying.

"Some players walk off the field and other have to be dragged off kicking and screaming," Turner said on October 14, 1983. That year, Niekro had posted an 11-10 record with a 3.97 ERA. Those weren't altogether bad numbers, but Niekro's vulnerability could be detected in the .275 average that hitters posted against him—the highest Niekro had allowed in his career. At age forty-three, Niekro had become too old for the Braves, a team that was looking to groom younger pitchers. As Turner asked, "Would we have been better off letting Phil come back and fall on his face next year? Would that have made it easier? The decision was unanimous."

Niekro had spent his entire career with the Braves, although he didn't reach the big leagues until he was twenty-five. His father, Phil Sr., was an Ohio coal miner who himself had played semi-pro ball until an arm injury ended his career. The elder Niekro taught his son to throw the knuckleball when he was in the seventh grade, and Phil became so proficient at making the ball dance, even his father would grow frustrated. "He'd just throw his glove down and walk away," Phil recalled, "but he'd be back the very next day practicing with me."

Niekro was offered scholarships by both the University of West Virginia and the University of Detroit, but he declined, expecting that "someone would sign me to a pro baseball contract." Niekro was wrong and spent a year working for the Continental Can Company in Wheeling, West Virginia, pitching on weekends against coal-mining teams. Finally, a scout noticed Niekro in 1958 at an open tryout conducted by the Milwaukee Braves. The kid with the unusual pitch was finally offered a minor league contract and a $500 signing bonus. Niekro gladly accepted and began working his way up the Braves' ladder. He made his debut with the Braves in 1964, but it wasn't until 1967 that Niekro became a part of the starting rotation. The knuckleballer was an instant success. That year Niekro led the National League with a 1.87 ERA and was so effective that the Reds' Pete Rose said, "Hitting Phil Niekro's knuckleball is like trying to hit a butterfly." Rose's teammate Bobby Tolan, who joined the Reds in 1969, agreed, "You swing, and then the pitch isn't there anymore."

Like most knuckleball pitchers, Niekro was at a loss to explain the dynamics of his signature pitch. He would simply dig his fingernails into the seams of the ball and release it—actually push it toward the plate—not knowing himself which way the ball would break. Some scientists have theorized the knuckleball's "dance" comes from a lack of rotation, thereby making the ball susceptible to wind currents, but Niekro said, "Some of the best games I'd ever thrown were in the [enclosed Houston] Astrodome. The pitch is a mystery to me."

Niekro had a long and successful run with the Braves, twice leading the National League in victories and in 1977 reigning as the National League's strikeout king, fanning 262

Johnny Sain, Boston Braves pitching star of the 1940s, served as the Atlanta Braves' pitching coach in 1977 and 1985–86. Sain disdained weight lifting and extensive running for pitchers, emphasizing instead frequent throwing on the side to develop arm strength but maintain flexibility.

Phil Niekro demonstrates the knuckleball grip that helped him win 318 games. Phil and his brother, Joe, (221 wins) learned the pitch from their father while growing up in Lansing, Ohio. The area also produced NBA Hall of Famer John Havlicek.

in 330 innings. In 1983 Niekro was certain that, despite his forty-four years, there were plenty of wins and strikeouts left in his arm. "I knew I could still pitch," he protested. "They basically asked me to retire myself, and I told them I wasn't ready for that," he said on leaving the Braves. "I'll find somewhere else to pitch." As an added incentive, Niekro needed only 32 more wins to reach 300 and almost certainly membership in the Hall of Fame.

The Yankees signed Niekro for the 1984 season, and he spent two years in the Bronx, winning number 300 on the final day of the 1985 season.

By 1984, as the team's slide accelerated, manager Joe Torre found himself looking for the door. On September 30, 1984, an hour before the Braves' last game of the season, Ted Turner approached Torre and told him, "See

THROUGH THE EIGHTIES, DARKLY

me in my office Monday morning, 11 A.M." The owner turned and walked away, and Torre already sensed a managerial change was on the way.

Torre had always known that he wasn't the choice of the Braves front office. General Manager John Mullen, scouting director Paul Snyder, and executive vice president Al Thornwell unanimously had selected Triple-A manager Eddie Haas and leaned on Turner to promote him, but Torre had been Turner's high-profile, ready-for-TV manager. After that Monday morning meeting, however, Torre was out of a job. "I didn't ask for a reason why," Torre said afterward. "A boss wanting to make a change is reason enough to make a change."

To the end, Turner liked Torre, but losses were losses, and losses meant fewer fans and lower ratings. Things had to change. Torre left an impressive legacy, however, as his .529 winning percentage from 1982 to 1984 was the best the Braves had had since moving from Milwaukee in 1966. Now the Braves were handing the reigns to Haas, a longtime organization man whose resumé included everything from scouting to managing in the

minors to serving as a coach for the Braves. Haas was about learn what happens to a team that has a few big-name players and not much else.

A Braves rookie stepped to the plate on the night of June 16, 1978, and sized up his opponent. Sixty feet away stood the Pirates' Bert Blyleven, a right-hander with one of the fiercest curveballs in the major leagues. Blyleven was especially dangerous against right-handed hitters, aiming his curveball at the batter's head, only to have the ball dip into the strike zone at the last moment, rendering it unhittable. Blyleven had heard of the Braves' rookie who was now in the batter's box: The kid was only twenty years old, and his name was Bob Horner. Blyleven had never faced him before, and he spent the first two at-bats doing a little reconnaissance. It didn't take long for him to realize Horner was big and strong, and quick. Even though Blyleven retired Horner in his first two at-bats, he knew the rookie could make trouble for him. In the third at-bat, Blyleven was proved right, as Horner slugged a mammoth home run.

That first game turned out to be a curse to

Bob Horner hit 215 home runs in his nine seasons with Atlanta (1978–86). Horner is one of only twelve players to hit four homers in one game (July 6, 1986, against Montreal).

The Game That Wouldn't End

O n July 4, 1985, the Braves were mired in fifth place in the National League West, 10½ games behind division-leading San Diego. But a sold-out crowd of just under 45,000 packed Atlanta-Fulton County Stadium nonetheless. Part of the draw was New York Mets pitching sensation Dwight Gooden, who was on his way to a 24-4 season, but the majority were there for the post-game fireworks, a Fourth of July tradition at the stadium.

The first problem was the weather. Rain delayed the start of the game one hour and twenty-four minutes. After the game finally did begin, another rain delay of forty-one minutes hit in the third inning.

It was well after midnight when the Mets came to bat in the ninth inning, trailing Atlanta, 8-7. But for the fifth time in his last nine tries, Braves reliever Bruce Sutter was unable to record the save. The Mets tied the game in the ninth, and when the Braves failed to score, the game went into extra innings. The Mets broke the tie in the top of the thirteenth inning, when Howard Johnson hit a two-run homer off of Terry Forster. But in the bottom of the inning, with two outs and a runner at

Rick Camp.

first, Braves left fielder Terry Harper hit a 0-2 pitch from Tom Gorman over the left-field wall to retie the game.

They played into the eighteenth inning, when the Mets scored again to take an 11-10 lead. In the bottom of the eighteenth, with two outs and the bases empty, Braves manager Eddie Haas brought out pitcher Rick Camp. Camp was the Braves' last hope. He was only 10-for-167 (.060) in his career, but Haas had no choice, for he was out of pinch-hitters.

Gorman was still pitching for the Mets and quickly worked the count to 0-2 against Camp. The next pitch, however, resulted in the most unexpected single moment in Braves history. Miraculously, Camp drilled a line drive over the left-field fence for his first and only career home run. Mets left fielder Danny Heep sank to the ground in disbelief. It was 3:12 A.M. and the game was tied once more.

The Mets struck for five runs in the nineteenth inning and held off the Braves for a 16-13 win. When Rick Camp struck out to end the game, it was 3:55 in the morning, making it the latest-ending game in major league history.

About 10,000 fans still on hand and expecting still to see a fireworks show. The pyrotechnics were launched at 4:01 A.M., waking the entire neighborhood. As one resident recalled, "I thought we were being attacked."

Bob Horner's career with the Braves was often controversial. A spring-training holdout in 1979, Horner also refused a minor league assignment in 1980 and spent two weeks on the suspended list before being reinstated.

Horner in many ways. For eight years with the Braves he never lived up to the expectations that had somehow engulfed him. Horner had walked off the campus of Arizona State University straight into the big leagues as the Braves No. 1 draft pick in 1978. "Bob Horner is destined for stardom—Cooperstown," Ted Turner had stated flatly. Horner had set a collegiate record that spring with 25 homers, and, on signing with Atlanta, stipulated that he skip the minor leagues entirely. "I wouldn't have it any other way," he coolly pronounced. That cockiness became part of Horner's personae, which made it hard for Braves fans to embrace him. Through the '80s, while the Braves continued to sink, he became the city's bad boy, aloof and indifferent—or so it seemed to those who didn't really know James Robert Horner.

"People say it looks like I don't care, that I'm not trying or that I'm not hustling or something like that," Horner told reporters, "but that's just the way I am. That's the way I play the game, and I'm not going to start changing now." And one fact was indisputable: Horner could hit. In that very first season, he smacked 23 home runs, and in his first three seasons hit 91 home runs. By 1983 Horner had totaled 158 home runs in 2,458 at-bats, placing him in the all-time top-ten list of most productive home-runs hitters. By going deep once every 15.6 at-bats, Horner joined the fraternity whose members included Babe Ruth (11.7) and Mickey Mantle (15.1). On July 6, 1986, Horner tied a major league record, hitting four home runs in one game, a feat accomplished by only ten other players at the time—including Milwaukee's Joe Adcock in 1954 and Boston's Bobby Lowe in 1894.

Teammate Jerry Royster called Horner, "the most misunderstood guy in baseball. He was the perfect guy to market, and instead it went the other way. He should've been the golden boy." Horner's vulnerability to injury was his downfall. He missed 380 games during his nine-year career with the Braves, with ailments that ranged from gastritis to a hyperextended elbow to pulled muscles to two frac-

tures of his right wrist suffered in August 1983 and May 1984, both of which ended the season for him.

"There are some people who might have a higher tolerance for pain than Bob," manager Torre conceded, "but that's not a knock on him. It would be different if you thought he was faking injuries, but the injuries he's had have been legitimate." "There's not a thing in the world I can do about [injuries]," Horner stated simply. But injuries devoured the rest of his career. He played in only thirty-two games in 1984 because of his wrist injury and missed fifty more over the next two seasons because of a chronic shoulder condition. Horner played in Japan in 1987, then made a brief comeback with the Cardinals in 1988. He left the game at age thirty-one with 218 homers.

In the spring of 1978, the Braves' farm system produced a seemingly ideal ballplayer: He was big and strong, could hit home runs, and even had a perfect baseball name—Dale Murphy. All that was left to do was to hurry him along to the Hall of Fame.

Murphy was the Braves' No. 1 draft choice in 1974, signed directly out of high school in Portland, Oregon, only two months after Hank Aaron had hit his 715th career home run. The Braves believed that Murphy, a catcher, would become the franchise's new superstar. He joined the Braves in 1978 after only three years in the minor leagues, but before making it to the majors he had to overcome a slight problem—he couldn't accurately reach second base with a throw from the plate, which created a mental block so troublesome that Murphy couldn't even toss the ball back the pitcher.

Dale Murphy is perhaps the most popular player who ever wore an Atlanta Braves uniform. His talent on the field was complemented by a committment to charity, which earned him the Roberto Clemente award in 1988.

Dale Murphy turned in a 30-30 season in 1983 with 36 home runs and 30 stolen bases. He also led the National League with 121 RBIs, earning him a second consecutive Most Valuable Player award.

The problem overtook Murphy in spring training in 1978 when he made a number of errors trying to throw out base stealers. Eventually, coach Chris Cannizzaro took Murphy to a remote field, where he made Murphy toss the ball, over and over, the ninety feet from home plate to second base. Still, accuracy eluded Murphy, whose father Chuck sidled up to him and said, "Don't worry, son, if they were trying to steal center field, you would've had them every time."

Murphy managed a smile, but both he and the Braves knew the team had too much invested in his future to risk that future over a seemingly unbreakable habit of overthrowing second. Murphy was converted into a first baseman. With peace of mind, he hit 44 home runs in his first two years, but it wasn't until he was moved to the outfield in 1980 that Murphy truly began dominating pitchers. That year he hit .281 with 33 home runs with 89 RBIs, and in 1982, not only did he lead the Braves to a Western Division title, but Murphy won the National League's Most Valuable Player Award, hitting 36 home runs, tying the Pirates' Al Oliver with 109 RBIs and winning the first of five Gold Glove Awards. Nolan Ryan was so impressed he said, "I can't imagine Joe DiMaggio was a better all-around player than Dale Murphy." "Dale is probably the best all-around player in either league, probably the most valuable commodity in baseball right now," Henry Aaron added.

Murphy won the MVP Award again in 1983—this time with 36 homers, an increased batting average of .302, and 30 stolen bases—and at twenty-seven became the youngest player to ever win back-to-back MVP honors. The future was a horizon of line drives and home runs, all belonging to Murphy. Chicago Cubs pitching coach Billy Connors said, "He's the best I've ever seen, and I've seen Willie Mays. I've seen Murphy win games every way there is, a base hit in the

Dale Murphy (right) with Eddie Haas, the Braves' hitting coach in the late '70s and early '80s and Atlanta's manager in 1985.

THROUGH THE EIGHTIES, DARKLY

And on This Winning Night . . .

Of all who have worn a Braves uniform or worked for the Braves organization, no one has touched the lives of as many Braves fans as Ernie Johnson.

Ernie's association with the team began in 1942, when he was signed as a right-handed pitcher out of Brattleboro (VT) High School by the Braves organization. After a stint in the military, Johnson worked his way up the minor league ladder, making it to Boston in 1950.

He moved with the Braves to Milwaukee in 1953 and was a part of the 1957 World Series Championship team. In his nine-year major league career, spent mostly as a long and middle reliever, Johnson compiled a highly respectable 40-23 record.

But it was after his career as a player that Ernie's biggest contribution to the Braves would be made. After a brief stint in the Braves' front office in the early sixties, Ernie became part of the broadcast team.

When the move to Atlanta came, Ernie was in place for a twenty-five-year stay as one of the South's most beloved voices. Working with Milo Hamilton through 1975 and with Skip Caray, Pete Van Wieren, and others since 1976, Ernie's homespun style radiated his warm personality.

Atlanta Journal columnist Ron Hudspeth once wrote, "With his soothing voice and over-the-back-fence delivery, Ernie Johnson is as comfortable as an old shoe."

Testimony to Ernie's popularity came in 1989 after he announced his retirement from full-time broadcasting. With September crowds averaging under 10,000, more than 40,000 fans turned out on "Ernie Johnson Night," as the long-time broadcaster was honored by the team he had served so well.

Ernie remains a part of the Braves family as a broadcaster on SportSouth telecasts. Thus, Braves fans still get to hear that familiar voice with their favorite sign-off, ". . . and on this winning night, so long everyone."

Top: Ernie Johnson.

Bottom: Braves broadcast team, 1994. (Left to right) Joe Simpson, Pete Van Wieren, producer Glenn Diamond, Don Sutton, Skip Caray.

ninth, a home run, a great catch, beating the throw to first on a double play. I've never seen anything like him before in my life."

What made Murphy so likable, though, was his personal warmth. A devout Mormon, Murphy was, in Ted Turner's words, "the original Mr. Goody Two shoes. He makes Steve Garvey look evil. The man doesn't drink, doesn't smoke, doesn't even drink Coca-Cola. If God's coming back, he's coming back as Dale Murphy." To this Murphy just smiled, embarrassed, and said, "Ted's such a great talker, he gets a little carried away. Not that I don't appreciate what he's saying, but there's no such thing as being too good. I don't want to be thought of as sickeningly nice. I don't know what to say when people say things like that."

The Braves, of course, respected Murphy's devotion to his church, but it nearly cost them. After his conversion to Mormonism by teammate Barry Bonnell in 1975, Murphy was ready to leave the Braves organization to complete two years of mandatory missionary work. A frantic Turner asked Murphy, who was already tearing apart minor league pitching, "What's with all this Mormon stuff? If you need some converts, take me and my kids. We could use it."

Unfortunately for Murphy, all his years of productivity could not reverse a trend of bad baseball. Between 1985 and 1990, the Braves finished last or next to last every season, as managers Eddie Haas, Bobby Wine, Chuck Tanner, and Russ Nixon all came and went with the tide of failure. But there was Murphy, productive through 1987, when he batted .295 with a career-high 44 homers and 105 RBIs. After that, the numbers softened, and his average fell to .226, .228, and .232 in his final three years in Atlanta. As difficult as it was for the Braves to accept, it was time for Murphy to leave, especially since they had another, younger right fielder ready to inherit his place. David Justice, killing time at first base, was part of a new generation of Braves who were on the verge of reclaiming the broken team.

On August 4, 1990, the Braves finally severed the ties to Murphy, trading him to the Phillies with pitcher Tommy Greene in exchange for pitcher Jeff Parrett, outfielder Jim Vatcher, and shortstop Victor Rosario. Murphy addressed his teammates before leaving, telling them, "I have a lot of feelings about this club that I'll leave behind. Those feelings won't go away overnight." Shortstop

Dale Murphy's clean-cut image made him a favorite with the media.

Glenn Hubbard handles a high throw, but it's too late to get Montreal's Tim Raines. Hubbard was Atlanta's second baseman from 1978–87, and was known for his quickness in turning the doubleplay.

Jeff Blauser spoke for the entire clubhouse when he said, "There's definitely an air of sadness here. Dale wasn't the only one with tears in his eyes." What hurt Murphy most, perhaps, was witnessing the Braves' surge a year later, in 1991, and not being able to participate. Murphy played hard for the Phillies, but his soul still belonged in Atlanta. As he put it, "It's a little strange, not winning all those years in Atlanta and now not being able to be part of all that excitement."

But age and injuries had diminished Murphy's skills. He caught on with the Colorado Rockies in 1993 but retired just one month into the season. He left with 398 homers, 27th on the all-time list, although Murphy refused to torture himself about not making it to 400. "I missed hundreds of hanging sliders that I should have hit," he said. "Mostly, I'll miss the game of baseball. I had a few tears this morning, as I guess most players do when they say good-bye to something that's close to them."

The six years between 1985 and 1990 were a long, bad blur. The only redeeming factor about this "great depression" was that it created a foundation for the Braves' revival—a place the franchise could call bottom. In

1985, new manager Eddie Haas had an immediate problem with the media, which had grown accustomed to Joe Torre's sharp-witted, insightful answers, not to mention his willingness to accommodate writers on deadline. On their way to losing ninety-six games, Pascual Perez jumped the team, and the rest of the Braves took advantage of Haas at one point by openly defying his edict that no player be allowed to drink in the hotel bar on road trips. "We're here, what are you going to do about it, Eddie?" one of the Braves said to Haas. Haas' internal problems aside, what wounded the front office most was the failure of prospect Brad Komminsk. He was propped up as the next Dale Murphy, but instead became part of the reason Haas was fired. With the team 21 games under .500, coach Bobby Wine finished out the '85 season.

Chuck Tanner, who had managed the White Sox, the A's, and Pirates for fifteen years—winning a World Series in Pittsburgh in 1979—was hired by Turner in 1986, but fared no better than Haas. Elsewhere, however, there were signs of hope. Bobby Cox had returned to Atlanta from Toronto, where he had been managing. This time, Cox served as general manager, and drafted left-hander Kent Mercker, who would become an important part of the Braves' rebirth in the '90s. On the field, the Braves lost eighty-nine games

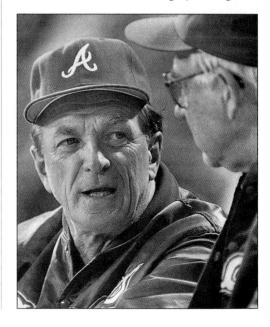

and suffered the embarrassment of trading reliever Steve Bedrosian to the Phillies, for whom he won the Cy Young Award in 1987. Although the Braves still had a few impressive names in the batting order—Claudell Washington, Bob Horner, Dale Murphy, Rafael Ramirez, Glenn Hubbard—there was nothing manager Tanner could do with his pitching. Often he would privately ask friends, "How am I supposed to win with this bunch?"

In 1987, another prospect failed. Shortstop Andres Thomas was supposed to hit, but all he gave Tanner was a glove the Braves didn't really need. There were another 92 losses, and by 1988, Tanner's tenure had reached its end. Only 39 games into the season—with the Braves already 15 games under .500—Tanner was replaced by Russ Nixon. The Braves were awful under Nixon, finishing with 106 losses, the second-worst season in Braves history, but Cox continued working his quiet magic. He drafted left-hander Steve Avery and traded veteran pitcher Doyle Alexander to the Tigers for a young right-hander with perfect mechanics, John Smoltz.

The Braves still had to endure two more years of poverty, but reinforcements kept arriving. In 1989, while the team lost 97 games and finished last, Tom Glavine was in his second season and posted an encouraging 14-8 record. Outfielder Ron Gant was learning about National League pitching, and in 1990 the Braves were ready—almost.

In 1990, the Braves finished last again, but now the rotation consisted of Glavine, Smoltz, and Steve Avery, a lefty with an enormous curveball. David Justice was displaying one of the prettiest swings in the game, Gant hit .303 with 32 home runs and 84 RBIs, and left fielder Lonnie Smith hit over .300 as well. And Bobby Cox was back in the dugout as manager, replacing Nixon and preparing the baseball community for the greatest surprise in a half-century.

Welcome to Bedrock

While the Braves struggled with their pitching in the early '80s, they could rely on one certainty: Summon Steve Bedrosian from the bullpen, and opposing hitters would have to face a 95-mph fastball. Bedrosian, nicknamed Bedrock by his Braves teammates, possessed one of the best fastballs of his day, and used it to win the Cy Young Award in 1987.

Unfortunately for the Braves, Bedrosian was pitching for the Phillies at the time, having been traded in 1986 with outfielder Milt Thompson for catcher Ozzie Virgil and right-handed pitcher Pete Smith. In his stellar 1987 season, Bedrosian recorded 40 saves and beat out the Cubs' Rick Sutcliffe for the Cy Young.

Before he left the Braves, Bedrosian led National League relievers with 123 strikeouts in 1982, posting 11 saves and a 2.42 ERA. Bedrosian saved a total of 30 games in 1983–84, before the Braves converted him to a starter in 1985. He posted a 7-15 record, and was traded to Philadelphia, where he pitched for three successful seasons, including 1988, when he saved 28 of the Phillies' 65 wins. He was again traded in 1989, this time to the Giants, who needed his fastball to help win the National League pennant. He later played for the World Champion Twins in 1991, before voluntarily sitting out the 1992 season with a circulatory problem in his right hand. In 1993 Bedrosian returned to the Braves as a free agent.

Steve Bedrosian.

THROUGH THE EIGHTIES, DARKLY

from chumps to champs

19

"Ecstasy, pure ecstasy."

—Catcher Greg Olson, after the Braves clinched the 1991 Western Division Championship

For six years, the Braves had been

the team the National League regarded as the easiest to beat, a sure pick-me-up for any team in a slump. Step off the plane, check into a posh hotel, and get ready for an easy series against a bad team. The Braves were so regularly outmanned, no opponent would feel they played decently unless they finished a four-game series with Atlanta with at least three wins. But 1991 is when Atlanta exacted its revenge, the year when all its young players matured at once, when all the bad baseball that had plagued the franchise suddenly turned around, and shutouts and home runs became the order of the day. The pitching staff, known collectively as the "Young Guns," finally began living up to its potential, and a nucleus of talented hitters began to

Greg Olson and John Smoltz celebrate winning the West.

deliver. It seemed as if every pitch the Braves pitchers threw had a purpose and that every line drive coming off a Braves bat would find the gap. Finally, the Braves decided to stop being abused.

Changes in the organization manifested themselves in subtle ways, at least at first. General Manager John Schuerholz, who had been lured away from the Kansas City Royals by team president Stan Kasten, signed third baseman Terry Pendleton, who was leaving the St. Louis Cardinals as a free agent. Then Schuerholz inked first baseman Sid Bream and shortstop Rafael Belliard, two more free agents who had just cut their ties with the Pittsburgh Pirates. The Braves now had a respectable infield defense and would never again lead the National League in errors as they had in 1990 with 158. Next on Schuerholz's savvy acquisitions list was outfielder Deion Sanders—or "Neon Deion," as he was known. The Yankees had just cut loose the high-octane, super-athlete who was so talented he would go on to share his skills with both the Braves and the NFL Falcons. Schuerholz then presented the 1991 Braves with one more gift—outfielder Otis Nixon, acquired from Montreal as spring training was ending. Suddenly, speed and defense, never strong suits of the Braves, were now two of their strengths.

Schuerholz did not need to find a manager. Bobby Cox was already in place before he was hired. This potentially awkward situation was quickly diffused by Schuerholz, who said, "If I had been looking for a manager, Bobby would have been first on my list." For five years, Bobby Cox had been the general manager, but returning to the field was something he readily accepted. "I've always been most comfortable being a manager," Cox said. "This is where I want to be." All Cox had to do was find a way to transform the Western Division's worst team into contenders. The Braves had gone through twenty-two straight losing months, and hadn't been above .500 in April since 1983. Cox's team might have looked crisp in spring training, but Florida has never been a useful barometer for predict-

ing a team's regular season success.

The Braves trailed the Dodgers 9½ games by the All-Star break, and while the rest of the league did not think it unusual for the Braves to be coughing and wheezing again, the disappointment in Atlanta was almost palpable. Despite his flawless delivery, John Smoltz was 2-11. "My teammates, my manager, and my coaches are sick of seeing this," he admitted. "It's not going to happen anymore." The Braves offense was weighted down by the prolonged slumps of Ronnie Gant, who was hitting .239, and Lonnie Smith, who was mired at .247. The Braves had faced the Dodgers in seven games before the All-Star break, losing five and creating such a profound deficit it was easy to imagine the Braves disappearing entirely in the second half of the season. Long summers weren't anything new in Atlanta.

With great pitching from Steve Avery, Tom Glavine, and, finally, John Smoltz, who won six of his first seven starts after the All-Star break, the Braves sliced seven games off the Dodgers' lead in the first twelve days after the All-Star Game. Incredibly, the Dodgers went 0-7 after the break, while the Braves swept the Cardinals, took two of three from the Cubs at

Terry Pendleton became the top free agent signed in baseball in 1991, winning the National League MVP award after hitting a league-leading .319 with 22 HR and 86 RBIs.

home, went on the road to take another two of three from St. Louis and beat the Pirates at Three Rivers Stadium before finally losing two straight. A euphoric Bobby Cox, almost dizzy from the blur of wins, called the Braves' run, "the most amazing week I've ever seen."

By August 10, the Braves were only 2½ games behind the Dodgers, and Tommy Lasorda's team was now taking notice. Outfielder Darryl Strawberry, who had signed with the Dodgers after eight turbulent years with the New York Mets, glibly observed that he had "never been concerned about Atlanta." To a team now on a serious roll, Strawberry's comment sounded too slick to be honest, and Braves catcher Greg Olson quickly cautioned that, "[Strawberry] better start rethinking what he said. We'll see who's talking in October."

It was only fitting that the regular season unfold with the Braves and Dodgers battling for a divisional crown. Even though it was a new rivalry—without the regional antipathy of the Dodgers-Giants or the Yankees-Red Sox—a tradition of Braves-Dodgers photo finishes had been established. In 1982 the race had gone down to the final day of the season, with the Braves winning the West by a single game. In 1983, the Dodgers had eliminated the Braves during the season's final weekend. Now, eight years later, Act Three was about to begin.

The Dodgers arrived in Atlanta on September 13, a half-game behind the Braves, and nearly 46,000 fans packed Atlanta-Fulton County Stadium. It was the biggest crowd of the year to that point. Enthusiastic fans were swinging their arms in the signature "Tomahawk Chop," and singing the Braves' war cry. It was an intimidating and simultaneously inspiring display for those who remembered the days when the stadium was a quiet, peaceful, and under-attended place where the Braves players would routinely get mugged. Now Braves fans were loud and tough. "They sit up in the stands and flip all kinds of fingers at me," Darryl Strawberry ruefully commented mid-series. "I smile and say, 'Lord, help these people. They've got problems.'" But even

First baseman Sid Bream returned from knee surgery and slugged a grand-slam home run in a key September series with the Dodgers.

Strawberry, whose exterior was hardened after so many years of listening to hostile Mets fans, had to laugh at one sign directed at his portly manager, Tommy Lasorda, who had recently become a pitch man for a diet drink. The sign, which mimicked his television commercials for the product, hung from the stands for all the world to see. It read: "I lost 9½ games in only nine weeks. And I owe it all to the Braves' plan."

The Braves found out what kind of clutch-player Strawberry could be, as he went four for four in the first game of the showdown series. Despite the howling in the stands, and despite the infield shift—the Braves devised to guard against Strawberry's tendency to pull the ball to the right, he nevertheless hit a home run, three singles, and had two RBIs. When it was over, the Dodgers had reclaimed first place with a 5-2 win. In the thirteen games the Dodgers and Braves had played in 1991, L.A. had won nine times. "On the field, they have been better than us," Tom Glavine was forced to admit, as game two of the series loomed as the most critical of the season. "Another loss and it would've been

FROM CHUMPS TO CHAMPS

The Turnaround GM

L ate in the 1990 season, with the Braves headed for another sixth-place finish, team president Stan Kasten made a decision about the ballclub's future. Bobby Cox would give up his front office duties to concentrate on managing, and a new general manager would be sought.

Kasten knew the qualifications his candidate would possess—experience, a winning background, energy, and leadership—and he had several people in mind. While in New York on business, Kasten ran into Kansas City Royals general manager John Schuerholz and decided to pick his brain on the situation.

The longer Schuerholz listened, the more interesting the Atlanta opening sounded. When he offered himself for the job, Kasten was overjoyed. "We couldn't have done better," Kasten said. "I'm sure of that."

Schuerholz had not been on Kasten's original list, but only because no one believed the Royals' general manager would ever leave Kansas City. From the Royals' very beginning in 1968, Schuerholz had been a primary architect of their success, starting as assistant farm director and rising to general manager by 1981. Under Schuerholz, the Royals were considered one of baseball's best organizations.

John Schuerholz.

Upon his arrival in Atlanta, changes began immediately. A new grounds crew was hired to transform the playing field from one of the worst in major league baseball to one of the best. Concessions were improved. Minor league spring training facilities were upgraded. And, of course, the Braves became winners.

Thanks to Bobby Cox, a deep and talented farm system was already in place. Building on that, Schuerholz added Terry Pendleton, Sid Bream, Otis Nixon, Deion Sanders, and Alejandro Pena in 1991; Damon Berryhill and Jeff Reardon in 1992; Greg Maddux and Fred McGriff in 1993; and Roberto Kelly in 1994. Using all available avenues (trades, the free-agent market, minor league free agents, and the amateur draft), Schuerholz has built the Braves into one of baseball's most admired and respected organizations.

The rapid success of the Braves in 1991 caught even Schuerholz by surprise. "We never dreamed it would happen this quickly," said Schuerholz, "but since it has, it's my job to make sure that we stay on top."

awfully tough for us from that point on," John Smoltz remarked, hinting at the pressure to win that was building up in the bullpen.

The second game of the series lasted eleven innings and took more than four hours to play, but the Braves' season was rescued when Ronnie Gant smoked a line drive single off Dodgers reliever Roger McDowell. With a 3-2 win, the Braves were back in first place. Steve Avery then threw a four-hitter on September 15, a 9-1 win that kept the Braves in first place. Veteran Sid Bream caught up with one of Ramon Martinez's fastballs, hitting a grand-slam in the first inning and all but dooming the Dodgers for the day. If Bobby Cox's team was feeling the strain of playing must-win games night after night, they didn't show it. In fact, Avery calmly observed, "This race is ours to win."

But the race was also the Braves' to lose. They were swept two straight in San Francisco, while the Dodgers took two from the Reds. Even worse news was that Otis Nixon had failed a drug test and would be suspended for sixty days, depriving the Braves of their leading base-stealer for the most critical stretch of the pennant drive. "This is not a big loss," Bobby Cox told reporters over and over, although privately, his concerns were real. The standings had the Dodgers in first place again, prompting a closed-door, players-only meeting. Cox's message to the players was not too complicated—stay calm, stay composed, the division title is within reach—and it was intended more to soothe the Braves than to incite them. The words sunk in, and the Braves went on to beat the Padres, 6-4, on September 18, although the Dodgers kept pace at home against Houston. The race was so close, National League president Bill White held a conference-call coin-flip to see who would be the home team in the event the Dodgers and Braves ended in a tie. The Dodgers won, as their general manager Fred Claire correctly called heads.

The race again focused on a Dodgers-Braves face-off. And once again, the Dodgers had to find a way to play around Avery, the left-hander whose curveball was improving with each

game. Mixing it with an especially tough fastball, Avery was an 18-game winner in 1991, and displayed his astounding skills against the Dodgers on September 20, shutting them out 3-0, boosting his lifetime record against the Dodgers to 5-0. "I can't understand why I match up with them so well," Avery bashfully said, as the Braves gave thanks that he did. The Braves were back on top by a half-game, but deeply frustrated when the Dodgers reclaimed first place the next night with a 2-1 win on Juan Samuel's ninth-inning triple. The Braves had been just six outs away from a 1-0 win, but the Dodgers tied the game in the eighth inning on errors by shortstop Rafael Belliard and third baseman Terry Pendleton—events so unlikely even Brett Butler called it, "a freak thing."

Maybe so, but the Dodgers stretched their lead to 1½ games when they beat the Braves 3-0 on September 22. L.A.'s Ramon Martinez was devastating with his fastball, and gave Darryl Strawberry another chance to tweak the Braves. "I could tell that some of their hitters were pressing up there," he said. "I was like that when I was in my first pennant race."

There were only twelve games left for the

FROM CHUMPS TO CHAMPS

Braves, eleven for the Dodgers, and L.A. extended its lead to two full games by beating the Padres while the Braves were rained out in Atlanta. The remaining games dwindled to nine, and the Braves were still two out, and about to embark on a six-game road trip on September 27. The Dodgers had an obvious advantage, as they had six games at home at Chavez Ravine, but the Braves weren't necessarily doomed. Six of their last nine games were against the Astros, the division's worst team. The Dodgers had to finish their season in Candlestick Park in San Francisco, where the Giants were waiting to break their hearts, just as they had in 1982. On the 155th game of the season, the Braves pulled to within a game of the Dodgers, beating the Astros 5-4 while the Dodgers lost to the Giants at home, 4-1. The Dodgers held that one-game lead, as the schedule kept evaporating. The turning point came for the Braves in Cincinnati on October 1, where, coming from six runs behind against José Rijo, they rallied against Rob Dibble, perhaps the hardest thrower among the game's relievers, as David Justice's

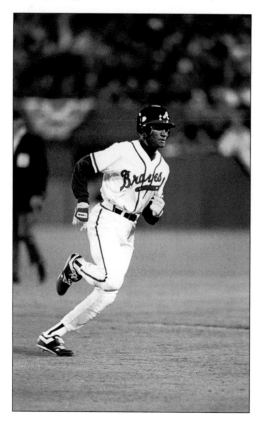

Otis Nixon tied a major league record with six stolen bases in a 1991 game and set a modern Braves record with 72 stolen bases in 1991.

two-run homer in the ninth led to a 7-6 win. Dibble's fastball has been clocked in excess of 100-mph, and that night he was throwing as hard as ever, but Justice was even quicker with his bat, hitting a line drive home run that was out of the park in an eyeblink. Although the Braves still trailed by a game, they believed that with the Dodgers headed for three games in San Francisco, the division really could be won.

As it turned out, the Braves pulled even before the Giants had a chance to work over the Dodgers. The Padres did Atlanta a favor, beating the Dodgers 9-4, while Tom Glavine won his twentieth game, a 6-3 win over the Reds on October 2. With three games left, the Braves and Dodgers were engaged in what was, essentially, a long-distance playoff series. If the two teams were still tied after the weekend, then there would be another playoff, nine innings, sudden death, face to face in L.A. But it never came to that. The next day, the Braves officially defied history, clinching a tie for the division title by beating the Astros, 5-2. But none of the 45,000 jubilant fans at Atlanta-Fulton County Stadium were about to leave. They instead wanted to experience the thrill of watching the Braves officially clinch the Western Division title, and eyes were glued to the Stadium's giant scoreboard TV. Incredibly, the Dodgers obliged, meekly surrendering to the Giants, 4-0. The moment L.A.'s Eddie Murray was retired on a ground ball to second baseman Robby Thompson, the Braves finally exorcised all those long humiliating summers, empty ballparks, and embarrassing seasons that no one wanted to remember.

Worst to first. As second baseman Mark Lemke had said of the 1991 regular season, "It was just one big party."

The Pittsburgh Pirates, winners of the Eastern Division, listened to all the Braves hype and smiled to themselves. The miracle Braves? Wait and see, the Pirates countered. We are not the Dodgers. Indeed, the Braves learned that October was a long way from the glory days of summer. October meant a one-week,

best-of-seven, intense, almost savage meeting of the National League's two best teams. There would be no room for slumps or mistakes, and certainly not for nervousness. Yet, after living on adrenaline for so long during the regular season, a strange metamorphosis took place in Game One of the National League Championship Series. The Braves became nervous.

"It was the first time for a lot of guys and I could see us being overly anxious," David Justice said. "But once we got into the third or fourth inning, it was a regular game for us." By then, it was too late though, because the Pirates were already ahead, 3-0. In the first inning, Glavine hung a curveball to Pirates' center fielder, Andy Van Slyke, who plated the Pirates' first run by crushing a long home run to right. In one swing, the Pirates distanced themselves from their embarrassing National League Championship Series loss to the Reds in 1990, where Van Slyke, Bobby Bonilla, and Barry Bonds combined to hit .191.

In 1991, the Pirates were using the Braves to prove a point: Pittsburgh, and not the little miracle machine from the West, was the best team in the National League. Van Slyke referred to his team as "focused." The Braves were in for a dogfight. Atlanta's best chance probably came in the fourth inning when Mark Lemke lined a ground ball under Gary Redus' glove at first base. The ball rolled into right field, and Lemke was assured of at least second on the two-base error. But he instead chose to gamble, trying to stretch to third base. Right fielder Bobby Bonilla gunned Lemke down with a perfect relay to Steve Buechele at third base. Bobby Cox later admitted, Lemke's judgment "probably looked wrong" especially since Terry Pendleton walked and Justice singled to center. Had Lemke held at second . . . well, the possibilities were inviting. All the Braves knew

was that Pirates' starter Drabek got fly balls from Ronnie Gant and Sid Bream, and all that was left for the rest of Game One was playing out the innings in a 5-1 loss.

The Braves turned to Steve Avery in Game Two, with the knowledge that another loss would give the Pirates an almost insurmountable advantage. But there Avery stood on the mound, taking deep breaths, staring down the Pirates like he was a twenty-one-year veteran instead of just being twenty-one. Avery was calm, just as he had been against the Dodgers, prompting Pirates manager Jim Leyland to admit, "We could've played another two hours and we still wouldn't have scored on Avery." In 8⅓ innings Avery struck out nine, allowed six hits, and matched the Pirates' left-hander, Zane Smith, inning for inning, zero for zero. Who knows how long the pitching duel might have lasted had the Braves not caught a break in the sixth inning.

With two out and David Justice on second base, Mark Lemke hit a chopper at third. The ball had plenty of top-spin and hit so high that Buechele knew there wasn't enough time

Second baseman Mark Lemke became the Braves' "Mr. October" in 1991. After hitting just .234 during the regular season, Lemke hit .417 in the World Series with a record-tying three triples.

to throw out Lemke. He decided his only play was to tag the onrushing Justice, later telling reporters, "If I catch it, Justice is out." But Buechele was shocked to look in his glove and see nothing—no ball, no play on Justice, only leather. The ball had taken a freak bounce over Buechele's head and gone sizzling into left field. "That's one of the stranger hits I've ever gotten," Lemke admitted later. The single scored the Braves' only run of Game Two, although Avery was so dominant, that was all he needed. But before the Braves would walk away with a 1-0 lead, they had to endure a scare in the ninth inning.

Bobby Bonilla started a Pirates rally with a double, and suddenly, Avery was staring at disaster. Barry Bonds was at the plate, as dangerous a ninth-inning hitter as there is in baseball. But Avery again triumphed, forcing Bonds to pop out to shortstop. Bonds was so frustrated upon returning to the Pirates' dugout, he smashed his bat on the artificial turf. The sound of wood splintering could be heard all over Three Rivers Stadium, and all the Pirates could do now was watch Braves' reliever Alejandro Pena, after allowing Bonilla to take third on a wild pitch, get Buechele to bounce to the mound and strike out pinch-hitter Curtis Wilkerson to end the game. This was Atlanta's first-ever postseason win after seven consecutive postseason losses (which had been gathered in postseason 1969, postseason 1982, and the first game of postseason 1991).

The NLCS returned to Atlanta for Games Three, Four, and Five, and the Pirates weren't thrilled with having to walk into the Chop Shop. "There's going to be a lot of energy in our ballpark," Bobby Cox predicted, and his words needed no translation. There would be thousands of Braves' fans chopping, waving their tomahawks, and singing the war cry. "The Chop" was new in 1991, a habit everyone fell into and loved, and the Pirates conceded there was nothing they could do to prevent being victimized. Andy Van Slyke said, "It'll be difficult coming into a situation like that. The fans will be coming at us like it's Custer's last stand."

"The Chop" worked on the Pirates for all nine innings in Game Three, and the war chant was at times so loud the stadium's organist simply refused to compete. The Pirates looked into the stands, mesmerized by the weight of thousands of souvenir red foam tomahawks waving at them, hypnotizing them. Even Ted Turner and his wife Jane Fonda were chopping wildly. Pirates manager Jim Leyland tried to downplay the effects of the Chop Shop, reminding reporters, "It's not the fans who are hitting the ball out of the ballpark or throwing the pitches." And he was right. It was the Braves, who, after spotting the Pirates a 1-0 lead in the first inning, scored four runs off John Smiley in the bottom half of the inning. In the rally there were doubles from Ronnie Gant, Dave Justice, Brian Hunter, and a two-run homer from Greg Olson. Four runs, and all Smiley could say later was, "The Braves are a very, very aggressive team. They took advantage of every mistake I made."

FROM CHUMPS TO CHAMPS

Ron Gant, sent all the way back to Class A Sumter in 1989, returned to become a key player in the Braves' back-to-back pennant years. In 1991, Gant joined Willie Mays and Bobby Bonds as the only major league players to record consecutive 30-30 (home runs and stolen bases) seasons.

All John Smoltz now had to do was protect the lead, and the closest Pittsburgh came to catching the Braves was in the seventh inning when they pushed to within three runs. But the Braves scored four insurance runs in the next two innings, and just to drive home their complete dominance of the game the Braves denied the Pirates a chance to score with the bases loaded and one out in the eighth inning. Alejandro Pena arrived from the bullpen and challenged every Pirate who stepped up to the plate with his overpowering fastballs. He out-maneuvered Orlando Merced with his heat, forcing him to foul out to Olson. He then struck out shortstop Jay Bell to end the inning. While the delirious Braves congratulated Pena in the dugout, Pittsburgh manager Jimmy Leyland called the series of events, "the turning point in the game." Suddenly, the Pirates were asking themselves hard questions. "You have to wonder if we're a bunch of gaggers," as Van Slyke put it.

Game Four represented a chance for the Braves to bury the Pirates. One more win in the Chop Shop and no one would have blamed the Braves for fast-forwarding their imagination to the World Series. But the Pirates, who were defending the Eastern Division crown for the second straight year, drew on their reserves of pride, gracefully handling a late-inning pressure situation. The score was tied at 2-2 in the tenth inning with Pirates on first and second. Mark Wohlers, whose fastball was even more impressive on the radar gun's clock than Alejandro Pena's, was facing pinch-hitter Mike Lavalliere, and with two out and an 0-2 count, it seemed Wohlers had won the battle.

Wohlers was confident his fastball was headed down and within the strike zone, right where Lavalliere couldn't touch it. At least, that's what he intended as he released the ball. Until this moment, it seemed Bobby Cox's gamble of not using Pena on a second straight night would pay a dividend: It was Cox's decision, twenty-four hours earlier, that after two innings' work "we weren't going ask Al to throw again unless we were ahead."

All the Braves asked of Wohlers was that he

keep the game tied going into the bottom of the tenth. The Pirates had actually started their rally against Kent Mercker as he issued a leadoff walk to Andy Van Slyke, and two outs later, watched as the Pirates center fielder stole second. Steve Buechele was intentionally walked, at which point Bobby Cox called on Wohlers to face Don Slaught, a right-handed hitter who was dangerous in situations such as these. But Pirates manager Jim Leyland countered with a left-handed pinch-hitter, Mike Lavalliere, a compact little catcher who was tough to strike out. Lavalliere talked about simply "surviving" the at-bat against Wohlers, adding that the only way to cope with a fastball better than 90-mph was to "not over-swing." He timed the pitch perfectly, lining a single to right-center that scored the winning run, and the Pirates emerged from the game with a 3-2 win.

With the series tied at two games apiece, the Braves knew they would have another long day against Pittsburgh's finesse artist, Zane Smith. Smith's ability was legendary in the National League, and if his control held,

Game Five could become a one-run affair. In fact, in the fourth inning of Game Five, David Justice made a base-running mistake that left the entire ballpark—fans, media, teammates—wondering if he had indeed touched third base or not. Third-base umpire Frank Pulli ruled that Justice had failed to touch third on his way to scoring on Mark Lemke's single to left. Justice, who had reached second on Gary Redus' two-base error, would have given the Braves a 1-0 lead, but he was called out when the Pirates appealed the play to Pulli.

"I absolutely did [touch]," Justice protested. "There's no doubt in my mind. [Third base-man Steve] Buechele was coming towards the hole, and I thought I was going to run into him. If I'd taken my usual turn around third and touched the base with my left foot . . . there was a chance I would run into him." Sidestepping Buechele, Justice attempted to touch the base with his right foot, nearly stumbling as he rounded for home. Tellingly, neither third-base coach Jimy Williams nor Bobby Cox argued with umpire Pulli. Williams in particular was tepid in his defense of Justice. "I can't tell you for sure that David hit [the base]," Williams said. "If he says so, I believe him. But if you're asking if I'm sure, my answer is no."

Denied the run, the Braves were powerless the rest of the day against Zane Smith, and when the Pirates scored off Tom Glavine in the fifth inning, the Braves were essentially dead—1-0 losers in Game Five. Although after the game Glavine remarked that "this [Series] is by no means over," there were only two remaining chances for the Braves, and both of them would have to be played in Pittsburgh. The Pirates had accomplished a near-miracle, winning two of three in the Chop Shop, and with Doug Drabek returning after suffering a strained hamstring muscle in Game One, it was the Pirates who might have let their minds wander to the World Series.

The Braves needed Steve Avery's help in Game Six, but Bobby Cox didn't want his young pitcher to feel the pressure of carrying

Welcome to the "Chop Shop"

The phenomenon started in spring training 1991, when Deion Sanders was picked up by the Braves after he'd been released by the Yankees. College football fans who had followed Sanders' career at Florida State came out to watch the converted ballplayer and brought with them "the Chop," which had been used at all Seminoles' games.

The Chop? Easy to learn, hard to forget. A mock tomahawk chopping motion, it involved a simple bending of the elbow with an extended arm and open hand and was not meant to offend or demean Native Americans, but to root on Sanders in the exhibition season. When the Braves went north, the Chop followed, and whenever Sanders came to bat, fans would start chopping. Soon, all the Braves received similar treatment, and fans would begin chopping at clutch moments during a game. Not long after, the excercise was accompanied by an Indian war chant. By the time the Braves met up with the Pirates, the Chop was recognized nation-wide and a local entrepreneur, Paul Braddy,

Ted and Jimmy.

capitalized on it by selling the Braves' concessionaires on the idea of a foam tomahawk fans could wave.

The idea caught on instantly in Atlanta—even Ted Turner and former President Jimmy Carter were seen chopping away—although the Chop was harshly criticized by Native American groups in Minneapolis during the 1991 World Series. It was Jimmy Carter who eloquently defended the Chop, commenting that, "With the Braves on top, we have a brave, successful, and courageous team, and I think we can look on the American Indians as brave, succesful, and attractive."

an entire organization's hopes and expectations on his shoulders. A pregame meeting was called. "I wanted to loosen [the team] up," Cox said, "and told them we definitely had the tools to win this thing. I also tried to make them laugh." A Pittsburgh radio station helped, too, running a contest for the best Braves joke. The winner said he'd just heard from Dave Justice, who had called, "just to touch base." On the field, though, there was little humor as Game Six got underway, just pure pitching talent as Avery went head-to-head with the Pirates' Doug Drabek.

Steve Avery was so precise with his curveball, so dominant with his fastball, that for eight innings the Pirates didn't get a runner past first base. "I've seen a lot of good pitchers . . . Gibson . . . Koufax," Pirates pitching coach Ray Miller said, "and if Avery's not up there with them, he will be soon." It was an impressive performance—by throwing eight shutout innings, Avery extended his playoff scoreless streak to 16⅓ innings, a League Championship Series record. "Steve is unflappable . . . and he's got all the qualities to be an All-Star for years to come," Cox was moved to say. "He's as good as I've ever seen." The Pirates' Drabek was almost as good, allowing only Greg Olson's RBI double in the top of the ninth. With the Braves ahead, 1-0, the Pirates were down to their last three outs in the ninth inning, and Alejandro Pena took the mound.

What followed were the tensest moments of the 1991 postseason, as Pena allowed Gary Varsho a leadoff single. Varsho was bunted to second and stayed there when Jay Bell flied to right. But with And Van Slyke up, Pena wild-pitched Varsho to third. With the count at 2-2, Pena threw five consecutive fastballs at Van Slyke, and twice the Pirates' outfielder sent screaming line drives, just foul, into the right-field bullpen. The tension at Three Rivers Stadium was so thick the sellout crowd remained on its feet for Van Slyke's entire at-bat—which finally ended when Pena shocked Van Slyke with a looping change-up over the outside corner. It was Olson who was responsible for out-thinking Van Slyke, telling reporters after the that game he had decided to "see what happened if we called a change-up." Van Slyke was so startled, he watched the pitch sail into Olson's glove. The third strike translated into a 1-0 win for the Braves, and ensured a Game Seven the next night.

Amateur baseball psychologists had a field day trying to decide who would have the advantage in the final game. Would it be the Braves, who had the superior pitching and the momentum from Game Six, or would it be the Pirates, who had the home crowd behind them and were fueled by the need to put the 1990 playoff loss to the Reds behind them? Those questions were answered in the first inning of Game Seven as the Braves scored three runs against John Smiley. Smiley's world began to unravel with a leadoff walk to Lonnie Smith, and he would soon allow Brian Hunter a two-run home run. In all, Smiley lasted just ⅔ of an inning, an even worse outing than in Game Three, when the Braves scored five runs in two innings. Incredibly, the fans at Three Rivers Stadium actually applauded Smiley was he walked off the mound, maybe out of pity, or maybe sensing the Pirates' season was over.

John Smoltz pitched Atlanta to its second consecutive shutout, a 4-0 win that gave the Braves their first pennant since 1958. At first, it was almost impossible for the Braves to digest what they had done: they limited the National League's top-hitting team to no runs in the final twenty-two innings, smothering Barry Bonds and Andy Van Slyke to a combined average of .200 with one home run and three RBIs. "[The Braves] just dominated us with their pitching," Pittsburgh

Atlanta-Fulton County Stadium acquired a new nickname after the "Tomahawk Chop" became the signature for Braves fans.

Opposite: Tomahawks of all shapes and sizes turned up at every home game and were also displayed throughout the city.

1991 World Series ticket.

manager Jimmy Leyland acknowledged. "There was no trickery involved. It was just pure power pitching."

As they marched on to their first World Series in thirty-three years, the Braves carried with them the ghosts of the past who had excelled but never made it to the Fall Classic: Rico Carty, who had won the National League's batting title in 1970 with a .366 average; Ralph Garr, the league batting champ in 1974 with a .353 mark; Buzz Capra, the league's ERA champion in 1974; Dale Murphy, who endured so many long summers; and the late general managers Bill Lucas and John Mullen. Dedicating their performance to them, the Braves took on the Minnesota Twins. The Series was a great one. Five of the seven games were decided by one run and three of them—including Games Six and Seven—went into extra innings.

The Twins had just beaten the Toronto Blue Jays in five games to win their second pennant in five years. They had beaten the Cardinals in the 1987 World Series, winning in seven games, and had postseason experience the Braves were lacking. Most strikingly, the Twins had also completed a worst-to-first journey, having finished in last place in the

American League West in 1990. But even though the Twins were coming off a great season, the Braves felt nothing could stop them, especially after the way they had dismantled the Pirates. Asked to assess the American League counterparts, Steve Avery casually remarked, "I'm sure the Twins have a good pitching staff, but I don't think there's a team in either league that can match our pitching."

The Twins simply nodded in response. No one questioned the Braves' excellence, but it remained to be seen how they would handle the high decibel level inside Minnesota's Metrodome—also known as the Thunderdome for the way noise bounced off walls and penetrated players' psyches and eardrums. "This place will be a little different for the Braves, that's for sure," Twins manager Tom Kelly cryptically echoed. Outfielder Kirby Puckett, who was named the American League Championship Series Most Valuable Player, agreed. "The Braves have never experienced anything like this," he commented. "If we're doing something with our bats, it'll be noisy and then it could be a tough evening for the Braves." Commenting on the '87 Series that his Cardinals played in Minnesota, Whitey Herzog offered this assessment, "We

Signs and banners during the 1991 pennant drive demonstrated the creativity of Braves fans. Tommy Lasorda and Darryl Strawberry of the Dodgers were favorite targets.

could have played until Thanksgiving and we still wouldn't have won a game in that place."

In preparation for their first game in the arena, the Braves went through a ninety-minute workout at the Dome the day prior to the Series opener. Bobby Cox chose to start Charlie Leibrandt in Game One, a calm thirty-five-year-old veteran who had played for the Kansas City Royals from 1984 to 1989 and was familiar with the Thunderdome. "I think Charlie will be more comfortable here right out of the chute," Cox said, explaining his choice. Cox had another reason for using Leibrandt: He would have Glavine, Avery, and Smoltz in place and rested for Games Two, Three, and Four, and each of his starters would be assured of having at least two starts if the Series went to seven games.

Just as the Braves feared, though, the Dome was almost as daunting as the Twins themselves. Leibrandt held his own for four innings, but then collapsed in the fifth when the Twins scored three runs and took a 4-0 lead. What did surprise the Braves was Minnesota shortstop Greg Gagne, who had hit only eight home runs all year and batted in the No. 9 spot in the Twins order, and who smoked a three-run blast off Leibrandt. Known mostly for his defense and powerful arm, Gagne said the homer represented "the biggest thrill of my baseball career." It also allowed Jack Morris to work comfortably, as he kept the Braves' left-handed hitters—Jeff Treadway, Terry Pendleton, David Justice, and Sid Bream—to just two hits in thirteen at-bats. By the time it was over, the Twins had won easily, 5-2, and were looking to right-hander Kevin Tapani to giving them a commanding 2-0 Series lead.

To get there, though, they had to handle Glavine, with whom they were acquainted only through scouting reports. His stats were impressive enough—in 1991 Glavine tied for the National League lead with twenty wins, the first twenty-game winner the Braves had since Phil Niekro in 1979, and the first Cy Young Award winner since Warren Spahn in 1957. Glavine threw a mean change-up and on his good days, never threw a strike above

the knees. Still, the weaponry was not enough to keep the Twins from ambushing Glavine in the first inning, as Chili Davis hit a two-run homer.

But the game's most significant play came in the third inning, with the Braves trailing 2-1. With Lonnie Smith at first and two out, Ronnie Gant drove a single to left. Smith slid in at third ahead of left fielder Dan Gladden's throw, but the play was not over. The ball got away from third baseman Scott Leius, Kevin Tapani picked it up and fired across the diamond to first, where Gant had taken too wide a turn. First baseman Ken Hrbek, all 6-4, 250 pounds of him, caught the ball and not only put the tag on the 5-11, 200-pound Gant, but nearly lifted him off the base. Incredibly, first base umpire Drew Coble called Gant out, despite the fact that Hrbek appeared to have forced him off the base. Gant was enraged. "It was so obvious . . . I felt the whole force of him pulling me off the bag. He's twice my size." Braves first base coach Pat Corrales likened Hrbek's play to "a wrestler's move." But Coble ruled that Gant's momentum had carried him off the bag and refused to change his mind. Even though Atlanta tied the game in the fifth inning, Glavine allowed Leius a solo home run in the eighth, enough for the Twins to take Game Two, 3-2.

History was clearly the Braves enemy at this point. Only ten teams of the forty-one that had fallen behind 2-0 in a World Series had recovered to win it all. But the Braves knew they had a not-so-secret weapon ready for Game Three—Steve Avery, whom the Twins had watched suffocate the Pirates. "The man can bring it, I'm aware of that," Kirby Puckett said. "I've watched Avery and I know you

FROM CHUMPS TO CHAMPS

don't have to meet him halfway with the fastball. He'll bring it right to you."

The Braves were also glad to be out of the Metrodome, a place Brian Hunter likened to "going to a nightclub and standing in front of the speakers all night." There were a few other factors the Braves were counting on, including Steve Avery and John Smoltz as the Games Three and Four pitchers and the fact that the Twins had historically been vulnerable on the road during World Series play. They lost all three games to the Cardinals in St. Louis in the 1987 classic and further back in 1965, in the first World Series in Twins history, they lost three games to the Dodgers in Los Angeles.

As it turned out, none of these factors came into play for Game Three: With home-run support from David Justice and Lonnie Smith, Avery departed in the eighth inning holding a 4-2 lead, and the Braves proceeded to clean out their usually dependable bullpen. Alejandro Pena allowed pinch-hitter Chili Davis a two-run home run in the eighth inning that tied that game at 4-4. The score remained tied into the twelfth inning when Mark Lemke faced Twins reliever Rick Aguilera with runners on first and second and two out. The Twins' bullpen, incidentally, had not allowed an earned run in 32.2 consecutive postseason innings dating back to the 1987 World Series against St. Louis. Aguilera, who was third in the American League that year with 42 saves, was an exceptionally hard thrower who also possessed a reliable split-finger fastball. That explained why Lemke was so defensive in his at-bat, telling reporters later, "I just tried to hit the ball somewhere. I said to myself, 'You don't need to hit a home run here. Don't even try to do it.'"

With an short, economical swing, Lemke dropped a soft fly ball in front of Dan Gladden in left field. Justice barely beat Gladden's throw to the plate, and the Braves were 5-4 winners, cutting the Twins' lead to two games to one. Atlanta was ready to unleash John Smoltz in Game Four.

1991 Atlanta World Series pin.

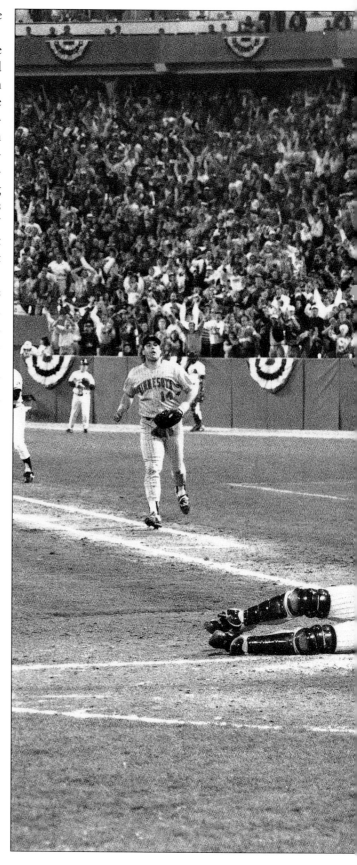

Game Three of the 1991 World Series. In the bottom half of the twelfth inning, David Justice slides home after Mark Lemke singled. Dan Gladden's throw to the plate is late and Justice is ruled safe by plate umpire Drew Coble. The 5-4 win over the Twins gave the Braves their first World Series win in their Atlanta history.

213

FROM CHUMPS TO CHAMPS

A Pena in the Pirates Side

One of the Braves' most important players in 1991 was Alejandro Pena, who was acquired in August of that year from the Mets and converted on all eleven of his save opportunities. But he didn't stop there: Pena saved three more games during the postseason, and even took part in a combined no-hitter with Kent Mercker and Mark Wohlers against the Padres on September 11, the first aggregate no-hitter in National League history.

Alejandro Pena.

Pena's finest moment came in Games Two and Six of the 1991 NLCS. In Game Two, with the Braves clinging to a 1-0 lead in the bottom of the ninth, Pena replaced Steve Avery with Bobby Bonilla on second with one out. He wild-pitched Bonilla to third, but then retired Steve Buechele on a grounder to the mound, and struck out pinch-hitter Curtis Wilkerson to end the game. In Game Six, Pena struck out Andy Van Slyke with the tying run on third and two out in the ninth inning, preserving another 1-0 win for Avery and setting the stage for Game Seven.

"Here, with the Braves, I get work. Here I can show everyone what I can do," Pena said, "I pitch now when it matters. I'm in the play-offs." But fate soon worked against Pena, as elbow problems diminished the effectiveness of his fastball. His record fell to 1-6, and his ERA swelled to 4.07 in 1992, even though he recorded 15 saves. Pena left the Braves and signed with the Pirates as a free agent in 1993, but he required surgery early in the season and developed an ulcer. Within two years, Pena had lost the magic he possessed with the Braves in the last two months of the 1991 season.

Once again, it wasn't the pitchers who were involved in the deciding moments, but Lemke, the umpires, and a television replay. With the score tied 2-2 in the ninth inning, Lemke hit a one-out triple off Mark Guthrie. After Jeff Blauser was intentionally walked, pinch-hitter Jerry Willard was sent to the plate to face former-Brave-turned-Twin Steve Bedrosian. Willard hit a fly ball to right, into the waiting glove of Shane Mack. As Lemke prepared to tag up, and as Mack prepared to fire the ball to the plate, the World Series' most hotly contested play began to unfold. Twins catcher Brian Harper caught the ball and turned to tag Lemke. Harper was certain he had tagged Lemke, completing the inning-ending doubleplay.

But to the delight of Braves fans, home-plate umpire Terry Tata called Lemke safe. "There was no doubt in my mind [Lemke] was in. Harper only [bumped] him with his elbow," he explained. Harper disagreed and argued so vehemently with Tata that he had to be restrained by teammates. Twins manager Tom Kelly remained in the dugout for the duration of the argument, bluntly telling reporters, "I thought Lemke was safe. Harper turned to tag and missed him." After the game Harper continued to claim, "I felt my shoulder touch his shoulder. I got very emotional out there. I said to Tata, 'He's out, he's out!' I really thought I got him."

By Game Five, the Braves were beginning to feel like the Series could be theirs. They took a 5-0 lead in the fifth inning, and by the time they had scored six more runs in the seventh, they were on their way to a 14-5 win. Everywhere the Twins looked, there was another line drive sizzling to a gap or another home run leaving the park. Mark Lemke hit two triples, Dave Justice hit the home run that put Atlanta ahead 2-0 in the fourth, and Lonnie Smith hit a home run for the third straight game. Tom Glavine won his first postseason game, but the real story was the Braves' offense, which sent a message to the American League champions. "Now the Twins know we can score a lot of runs," Ronnie Gant said. "And it puts some pressure on them."

Greg Olson slides home safely on Rafael Belliard's run-scoring single in Game Three of the 1991 World Series. This represented the first World Series run ever scored in Atlanta by a Brave. The Braves went on to win Game Three, 5-4, in twelve innings, but still trailed in the series, 2-1.

The Braves were going to need that pressure, because they were headed to Minneapolis' Thunderdome for Games Six and Seven. Even though they only needed one more victory, it was the Twins who felt confident, knowing the Dome and its high decibel level would be their ally. "The Metrodome is so much different than playing in Atlanta," Minnesota second baseman Chuck Knoblauch said "They make that tomahawk chop thing more than it actually is. You can't even see it when you're on the field. It has no effect. The Dome does."

If anyone was immune to the Dome, though, it was Steve Avery, who time and time again had proved how calm he could be. "You dream about pitching a game like this," he said. "The last three I've pitched, we were down, we desperately needed the win. I don't look at this as any different." But the Twins jumped him for two runs in the first inning, on a run-scoring double by Kirby Puckett and RBI single from Shane Mack. Even though a 2-0 deficit was hardly insurmountable for the Braves, it did indicate that Avery was working without his meanest fastball and would not dominate. Yet Terry Pendleton

tied the game at 2-2 with a two-run homer in the fifth, and the score was tied 3-3 going into extra innings. Bobby Cox arrived at a crossroad in the tenth inning when he decided not to push Alejandro Pena to a third inning's work. Pena had kept the Twins scoreless in the ninth and tenth innings, but in protecting against the possibility of using Pena again in the event there was a Game Seven, Cox summoned Charlie Leibrandt for the eleventh inning.

This decision raised a few eyebrows, since Leibrandt, a lefty, would be facing Puckett, a right-handed hitter whose average against left-handers during the regular season was .406, the best in the majors. Cox countered by pointing out that Leibrandt had struck out Puckett twice in Game One. But there was only a finite number of times Puckett would be fooled by Leibrandt's finesse, and the Braves' luck ran out in the eleventh. Puckett rocketed a 2-1 change-up over the wall in left-center, a home run that not only gave the Twins a 5-4 win, but set the stage for Game Seven.

The pitching matchup featured power vs.

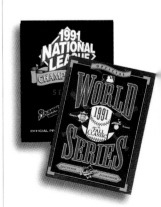

1991 NLCS program and World Series scorebook.

FROM CHUMPS TO CHAMPS

power—John Smoltz against Jack Morris. "This is the kind of situation I've played out in my mind when I was younger," said Smoltz, who went 12-2 in the second half of the regular season. He wanted the ball, but so did Morris, a fourteen-year veteran who dismissed all pregame analysis. "Let's get it on," he said simply.

Every moment was huge, every inning was a miniature apocalypse. The Braves were about to make history, win or lose, a fact they were reminded of by Phil Niekro, who had become the manager of the club's Triple-A affiliate in Richmond. "No matter what happens in Game Seven, win or lose, you hold your heads high because you've done something that no Braves team has done in thirty or forty years." For eight innings, the Braves and Twins staged a game dominated by the two pitchers. No one scored. No one came close. But in the eighth, things changed.

Lonnie Smith led off with a check-swing single. Playing hit-and-run with Terry Pendleton, he was moving as the ball was driven up the gap in left-center. Unfortunately, Smith only made it to third, thanks to a fake doubleplay conducted by second baseman Chuck Knoblauch. Smith, who initially declined to be interviewed, later admitted he hadn't seen where Pendleton's hit had gone, and, deceived by Knoblauch, lost precious seconds around second base. That moment had represented the Braves' best chance to win the World Series, and the rally soon fizzled. Ronnie Gant hit a harmless grounder to first, and both Smith and Pendleton did not dare advance. Morris then issued an intentional walk to Dave Justice. When Sid Bream hit a one-

bouncer to Kent Hrbek at first base, the Twins began the inning-ending double play. Incredibly, the Braves walked off the field without a run, despite having had runners on second and third and none out.

The end came for the Braves in the tenth inning when Dan Gladden led off with a double against Alejandro Pena and was bunted to third by Knoblauch. The Braves had no choice but to intentionally walk both Kirby Puckett and Kent Hrbek to load the bases and hope that Gene Larkin, the pinch-hitter standing at the plate, would hit into a double play, just as Bream had done a half-inning earlier. Larkin was smart enough to know a fastball was coming from Pena, and when he got it, he lifted it over Brian Hunter's head in left field. Hunter never bothered to chase it, letting it drop as the Twins celebrated a 1-0 win and their second World Series championship in five years.

As for the Braves . . . well, it took a while for their accomplishments to sink in, but they agreed unanimously that 1991 had wiped away years of disappointment. All of Atlanta agreed, too. Not only had the Braves set an attendance record with 2.1 million fans, but almost 750,000 people showed up for a downtown parade after the Series. They came to see Terry Pendleton, the National League's batting champ and Most Valuable Player; Tom Glavine, the Cy Young Award winner; Ronnie Gant, who finished second in the league in homers; pitchers Avery, Smoltz, Bream, and Kent Mercker (who had pitched with Alejandro Pena and Mark Wohlers against the Padres on September 11 and delivered the first no-hitter by committee in National League history). And the crowd came to see Bobby Cox, who told the masses, "You are all wonderful."

As happy as everyone was, though, there still remained the matter of unfinished World Series business. The Braves promised 1992 would take care of that.

Braves owner, Ted Turner; his wife, Jane Fonda; and chairman of the board Bill Bartholomay enjoy a successful moment for Atlanta in the 1991 World Series.

Opposite: An estimated 500,000 fans turned out for a Peachtree Street parade celebrating the Braves' "worst to first" season and near-miss in the 1991 World Series. Pictured are Mark Lemke (left) and David Justice (right).

instant replay

20

*"You won't see a lot of rah-rah from this team
until we get back to the World Series."*

—Tom Glavine, after the Braves clinched their second straight Western Division title

Incredibly, by May 27, 1992, Atlanta

was in last place in the West, seven games behind the Giants, with a 20-27 record. So many of the factors that helped the Braves win the pennant in 1991 were now working against them. David Justice was hitting .048 in April, and Mark Lemke, one of the heroes of the 1991 World Series, was barely rising above .200. Alejandro Pena's elbow was in trouble, and so was his fastball, suddenly down to 85-mph after having exceeded 90-mph in 1991. The identity of the bullpen stopper seemed to change every day, from Pena to Juan Berenguer to Mike Stanton and then back again. Bobby Cox played musical chairs with batters Deion Sanders, Otis Nixon, Ronnie Gant, and Justice, pleasing no one and making everyone jittery.

John Smoltz displays MVP trophy (1992 National League Championship Series).

This was the flip-side of last October's adrenaline rush. Most baseball experts had picked the Braves to repeat in '92, but that was assuming that everyone would play as passionately as they had in '91. Cox had waited six weeks for the Braves to get over the World Series disappointment, and heading into June he was beginning to worry the Braves would find it impossible to recapture that passion of last season. Cox couldn't call a team meeting and demand the Braves snap out of it, nor could he ask that a clubhouse leader step forward. Cox's only option was to wait and let the two-month funk run its course. He was hoping for a great game, or even a great play, to jump-start the Braves. That turning point finally occurred in the ninth inning of Game No. 52, on June 2, against the Phillies.

The game was tied 3-3. When Terry Pendleton stared at reliever Mitch Williams, he was certain of two facts: First, that a fastball was coming. Second, that neither he nor Williams had any idea where the ball would go. (Williams had rightfully earned the nickname "Wild Thing" because of his lack of control.) It's a dangerous life, standing up against a 97-mph bullet that could kill you, but Pendleton did his best to track the ball, prepared to get out of the way. On this night, though, Williams' fastball behaved beautifully, crossing over the plate just where Pendleton could really punish it. He sent the ball deep to left-center, a two-run homer that capped a two-inning rally, giving the Braves a total of four runs since the eighth inning. The Braves beat the Phillies 5-3, a key win that foretold everything about the future of the 1992 season.

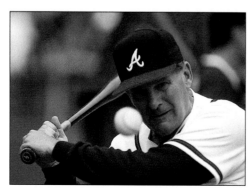

Cox had never worried about Pendleton, the National League's MVP in 1991. It was the rest of Braves who needed to wake up. And they did. Starting on May 27, they won 21 of 24 games, a stretch during which Tom Glavine won five straight and John Smoltz won four of five decisions. Although Cox couldn't know it at the time, June was the month the Braves finally would let go of the frustrating memories of the 1991 World Series, as they went 19-6 and never looked back. The Braves were so efficient in June and July that they tied a franchise record with a 13-game winning streak between July 8-25, finally moving into first place on July 2 and never surrendering it (except for a two-day stint out of the top spot, July 31–August 1).

The Reds were the division's only challenge to the Braves, and they tried desperately to make it a race. But they, too, had trouble matching the Braves' pitching, and a three-game series in early August quickly ended Cincinnati's last stand. They arrived at Atlanta-Fulton County Stadium a half-game behind the Braves, knowing they would have to face Tom Glavine, Steve Avery, and John Smoltz. Reds' manager Lou Piniella countered with Tom Bolton, Tim Belcher, and Greg Swindell, and he was more than happy to tell reporters it was the Braves, not the Reds, who were carrying the emotional baggage to the ballpark. "I think there's more heat on Atlanta," Piniella said. "Just about everyone has conceded the division to them."

Perhaps, but the Reds still hoped to wound the Braves' psyches by winning the first game of the series. They were on their way, too, taking a 5-2 lead into the eighth inning against Glavine, when they turned matters over to their bullpen. Reds reliever Norm Charlton stood on the mound, just two innings from a win, a return to first place, and an huge spiritual gain on the West's tough guys. If this was the season's most critical game, then its most critical juncture came in the eighth inning, when the Braves tied the score. In three separate at-bats in which Charlton was ahead in the count 0-2, he was beaten. First by Terry Pendleton, who lashed an RBI single. Then

In his second tour of duty as the Braves' manager, Bobby Cox led the team to successive National League pennants in 1991 and 1992.

by Justice, who lined a run-scoring double, and finally by Greg Olson, whose sacrifice fly made the score 5-5.

Incredibly, Piniella allowed the left-handed Charlton to face the Braves in the ninth inning, too, and they resumed their attack. With two out, Otis Nixon walked, stole second, and waited for the Reds to issue an intentional walk to Pendleton. It was an obvious and logical strategy, Nixon and everyone else in the stadium thought, one which would put runners on first and second and create a force play at any base. Not only that, but Pendleton was on his way to hitting .357 against left-handers in 1992 and was tied for the sixth-best average in the National League that year. With Ron Gant in a slump at the time and generally less dangerous than Pendleton, why would Piniella even consider anything but an intentional walk?

Piniella had gained a reputation over the years for being a notorious hunch-manager, and something told him Charlton could beat Pendleton. Maybe it was Charlton's splitter, or maybe it was just luck, but Piniella made his decision and let the game's outcome ride with the fates. So much for hunches, Piniella

must have thought, as Pendleton crushed a two-run home run, giving Atlanta a 7-5 victory that all but devastated Piniella's Reds. Pendleton later admitted he was surprised Charlton had been so careless with his splitter, leaving it up in the strike zone. "I'm not trying to be arrogant or cocky," Pendleton said, "but if it was me pitching, I would have been more careful."

Piniella, whose temper was even more legendary than his hunches, snapped at reporters after the game. "You saw what happened. Just write it. What the hell am I going to tell you guys?" Piniella had good reason to come unglued as his Reds were beginning to fade in the West. They also lost the remaining two games of the series and left town 3½ games out. That's as close as they got to the Braves in the closing two months, prompting Cincinnati general manager Bob Quinn to correctly observe that, "That [7-5] loss was the most pivotal loss of the season. The momentum from the game was like a tidal wave."

The Braves were on their way to the National League Championship Series. They used August and September to fatten their already impressive statistics. As a team, Atlanta finished eight games ahead of the Reds, and their 98 wins were the most in the major leagues. The pitching staff led the majors in ERA (3.14) for the first time since 1958, with 24 shutouts. Individually, Tom Glavine won 20 games for the second straight season, John Smoltz led the National League with 215 strikeouts, and Terry Pendleton drove in a career-high 105 runs while batting .311. The numbers said the Braves were ready for a rematch with the Pirates, who also dominated their division. Despite the frustration of two National League Championship Series defeats in two years, the Pirates nevertheless won 96 games, finishing nine games ahead of the second-place Montreal Expos.

Even though outfielder Bobby Bonilla had left Pittsburgh to sign as a free agent with the Mets, the Pirates' offense was still dangerous. Barry Bonds had hit 34 home runs with 103 RBIs and led the National League with a .624 slugging percentage. Teammate Andy Van

Ron Gant experienced a sub-par season in 1992, hitting .259 with only 17 home runs and 80 RBIs. Gant's first career grand slam came in the National League Championship Series against Pittsburgh's Bob Walk, highlighting a 13-5 Atlanta win in Game Two.

INSTANT REPLAY

Slyke tied with Terry Pendleton for the league lead with 199 hits, and finished second with a .324 average. But now all the calculators would be reset to zero because October had arrived, and with it, a National League Championship Series déjà vu.

The Braves tried to hide their glee, but in the first inning of Game One at Atlanta-Fulton County Stadium John Smoltz—who was 1-6 with a 3.66 ERA in his last eleven regular season starts—dropped three monstrous curveballs to strike out Barry Bonds, and the Braves' miracle machine was up and running. Nothing went right for the Pirates after that. Pittsburgh's pitching ace Doug Drabek lasted less than five innings and allowed four runs and five hits. This was the game, ironically, that the Pirates thought they could sneak from the Braves, considering Smoltz's second-half struggles. But Smoltz breezed through the Pirates' batting order, the easy outs blurring one into the next.

Smoltz, in fact, flirted with a no-hitter until the fifth inning. But by then, the Pirates were confronting a much deeper dilemma: what to do about the Braves' lineup, which had already ambushed Drabek for a 1-0 lead in the second inning and was laying in wait in the fourth inning. David Justice walked, then scored as Sid Bream crushed Drabek's curveball into the gap in left-center. Down 2-0, the Pirates froze as Gant pushed a perfect bunt down the first base line. The ball was fielded by Orlando Merced, dropped, and then thrown directly into Gant's ribs as he crossed first, giving the Braves a 3-0 lead.

In the fifth inning, the Pirates' Jose Lind bounced an infield single behind second base with two out. Drabek followed, only to be struck out by Smoltz. In the bottom of the same inning, Drabek lost a one-pitch war to Jeff Blauser, a 3-2 fastball that Blauser sent screaming into the night for a home run. Suddenly, the Braves were ahead 4-0, and it was obvious that Smoltz—who had responded to pressure in Game Seven of the 1991 World Series—wouldn't collapse in this Championship Series.

"Compared to Game Seven of the Series, this was a piece of cake," Smoltz said, following the Braves' 5-1 win in Game One. "I enjoy being able to pitch in games like this, but I gained a lot from last year." The Pirates could only nod in sad agreement. "We didn't have one key situation all night," Barry Bonds lamented. "Smoltz had great, great stuff."

Game Two looked even brighter for the Braves, especially as they watched Steve Avery limit the Pirates to only two hits in six innings. Avery took a League Championship Series record of 16⅓ consecutive scoreless innings into the game, a pleasant reminder that the Pirates were virtually incapable of hitting him in the 1991 Series. The Pirates' only hope was in left-hander Danny Jackson, who had been acquired from the Chicago Cubs in July, and who was now called on to stop the Braves. But Jackson was 0-4 with a 4.19 ERA against Atlanta in 1992, and he had not developed any secret weapons for Game Two. He was pummelled by the Braves, allowing four runs before being knocked out in the second inning. The Braves' run began with back-to-back RBI singles from Damon Berryhill and Mark Lemke, and when Avery himself crushed a long sacrifice fly to center field, the Pirates' desperation seemed almost palpable.

Still, Atlanta's most punishing blows weren't delivered until the fifth inning. The Braves had loaded the bases with two outs, when Bob Walk's 2-0 pitch to Ron Gant failed to reach catcher Don Slaught's glove. Gant nailed it with the sweet spot of his bat and stood at home plate, watching his grand-slam home run disappear from sight. Actually, the Pirates were beaten as early as the first inning, when Avery struck out Barry Bonds. And when Bonds stepped up to the plate again in the fourth inning, he popped to second. When he finally singled in the seventh inning, the crowd at Atlanta-Fulton County Stadium stood and cheered him, with more than a hint of mockery. Bonds tipped his cap, in acknowledgment, returning the sarcasm.

By the time Game Two was over, the Braves had taken it, 13-5. "We were obviously embarrassed out there," Jim Leyland confessed. "The only good thing is that it's over." The Braves seemed somewhat sympathetic to the Pirates' unraveling. "It's like they're trying

Prime Time

There is probably no player in Braves history who has attracted controversy as easily as Deion "Prime Time" Sanders. A tremendously gifted athlete, Sanders simultaneously starred in two sports, combining a career as an All-Pro defensive back in the NFL with that of a major league baseball player. Signed as a free agent by the Braves prior to the 1991 season, Sanders immediately added speed to the Atlanta lineup. In 1992, playing only 97 games, Sanders led the National League in triples with 14.

But it was Deion's own agenda that seemed to best define him. Continually creating situations where one career (baseball) vied with the other (football), Sanders seemed unable to satisfy either employer. In 1992, he tried to work for both on the same day. After playing for the Atlanta Falcons in a game at Tampa Bay, Deion jetted to Pittsburgh for Game Five of the NLCS, but was too dehydrated to see any action for the Braves.

Deion's flashy style of play was called charismatic by some, egocentric by others. Although a self-described team player, Sanders jumped the Braves for three weeks in 1993, unhappy with both his contract and his playing time. Although active in several Atlanta charities, Deion would not participate in team-sponsored player appearances. He would sign autographs for Falcon fans ("They appreciate me"), but wouldn't for Braves fans ("They don't understand me").

This enigmatic and often contradictory nature of Deion was a contributing factor in the 1994 trade which sent him to Cincinnati for Roberto Kelly. Said one teammate, at the time, "You may love him or you may hate him, but you'll never forget 'Prime Time.'"

Deion Sanders.

to carry more on their shoulders this year than the last three years," Avery said. "I think the pressure is on them now, like they're swinging at pitches they normally wouldn't. Hitting isn't an easy thing, and when it becomes a mental thing, too, it's that much more difficult."

That axiom was never so obvious as in Game Three, only it was the Braves who learned the truth of it. They were facing Pirates knuckleball specialist Tim Wakefield, an infielder turned pitcher, who, for reasons not even he knew, could make a knuckleball dance like a vision. Wakefield had been recalled from the minors in July and, like a savior, posted an 8-1 record with a 2.15 ERA. The Braves knew it would be a long, irritating night, so the front office asked Richmond pitching coach and former major league knuckleballer Bruce Dal Canton to throw batting practice. There were no last-minute secrets to learn about the knuckleball, but Bobby Cox made the request so his batters wouldn't be completely disoriented when facing Wakefield.

The Braves were no strangers to Wakefield, having lost to him 4-2 in August, and they were well aware of his credentials. "It's like a butterfly coming at you," Otis Nixon said of Wakefield's knuckleball. "Can you imagine being on a trampoline and catching a ball while jumping up and down? With a good knuckleball, that's what it's like," Sid Bream added.

The Pirates were staring at a possible 3-0 game deficit when they turned to Wakefield, who calmly proceeded to muzzle the Braves. After scoring 18 runs in the first two games, Atlanta could only manage solo home runs by Sid Bream and Ron Gant. But the Pirates were having an equally difficult night with Tom Glavine, and the score was tied 2-2 going into the bottom of the seventh inning. That's when Glavine allowed first baseman Gary Redus a one-out single to center, after which shortstop Jay Bell smoked a double to left. With runners on second and third, Bobby Cox headed to the mound to rescue Glavine. "Tommy made some bad pitches late in the game," Cox later admitted. But by now it was too late.

Mike Stanton arrived from the bullpen with orders from Cox to somehow contain Van Slyke. "My only thought was, 'I don't want to be walking back to the dugout,' " Van Slyke said. He took an inside corner fastball, sent it deep to center, and as Redus tagged up and scored, the Pirates had a 3-2 lead. All that was left for the Pirates was to sweat out the last two innings, as Otis Nixon's two-out double in the eighth was followed by Jeff Blauser's long foul ball to left—missing the foul pole by maybe six feet. "I thought it was just a pop-up," Wakefield admitted. "I was shocked, really shocked, to see it go that far."

And in the ninth, Wakefield saw Justice at the plate—and remembered his second-inning single, his fourth-inning missile to first, and his seventh-inning near-single between first and second. "I wasn't going to get beat with my second or third pitch," he decided. That meant another knuckleball: all fingertips, no wrist, no spin. And for the Pirates, 3-2 winners in Game Three, it meant no doubt.

In Game Four, Otis Nixon's four hits led the Braves to a 6-4 triumph, giving the Braves a three-games-to-one lead. The Braves wanted this game, but the Pirates needed it. The most enduring image of the game was of Barry Bonds, not just kicking the dirt at home plate, but attacking it with all the anger and embarrassment the Pirates felt. With one out and the tying run on second in the seventh inning, Bonds had struck out against Mike Stanton and was booed heartily by fans at Three Rivers Stadium as he left the batter's box in a dust-storm.

The fans had just watched Doug Drabek get knocked out in the fifth inning, failing to hold a 3-2 lead. Drabek, who was similarly roughed up in Game One, had allowed seven hits in 4⅓ innings. "I didn't finish anyone off," he later admitted. "I'm disappointed in myself." Manager Jim Leyland didn't bother to disagree with Drabek, saying, "It was our pitching that hurt us tonight." Bonds' disappearance had been just as damaging to the Pirates, especially in that fateful seventh inning. With one out, Andy Van Slyke had overpowered Smoltz with an RBI double to right, cutting the Braves' seemingly-safe 6-3 lead to 6-4. Then Mike Stanton arrived and went to war with Bonds.

Stanton got to two strikes and threw the fastball as hard as he could. Bonds responded by swinging with enough fury to send the ball over the wall . . . if he had connected. By the game's end, Braves pitchers had limited Bonds to just one hit in 11 at-bats. With a 6-4 win secure, Smoltz, who struck out nine batters in 6⅓ innings, could afford to be diplomatic. "Barry's not really in a slump," he said. "We're just pitching him very carefully. And until whoever's hitting behind him in the lineup can hurt us, we'll attack them the same way."

The Braves were only one win away from the World Series, with three chances to get there. Logic dictated that the Pirates wouldn't touch Steve Avery's curveball in Game Five, and that journeyman Bob Walk would be no match for the Braves, against whom he was only 5-9 lifetime, with a 4.93 ERA. Logic— and history—also indicated the Pirates' situation was hopeless, as no National League team had ever recovered from a 3-1 deficit in the playoffs. Imagine then, the Braves' disbelief as Avery lasted only one-third of an inning. That's all it took for the Pirates to eliminate Avery, starting with Gary Redus' bloop double over first base. Avery—who threw six shutout innings against the Pirates in Game Two—was in the game for all of thirty pitches, in which time he allowed four runs, five hits, and successive doubles to Bonds, Jeff King, and Lloyd McClendon.

"I just didn't have it, and if you don't, they'll hit you every time," Avery later told reporters. "I really have no explanation. You never think it's going to happen to you, but sometimes it does." By the time Barry Bonds walked to the plate in the first inning, the crowd at Three Rivers Stadium sensed the left fielder's awful luck was about to change. Avery pitched two

Souvenir foam tomahawk used by fans in the Chop.

In 1992, record base-stealer Otis Nixon made the catch of the year against Pittsburgh.

1992 National League Championship ring.

strikes, but when he tried to slip a fastball by Bonds, the ball went sailing up the gap in right-center—an RBI double that ended Bonds' October slump. Rounding second base, Bonds later said, "I wanted to tell all the fans, 'yeah, the jinx is over.' "

Walk defied history, allowing the Braves only three hits, and kept the Series alive for a Game Six and possibly a Game Seven. The Pirates knew those last eighteen innings were in Atlanta's home park, but they'd crushed the Braves in Game Five, 7-1, and were ready to believe in miracles, too. Or at least, they were trusting Tim Wakefield's knuckleball.

If the Braves were shocked by Game Five, they were embarrassed by Game Six. By the fifth inning some fans were jostling at the exit ramps, having seen enough. Tom Glavine's eight-run, eight-batter, zero-outs second inning—which he bluntly called "a nightmare"—ensured there would be a seventh game between the Braves and Pirates for the second straight year. Only this time, the Braves weren't the ones feeling blessed by the gods. In Games Five and Six, Glavine and Steve Avery had allowed 12 earned runs in just 1⅓ innings, and even though Pirates manager Leyland tried to be polite, saying, "There's no such thing as momentum in baseball," the Pirates discovered the Braves could be conquered, even at home.

While Tim Wakefield's knuckleball again wiggled impressively—he was hurt only by two Justice home runs—Glavine was in such trouble that the game was over in the second inning. Barry Bonds led off the top of the second with a long home run to right, sending a warning to the Braves. Glavine tugged on his cap, looked into Damon Berryhill for the next sign, and proceeded to suffer a mugging of the worst kind. Jeff King singled. Lloyd McClendon singled. Don Slaught doubled to right-center, scoring two runs. Jose Lind bounced to short, but Jeff Blauser—attempting to nail Slaught on his way to third—hit Slaught with the throw. Slaught scored. Wakefield bunted. Glavine threw too late to third. Gary Redus doubled home one more run. Jay Bell crushed a three-run home run to left.

In the space of twenty pitches, the Pirates had taken an 8-0 lead on the Braves, and any further thought of the Braves winning Game Six was pointless. The Braves wrote it off, a 13-4 rout, and tried to prepare for Game Seven. For twenty-four hours, the entire city of Atlanta was frozen in anticipation—and worry. Could the Braves possibly recover? As it turned out, the real Game Seven question was: Would the fans recover from what baseball observers say was perhaps the best ending to a postseason game ever?

The telling moment of Game Seven came in the ninth inning, as the Braves were three outs away from a 2-0 loss, with Doug Drabek finally outpitching John Smoltz. Drabek faced Terry Pendleton leading off the ninth, having held him zero for fifteen in Championship

Top right: Sid Bream slides home as throw arrives from Barry Bonds to Pirates catcher Mike LaValliere in Game Seven of 1992 National League Championship Series.

Center right: Umpire Randy Marsh rules Bream safe, giving the Braves a 3-2 win in the game, and a 4-3 win in the series.

Lower right: Bream is swarmed by his World Series-bound teammates.

Francisco Cabrera is doused by David Justice after delivering the game-winning hit in Game Seven of the National League Championship Series against the Pirates. Cabrera was an unlikely hero, having played in only twelve games during the regular season.

Series play. But Pendleton doubled to right, after which David Justice's grounder to second base was mishandled by Jose Lind. Lind was on his way to a Gold Glove Award that year and had made only six errors all season, but for some reason he lost the ball. "I backed up on the ball," he admitted. Lind took four steps, got the ball . . . and watched helplessly as it rolled away.

The Braves decided not to sacrifice, despite Sid Bream's far-below-average running speed and vulnerability to doubleplays. Luckily, Drabek walked Bream on four pitches. By now Leyland could see Doug was tired. Bob Walk, who had pitched nine innings two days earlier, was warming up in the pen, but it was Stan Belinda who was summoned. With bases loaded, Belinda almost pulled the Pirates through the emergency. Ron Gant's sacrifice fly cut Pittsburgh's lead to 2-1, and even though Damon Berryhill drew a walk to reload the bases, Belinda got a soft pop-up to second from Brian Hunter.

The only player left, aside from light-hitting infielder Rafael Belliard, was pinch-hitter Francisco Cabrera, who had faced Belinda only once in his career, on July 29, 1991, and had hit a home run. Cabrera had already

proved to the Braves how tough he could be in late innings, having crushed a ninth-inning, two-out, three-run home run off the Reds' Rob Dibble in August 1991 that had resulted in a Braves' win in thirteen innings. Now Cabrera was ready to make history again. On a 2-1 pitch, he lined a base hit to left, scoring Justice with the tying run. But Barry Bonds made a stunning, full-sprint retrieval of the ball and without breaking stride, threw an on-the-fly strike to catcher Mike LaValliere. The Pirates were trying to stop Bream from scoring the season-ending winning run from second.

Another step, and Bonds would have thrown out the heavy-legged Bream at the plate, and the Pirates would have emerged from the inning still tied at 2-2. But Bream just barely beat LaValliere's tag, and the ballpark exploded. The Braves piled on top of each other at home plate, crushing high-fives to each other, oblivious to the TV cameras in their faces. A few Pirates remained in the dugout for several minutes, too stunned to walk away. Bonds dropped to one knee in left field and stared at the ground. Andy Van Slyke simply sat down in center field. He was the last Pirate into the dugout.

The Braves ran wildly through the infield, into the outfield, delirious, their fists in the air in wild celebration—shouting and crying—although the noise they made was lost in the thunder that filled the ballpark. Helmeted police on horseback rushed to the field to protect the Braves from a throng of cheering fans, although that was hardly necessary. The shock of the Braves' 3-2 win in Game Seven was so overwhelming that no one in the park moved. Instead, more than 50,000 remained in their seats for ten minutes, fifteen minutes, a half-hour, chanting the Braves' war cry, chopping and pleading for curtain call after curtain call from the Braves. Bedlam reigned in the streets of Atlanta as fans celebrated throughout the night. The final moments were so humiliating for the Pirates, manager Leyland said, "This is probably the hardest lesson I've ever had to handle, and I'm not sure I'm handling it well."

Leyland's voice broke while speaking to reporters, and twice he had to stop speaking to regain his composure. "I'm probably still in shock," Leyland said quietly. "It's a little tough to tell your players three years in a row, 'Thanks for the effort.' This is a real heartbreaker." Even Bobby Cox sent his sympathies to the Pirates, saying, "My heart goes out for them. They busted their butts the whole series, but it just didn't work out." In the end, the Braves seemed fated to win the pennant for the second straight year, the first National League team to do so since the 1977–78 Dodgers.

In the World Series the Braves would face the powerful Toronto Blue Jays in baseball's first international World Series. The Jays had outfielders Joe Carter and Dave Winfield, second baseman Robby Alomar, pitchers David Cone, Jimmy Key and . . . Jack Morris. The same Jack Morris who had beaten the Braves

Braves shortstop Rafael Belliard starts a doubleplay in Game One of the 1992 World Series against Toronto.

as a Minnesota Twin in Game Seven of the 1991 Series.

There Morris was again in Game One of the 1992 Series, a free-agent enlistee with Canada's first pennant winner. The Braves countered with Tom Glavine, who, after allowing Carter a solo home run in the fourth inning, limited the Jays to just one hit the rest of the game. Glavine watched Carter's home run disappear, and almost instantly his internal monologue began. "I told myself, 'A solo home run is not going to beat you,'" Glavine recounted later. "I told myself not to change my game-plan just because Joe had taken me deep."

Still, the Braves' dilemma lingered: how to defeat Morris? The sixth inning yielded the answer. Even though Morris had spent the early innings, "getting us to chase a lot of bad pitches, making us look bad," as Cox put it, he was undergoing a subtle but unmistakable decline. The forkball that was so wicked suddenly dropped too much out of the strike zone to tempt the Braves. Morris walked two batters in the fourth inning, two more in the fifth, and even though he wriggled out of both crises, he walked into more serious trouble in the sixth—when he walked David Justice and allowed Sid Bream an opposite-field single between short and third. After Ron Gant grounded into a fielder's choice, Morris threw a 1-2 forkball to Berryhill. Morris knew he was in a jam the moment the last seam left his fingers. "I was able to stay back and drive it," Berryhill explained. Not just drive it, crush it. The ball was immediately launched in a huge arc, and Morris' head jerked, watching the ball fly far over the right-field wall. That home run was all Glavine would need, as the Braves took Game One, 3-1.

Game Two could have belonged to the Braves, too, and all they had to do was survive the ninth inning. They were ahead, 4-3, and the Blue Jays were down to their last two outs—until Braves reliever Jeff Reardon walked pinch-hitter Derek Bell before facing another pinch-hitter, Ed Sprague. Reardon offered Sprague the exact pitch he was looking for, the fastball in the lower half of the

David Justice hit 11 of his 21 home runs in the final 43 games of the 1992 season, as the Braves pulled away to win the National League West by 8 games over Cincinnati.

strike zone, and Sprague sent it out of the park. After the Braves' stunning 5-4 loss, Reardon said, "It's pretty tough to have that happen to you in a World Series. I normally get people out with high fastballs and it didn't happen that way tonight. That [low fastball] was a mistake."

The Braves accepted that explanation, although in Game Three, Reardon was again answering hard questions. The score was tied 2-2 in the ninth inning, and the Jays had the bases loaded and one out. At that moment, the Braves were wishing they had made more of some missed opportunities from earlier in the game: for example, David Justice's blast to the center-field wall off Juan Guzman in the fourth inning was acrobatically snared by Devon White. Terry Pendleton, on first base and thinking Justice's hit was at least a double, was stunned to discover he had overrun Deion Sanders at second, who was tagging up on the play. Pendleton was called out by umpires for passing Sanders, who himself was actually tagged out trying to slide back into second. It should have been a triple play— only the second in World Series history and the first since 1920—but second-base umpire Bob Davidson called Sanders safe. But even given another out to work with, the Braves still didn't score in the inning against Guzman, and they were paying for it in the ninth.

Reardon actually got two sliders past Toronto's Candy Maldonado in the bases-loaded crisis that in Maldonado's words, "made me look real bad." He swung and

1992 Atlanta Braves World Series pin.

INSTANT REPLAY

Flag Flap

The 1992 World Series created the first international incident in baseball history when a U.S. Marine color guard inadvertently presented the Canadian flag upside down before Game Two in Atlanta.

The reaction in Canada was heated and Prime Minister Brian Mulroney was "dismayed and upset" at the Marines' mistake. In an editorial, the *Toronto Sun* wrote that the incident "speaks to the appalling ignorance many Americans suffer whenever it comes to dealing with any country other than their own."

"On behalf of all Americans I simply want to apologize to the people of Canada," President George Bush said, "If that had happened in Canada and we had seen the United States flag flown upside down, every American would have been very, very upset. Certainly nobody would ever do anything like that on purpose."

Game Two, 1992 World Series, Atlanta.

One of the members of that Georgia-based Marine guard, Sgt. David Day, said the soldiers were unaware why so many flashbulbs went off as the Canadian anthem was being sung. "The photographers were going nuts and I thought, 'Man, we must look good,'" Day said. "I didn't know until we walked off the field, and my wife said, 'You guys had the Canadian flag upside down.' I said, 'No way. How could something like that happen?'"

The Commandant of Marine Corps asked the Blue Jays for a second chance to present the Canadian colors before Game Three in Toronto, a request that was granted. A four-man Marine detachment from Buffalo, New York, was flanked by four Royal Mounted Police, who presented the Stars and Stripes—the crowd received the Marines warmly, and there were no further incidents.

missed at both, and Reardon reasoned he would try again. "I was trying for the strikeout, getting the pitch down," Reardon said. It never happened. Reardon hung the pitch, left it so exposed in the strike zone that all Maldonado had to do was take an easy swing and let the bat do the work. The ball sailed over the infield, helping the Jays to another win, 3-2, and a 2-1 Series lead. "This is the worst thing that has ever happened to me in my career," Reardon said later.

As much as the Braves wanted to sympathize, they knew they were running out of innings. Their next chore in Game Three would be to neutralize Toronto lefty Jimmy Key, a strike-zone surgeon who won not with a great fastball or curveball but with awesome control. At one point, Key retired sixteen straight Braves, and they could only hope Tom Glavine in turn would be as oppressive. He almost was, allowing the Jays only two runs. In the eighth inning the Braves finally made Key sweat, after Ron Gant's leadoff double and Brian Hunter's push-bunt to third.

With runners on first and third, none out and a two-run deficit, the obvious move would have been to bunt, but Bobby Cox decided against it, choosing to instead play for a big inning. Damon Berryhill was free to hit, but he was impressed with the ease in which Hunter was able to surprise the Jays' infield with a bunt. So Berryhill tried likewise to bunt, defying Cox and ultimately self-destructing. He popped the ball into the air, allowing Jays catcher Pat Borders an easy play at home plate.

"I have no idea what Berryhill was thinking," Cox said stiffly. Berryhill shrugged and said, "I've attempted it a few times and never popped up. Tonight was the worst thing that could happen." The Braves eventually got one run on Mark Lemke's bouncer off Key's glove, and even after Nixon reached on Duane Ward's strike-three, wild-pitch splitter, the Braves weren't dead. Not until Jeff Blauser lined a sharp grounder at John Olerud to end the inning. That's when Tom Henke came in and retired the Braves 1-2-3 in the ninth, and with a 2-1 win over the

Braves and 3-1 lead in Games, sent the Blue Jays straight into Game Five.

The universe was in perfect order for the American League champions: they had the SkyDome, the October Man, Jack Morris, and the Series. All that was missing was nine innings, and they were just a formality. The Braves' memories flooded with images of 1991, when Morris ruined their dream. "I'm not making any promises, no guarantees," Morris would only say this time. "Let's just see what the game brings." There were four innings of civility, where the scored was tied 2-2, then a avalanche of line drives.

Perhaps it was just the law of average finally manifesting itself, as too many Braves had been invisible for too long. Collectively, the team was batting only .185 with just one home run. Gant and Justice were batting .167, Nixon and Pendleton were at .188, Mark Lemke was at .154. All them played a role in sabotaging Morris, but it was Lonnie Smith who opened the greatest wound, crushing a grand slam in the fifth inning. In fact, the Braves exposed Morris as a talented but suddenly hittable pitcher, as he was 0-3 in the 1992 postseason having allowed 19 runs in 23 innings. And for all his October mystique, there he was at his locker, humbly telling reporters, "I did the best I could."

It wasn't just Smith who crushed Morris' fastball in the fifth, it was Otis Nixon who rejected Morris' stuff, too. Nixon singled to center, stole second, then scored when Deion Sanders beat up a fastball for a single as well. Moments later, Sanders was on third when Terry Pendleton hit another Morris fastball, this time a ground-rule double inside first base.

By now, Jays manager Cito Gaston had to understand the reality before him. Morris wasn't just mediocre: he was costing the Jays a chance to end the Series. "Did I leave Morris in too long?" Gaston said, repeating the question. "I guess the results will show that I did. But I believe in Jack. Without Jack, we wouldn't have been here." Gaston knew the risks of intentionally walking David Justice to load the bases, then letting Morris face Lonnie Smith. Gaston saw, foul ball after foul ball,

that Morris was losing this battle, too, and that as Nixon said, "it was only a matter of time" before the inning exploded.

With a 1-2 count against Smith, Morris tried another fastball. "Up and away," he said ruefully. "If I had to do it again, I might've thrown it another couple of inches up, maybe gotten him to pop it up." It was a mistake by Morris, and it was Smoltz who said, "We all knew we'd have to capitalize on any mistake Jack made." Smith swung, sending Joe Carter on a desperation-chase to the right-field wall. "I hit it good," Smith later said. "I knew it was good enough."

Good enough for a 7-2 win in Game Five, meaning the Series would return to Atlanta for Games Six and Seven. Home. No Brave needed to be told the advantage this meant to them. "We felt all along that if we could get this thing back in our park then we could do something good," Nixon said. And to make sure the Jays understood their handicap, the Braves pumped Placido Domingo and Mario Lanza through the PA system during batting practice, a direct retaliation for the elevator music the Braves were forced to listen while they took batting practice in the SkyDome.

Steve Avery set a League Championship Series record in 1992 for most consecutive scoreless innings thrown. When he shut out the Pirates for the first six innings in Game Two, it gave him 22⅓ straight innings without allowing a run, easily breaking Oakland's Ken Holtzman's old record of eighteen.

The Braves started Steve Avery, and faced Dave Cone. Cone was no stranger to the Braves, having played for the New York Mets for six years before being traded to Toronto that summer. Actually, Cone was a lock to win the National League's strikeout crown had he not left the Mets, instead losing by one strike-out to John Smoltz. The Braves knew Cone to be a gifted pitcher who could throw a 92-mph fastball, slider and splitter, and on some nights all of them could be unhittable. But Cone was also prone to anxiety on the mound, when he would overthrow the fastball or else bounce the splitter in the dirt. This was the Braves' best hope, since Avery was starting on three days' rest and from the outset it was obvious his fast-ball hadn't been sufficiently replenished.

The Jays took a 1-0 lead in the first inning after Devon White singled, stole second, and later scored when David Justice misplayed Joe

Carter's line drive. Even though the Braves tied the game in the third, Candy Maldonado slugged a solo home run in the fourth inning, giving Toronto a 2-1 lead. Bobby Cox decided Avery wouldn't be able to contain the Jays any longer. Pete Smith started the fifth inning, keeping Toronto scoreless for the next three innings, an enormous contribution considering Cone never did have his meltdown. In fact, the Braves were down to their last three outs, trailing 2-1 when they produced yet another miracle. With the Jays relying on closer Tom Henke, Jeff Blauser singled to left and was bunted to second by Damon Berryhill. Lonnie Smith drew a walk. Francisco Cabrera was next, making his first plate appearance since breaking the Pirates' hearts, and the line drive off his bat was, for an instant, a clone of the one that beat the Pirates' Stan Belinda. But this time, Candy Maldonado made a stumbling, off-balance catch while back-peddling, testimony to how hard Cabrera had hit the ball.

The Braves last chance was Otis Nixon, and they appeared doomed when he bounced a ground ball between third baseman Kelly Gruber and shortstop Manny Lee. Somehow the ball rolled through the infield, an RBI single that tied the game at 2-2, and even though that's as far as the rally went—meaning extra innings were on the way—the Braves were sure their karma had changed.

Only, no one expected Charlie Leibrandt to have to face such a difficult eleventh inning crisis by himself. He had created his own problems with one out by hitting Devon White, then allowing Robby Alomar a single. The telephone rang in the Braves' bullpen, delivering instructions to warm up Jeff Reardon. Leibrandt got Joe Carter to fly to center, and with the free-swinging Dave Winfield up, Reardon probably should have replaced Leibrandt. Yet Bobby Cox never left the dugout, ignoring Reardon and hoping for the best from Leibrandt. It was obvious Reardon's earlier failures in the Series had made Cox wary of him, although the manager later said he was "saving Reardon for the twelfth inning." But it never came. Winfield lashed

one of Leibrandt's changeups down the left-field line, a two-run double that gave the Jays a 4-2 lead. Leibrandt said, "I felt I had to go with my best pitch," but there was no point in second-guessing. There were still three outs left in 1992.

Incredibly, the Braves rallied one more time. Jeff Blauser led off the bottom of the eleventh with a single off Jimmy Key, who was working his second inning of relief. Damon Berryhill bounced what should have been a doubleplay ball at Alfredo Griffin, but the ball took a bizarre hop over Griffin's head and into the outfield. Key watched in disbelief, as did all the Jays, and the usually stoic left-hander said, "When I saw that I said to myself, 'Oh, no, here we go again.' "

Rafael Belliard bunted both runners over, and Brian Hunter's grounder to Joe Carter scored one run and advanced Smoltz (who had entered the game as a pinch-runner for Berryhill) to third. The moment now belonged to Nixon, who was facing relief right-hander Mike Timlin. In his mind, Nixon was replaying the seventeen bunt hits he had collected in 1992, thinking that an eighteenth would the perfect way to not only tie the game but keep the inning alive. Nixon tried, placing it down the first base line. Had it been a few more feet to Timlin's left, closer to the line . . . who knows? But Timlin picked the ball up, flipped to Carter, and in one surreal moment the Braves' season came to an abrupt and painful end.

It was easy enough to think of the ninety-eight wins, but after two straight World Series losses, the regular season numbers, the Western Division crown, even the National League pennant failed to truly satisfy the Braves. As Tom Glavine put it, "Everything was all right until I saw the Blue Jays jumping around at their parade. That's when it hit me. There you are at the brink of realizing a goal and you don't do it. It's very disappointing."

The Braves had only option available: win another Division in 1993 and become October's guest all over again.

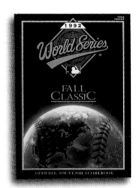

1992 World Series souvenir scorebook.

the great race

21

"Confidence. That's it. Everybody on the team believed in themselves. Even when we were seven or eight games behind, these guys were surprised they weren't in first place."

—Braves pitcher Greg Maddux, on the last day of the 1993 regular season, when the Braves clinched their third-straight Western Division title

Every year, it seemed, the Braves played a game of chicken with the standings, seeing just how far they could drift from first place and still win the West. In 1991 the Braves were 9½ games out at the All-Star break. In 1992 there was a slight improvement, as the Braves were out of the cellar by late May. But in 1993, Bobby Cox's team looked as if it had signed its own suicide note, spotting the Giants a ten-game lead on July 22. The Braves had just squandered a three-run lead to the Pirates, and their situation looked bleak. Even with a respectable 55-42 record, the Braves couldn't catch up with the Giants, who seemed determined not to give other division teams any breathing room. "People ask me all the time if we can hold onto this lead," San Francisco manager Dusty

Top: Greg Maddux (left), Steve Avery. Bottom: Tom Glavine (left), John Smoltz.

Baker said to a reporter, "I tell 'em, 'Shoot, I'm thinking about increasing it, not about it going down.' "

But privately, Baker was deeply concerned about the Braves. Their pitching, the best in the National League in 1992, had improved in the off-season with the signing of Cy Young Award winner Greg Maddux. Maddux accepted the Braves' five-year offer for $28 million, nearly $6 million less than the Yankees were willing to pay. "Atlanta is where I want to be," Maddux said simply, in response to questions about his decision. In 1992 Maddux, who was gifted with rare ability to both finesse and overpower a hitter, was 20-11 for a Cubs team that finished eighteen games out of first place. Euphoric Atlanta fans could only dream of how unbeatable Maddux would be pitching for the Braves, and, in fact, that spring it must have seemed possible to general manager John Schuerholz that the Braves could win not only 100 games, but perhaps 110.

They started off slowly in April, going 12-13, but each subsequent month the Braves were above .500. Although they were hitting a mere .245 in mid-July, the lowest in the majors, there wasn't any one factor that had contributed to the Braves' undistinguished performance other than the Giants' prolonged hot streak. That's baseball. "What I can't understand is how everyone thinks we're supposed to breeze through the season," Tom Glavine said at the time. "You know, win all 162 games and our pitching staff not give up a run. But that's not being realistic . . . there are a lot of good teams in this division, too." "We still believe in ourselves," Terry Pendleton insisted, "We know we can still do it."

Maybe so, but by mid-July Schuerholz had decided it was time to act. He obtained first baseman Fred McGriff from the Padres in exchange for three minor league prospects: outfielders Melvin Nieves and Vincent Moore, and right-handed pitcher Donnie Elliott. McGriff instantly added home-run power to the Braves' lineup. Slugging 36 home runs for the Blue Jays in 1989 and 35

home runs for the Padres in 1992, McGriff was the only hitter since the deadball era to lead both leagues in homers. "What bothers me is that San Diego didn't get more for him," San Francisco general manager Bob Quinn said, commenting on Schuerholz's coup.

Yet what the Padres really wanted was inexpensive young players. The San Diego front office had become intent on trimming its costs, and with the exception of five-time batting champion Tony Gwynn, had traded all its high-priced stars to improve the bottom line. No matter how talented McGriff was, he was earning $4.25 million, and therefore expendable—which was just fine with the Braves. "Fred McGriff has brought something to this team," Deion Sanders said. "He sits in the batter's box, and you know every pitch could be gone. You don't want to sit around and watch, you want to join in."

In his six previous seasons, McGriff had hit 191 home runs, more than any other major leaguer. More than Mark McGwire, Jose Canseco, Joe Carter, Darryl Strawberry . . . more than any of them. McGriff had hit at least 31 home runs each year since 1989, during which time his average never dropped below .269. His RBI total remained at a steady 94 per year.

On July 20, McGriff first strolled into Atlanta-Fulton County Stadium, greeting the players he knew and introducing himself to the players he didn't. Suddenly a security guard burst into the clubhouse, screaming, "Fire, fire! There's a fire upstairs. Everybody get out on the field!" Scrambling out of the clubhouse and onto the infield, McGriff and his new teammates were horrified to see flames consuming eight luxury boxes and part of the press box. At that moment Ted Turner, who was on hand to welcome McGriff, leaned over Terry Pendleton and said, "There's our omen. We're going to win this thing."

And he was right: McGriff homered in his first game with the Braves, a two-run blast against the Cardinals that helped turn an early 5-0 deficit into an 8-5 win. "Like lightning

Mark Lemke (left) and Jeff Blauser (right) pose safely on the field as fire consumes eight luxury boxes and part of the press box at Atlanta-Fulton County Stadium on July 20, 1993. The date also marked the arrival of Fred McGriff, acquired in a trade from San Diego.

striking," was how Pendleton recalled the moment of McGriff's home run. Installed as the No. 4 hitter, and with no complaint or protest from Justice, McGriff went on to hit five more home runs in the next seven games. Soon the Braves began averaging six runs a game, and it wasn't long before Dusty Baker's fears were realized: the dormant Braves were alive and ready for a fight. The first test of the rejuvenated team came on August 23, when the Braves arrived in San Francisco for a three-game series, 7½ games out. "We know what we have to do," Pendleton said flatly. "We have to sweep."

In the first game Steve Avery picked up his fourteenth win, defeating the Giants, 5-3. Tom Glavine then out-pitched Bryan Hickerson, 6-4, as Pendleton, Justice and Ron Gant all went deep, prompting the Giants' Baker to observe, "We appear a little tight." And in the series finale, the Braves hit six home runs—two apiece by McGriff and

Justice—in a 9-1 public flogging of Giants right-hander Billy Swift. "Atlanta is trying to catch us; we're not trying to catch them," Barry Bonds caustically reminded his teammates. But the Braves knew they were on a roll, and that they had just turned the table on San Francisco. "That's where it all started," Greg Maddux would later say about the Braves' run for the championship. The Giants still led by 4½ games, though that lead shrank even further when the Braves routed Swift again in the first game of a three-game rematch in Atlanta. This time the score was 8-2, as Maddux won his sixteenth and the Braves came within 3½. By September 10, the Braves were neck-and-neck with the Giants, and a week later Atlanta had completed a miraculous recovery, having pulled safely out in front with a four-game lead. But the Giants, who had lost eight straight at Candlestick Park, rebounded by winning eleven of twelve, and on the second-to-last weekend of the season, as they inched back to within 1½ games of Atlanta, Barry Bonds hit four home runs in three games against the Padres. In Game No. 157, the Braves lost to the Astros, 5-2, as Pete Harnisch's sixteenth win was preserved by Doug Jones, who struck out Jeff Blauser with the bases loaded. The Giants then beat the Colorado Rockies, 6-4, leaving the two teams tied, each with 100 wins. "I think I know how Lazarus felt," Baker remarked.

The next day, the Giants lost to the Rockies in front of thousands of Braves fans who followed the game on the scoreboard's DiamondVision screen. Secure in the knowledge that first place was still theirs for the night, the Braves beat the Astros 6-3 as Glavine won his twenty-first game, giving Atlanta a one-game lead with four to go. Preparing for a possible Braves-Giants first-place tie, the National League called for a one-game playoff; the home team would be determined by a flip of the coin. The Braves lost the toss when John Schuerholz (advised by his thirteen-year-old son Jonathan), called heads. Monday awaited in Candlestick, and no matter what the result, the winner would have to fly to Philadelphia on Tuesday and be ready to start the National League Championship Series on Wednesday.

In Game No. 159, the Astros knocked out John Smoltz after four innings, en route to a 10-8 decision over the Braves. A few hours later, the Giants opened a four-game series in

The middle of the Braves' 1993 batting order. Left to right: Ron Gant (36 homers, 117 RBIs), Fred McGriff (37 homers, 101 RBIs), and David Justice (40 homers, 120 RBIs).

Los Angeles against their rivals, the Dodgers, with a 3-1 victory that lifted the Giants back into a tie for first. On Friday, October 1, Game No. 160, the Braves beat the Colorado Rockies, 7-4, as Avery picked up his eighteenth win and Pendleton smacked a home run and five RBIs. But that night, Barry Bonds single-handedly kept the Giants even with Atlanta. L.A. took a 4-0 lead, although Bonds closed the gap with a three-run homer off Ramon Martinez, tying the score at 4-4 in the third inning. In the fifth, with runners on second and third, Tommy Lasorda brought in rookie left-hander Omar Daal, but decided not to intentionally walk Bonds. "The bases loaded is too tough a situation to put a pitcher in," Lasorda explained. He paid for that decision as Bonds hit another three-run homer, and again in the seventh, when Bonds returned to hit the decisive, run-scoring double off Steve Wilson as the Giants won, 8-7, to preserve the tie.

"That right there is what MVPs are all about," Dusty Baker said after Bonds' astounding performance. But the Braves had their own candidates, Fred McGriff and Terry Pendleton. Pendleton, the tough third baseman, went two for four with a triple and three RBIs as the Braves pounded the Rockies the next day, 10-1. But across the continent the Giants' Rod Beck had orchestrated a 5-3 win over the Dodgers with two strikeouts and a ground ball in the ninth. Both teams were tied going into the final day of the season.

There they were on October 3, 1993: the Braves and Giants, both with 103 wins, neither one a champion yet. This race had been so focused and intense and required so much adrenaline and so much energy that no one had mentioned the Phillies or the National League Championship Series for weeks. The race with San Francisco was a crucible for the Braves, a way of cleansing the memories of Game Seven of the 1991 World Series and Game Six of the 1992 World Series, and they could think of nothing else. The Braves had never encountered a team as relentless as the Giants, or an opponent as tenacious as Barry Bonds, and there was one day left to beat him.

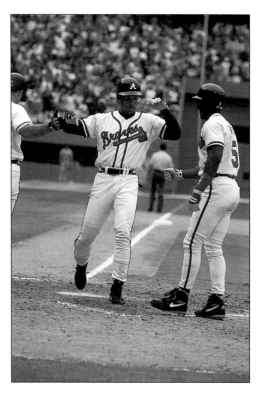

In 1993, David Justice became the third left-handed batter in Braves history to hit forty home runs in a season, joining Eddie Mathews and Darrell Evans.

Because their game with the Colorado Rockies would begin three hours earlier than the Giants' game against the L.A. Dodgers on the West Coast, Fred McGriff wanted to press the Braves' psychological advantage in the cross-country game of nerves.

"We've got to throw a win up there early so they see it," he said. There was no doubt the Giants were watching. As was Tommy Lasorda. His Dodgers had one last chance to hurt the Giants the way they had hurt him in 1991. Lasorda treated this game like his own nine-inning World Series, reminding the Dodgers of how the Giants had acted as spoilers through the years. "Let's break their hearts this time," Lasorda said. "Winning this game will make my year." But back in Atlanta, the Rockies weren't about to lay down, either. "Don't count your money yet!" Colorado outfielder Daryl Boston shouted at the Braves during batting practice.

The Rockies fought fiercely, knocking out Tom Glavine in the seventh inning and cutting the Braves' lead to 4-3 when second baseman Roberto Mejia homered off Glavine. Bobby Cox then summoned Steve Bedrosian, who struck out pinch-hitter Alex Cole. In the bottom of the seventh, David Justice hit his fortieth home run, driving in his 120th run, making him only the fourth player in Braves' history—along with Hank Aaron, Jeff Burroughs, and Dale Murphy—to hit 40 homers and drive in 100 or more runs in the same season. That's all the room reliever Greg McMichael needed as the Braves finished with a 5-3 win. But no one celebrated yet. Instead, the Braves retreated to the clubhouse to watch the Giants-Dodgers on ESPN, and in the stands, the fans were invited to stay and watch the game on the DiamondVision.

With the Braves huddled around the TV, the Dodgers took a 3-0 lead from Giants' starter Salomon Torres in the fourth inning. Dusty Baker had taken a risk relying on a rookie for such a critical game, and he knew it. "I've got to come get you, man," Baker said as he walked to the mound. "I don't want to, but I've got to." The Giants crept to within 3-1 in the fifth, but with reliever Dave Burba on the mound, the Braves suddenly rejoiced. Dodgers' catcher Mike Piazza smoked his thirty-fourth homer of the season, and after first baseman Eric Karros walked, Cory Snyder also homered. That gave the Dodgers a 6-1 lead. When Dave Righetti was brought up, he allowed Piazza a three-run homer in

Greg Olson, signed as a minor league free agent in 1990, became the Braves' top catcher for the next four seasons. Olson may be best remembered for a jarring home plate collision with Houston's Ken Caminiti in 1992, in which Greg suffered a broken ankle.

the eighth, the Braves finally knew the West was theirs. "It's over," Justice said, "Bonds can't hit an eight-run homer."

The Braves respected the Giants for winning 14 of their last 17 games, and sympathized with their long-time nemesis, Barry Bonds. Despite leading the league with 46 homers, 123 RBIs, and the fourth-best average (.336), Bonds still wasn't a champion. He took the defeat with grace, but vowed to never yield to the Braves, ever. "Only good thing about it is, I didn't have to see them on the field, didn't have to see them parade around like the last two years," Bonds said. "But they know I'm coming after them."

Hours later, after the clubhouses had emptied, the phone rang in Dusty Baker's office.

"Dusty. Tommy." It was Lasorda.

"Hi, Tommy."

"Dusty, I want you to hold your head high. You did a good job."

"I hear you."

"I feel bad it had to end this way for you when you won 103 games, but we had to play hard."

"I wouldn't have expected any different."

"Now you know how we felt in '91," Lasorda said softly, hanging up.

Both Baker and Lasorda had now shared the experience of losing to the Braves. Statistically, Atlanta was untouchable, as McGriff, Justice, and Ron Gant gave the Braves the first trio of 100-plus RBI men since Aaron, Cepeda, and Carty in 1970. The pitchers won the league ERA crown for the second straight year. Jeff Blauser became the first Braves shortstop since Alvin Dark to hit .300. There was a franchise attendance record, 3.8 million. And of course, there were 104 wins, another club record, each one a battle scar. "This is most rewarding of our three consecutive divisional titles," Bobby Cox said, "because of the number of games we had to win." But another National League Championship Series awaited. And after that, another World Series. How much adrenaline could one team possibly manufacture?

Maybe it was all to be expected, the Phillies' 4-3 win in Game One of the National League

Championship Series, as third baseman Kim Batiste lined the game-winning single off Greg McMichael. Even though it lasted ten innings, Atlanta was in trouble as soon as Curt Schilling struck out the first five hitters in the Braves' lineup. Nixon, Blauser, Gant, McGriff, and Justice all went down, answering any lingering questions about the adrenaline hangover. The Braves were understandably tired and were a lucky to make it to extra innings. They were down, 3-2, in the ninth before Bill Pecota drew a leadoff walk from Mitch Williams. Then Mark Lemke hit a perfect one-bouncer at third baseman Kim Batiste, who was poised to start an around-the-horn doubleplay and all but extinguish the Braves for Game One. But Batiste threw the ball away, and the Braves eventually tied the game on Otis Nixon's grounder to short. Batiste redeemed himself in the tenth, singling home Philadelphia first baseman John Kruk after his one-out double.

With enough sleep and a chance to distance themselves from the Giants, the Braves were far more interested in Game Two. They faced Tommy Greene, who was 10-0 in Veterans Stadium, and ready to take on Greg Maddux.

The Braves, old hands at the postseason,

sensed Greene's nervousness as soon as he threw ball one to Otis Nixon in that first inning. Ball two came moments later, and then ball three and ball four, none of them close. There was an uncomfortable sensation in the Phillies' dugout, even as Greene was striking out Jeff Blauser and getting Ron Gant to ground out. Then Fred McGriff stepped to the plate. Greene made the mistake of challenging him on the very first pitch, a fastball that was supposed to tease the outside corner, but instead found the middle of the plate. McGriff's body tensed as the fastball arrived, and he nailed it perfectly, catching the ball about three inches from the top of the barrel. McGriff knew the ball was history the moment he connected, and so did the rest of the Braves. No one moved at the Vet; the home run was that impressive. And McGriff's 438-foot home run probably would have pushed past 500 feet if it hadn't landed in the stands in the upper deck.

McGriff later said his only reaction was, "I got it." There was no arrogance in that proclamation, nor did any of the Braves gloat in their humiliation of Greene. Terry Pendleton, in fact, didn't even bother to watch the ball's long arc. Instead he turned away to practice his swing in the runway between the dugout and the clubhouse. "I knew the ball was out, so there really wasn't any point in seeing where it landed," Pendleton said. What mattered were the two runs, the early lead, and the fast exorcism of Game One. The Braves never panicked at a 1-0 deficit in the series, and after dealing with Doug Drabek and Jack Morris in previous Octobers, were ready for Greene, too. "I made some mistakes and the Braves capitalized," Greene said of the savage seven-run attack that forced his exit in the third inning. "Everything I got over the plate, they seemed to hit out." The two runs in the first inning were followed by six more in the third, resulting in a 14-3 Braves win in Game Two, probably the best medicine they could have had in the early stages of the National League Championship Series.

In Game Three, Tom Glavine watched his fastball go one-on-one with John Kruk's bat

After several seasons as a utility man, Jeff Blauser became the Braves' regular shortstop in mid-1991. In 1993, Blauser became the first Braves shortstop since Alvin Dark (1948) to hit .300.

THE GREAT RACE

in the sixth inning, and it took less than a second for Glavine to know who had won. A smart pitcher, Glavine knew Kruk had hit a home run to left, and that if the Braves were going to win this game, he would have to collect his composure and his fastball in a hurry. "I told myself, 'Don't get mad about the home run, channel it in the right direction,'" Glavine said after Kruk's homer gave the Phillies a 2-0 lead. "Hold 'em right here.'" There was no panic in the Braves' dugout, no panic at all. The team had long since eliminated that word from their National League vocabulary and they were waiting for redemption against the American League. "We just don't want to win it this year—we *need* to win the Series," Glavine said. "Getting there won't be enough, not this year."

It was easy to understand the Braves' emotional burden, which made their composure all the more admirable. As Kruk circled the bases, the Phillies were high-fiving each other in the dugout, dreaming of a World Series, too. They resembled the Braves of 1991, as they had gone from worst in 1992 to first in 1993. The Phillies' roster was full of crazy, sloppy players like Kruk and Lenny Dykstra and Curt Schilling, and they were fearless in late innings, too. But Glavine calmly got Dave Hollins to fly to right, induced comfortable ground balls to second from Darren Daulton and Pete Incaviglia, and, just like that, the moment had slipped away from the Phillies. Glavine gave what he called "a little confidence-booster" to his teammates, letting them know they didn't have to deal with too big of a deficit. A 2-0 lead was nothing for the Braves to overcome, and they crushed Phillies starter Terry Mulholland in the sixth inning. In the span of five batters, Mulholland allowed four hits and a walk, including David Justice's two-run double over Pete Incaviglia's head in left.

That made the score 5-2, and the Phillies had no further use for their bats. The Braves were en route to a 9-4 win, and with the next two games in Atlanta, it was possible for them to imagine snuffing out the Phillies' fire at home. But the Braves still had to cope with

the unpredictability, not to mention the danger, of Mitch Williams in Game Four. His moment—the Braves' moment, really—came in the ninth inning with runners on first and second, nobody out, and Williams ready to either blow the Braves away or turn Game Four into a bad dream for the Phillies. He had been trusted with a 2-1 lead, but the Braves inevitably found life. Williams' first pitch allowed Bill Pecota a broken-bat single to start the inning, and the Braves didn't notice that Pecota's bat didn't just splinter, it was demolished by the force of Williams' fastball. All that mattered was that there was a runner on first and a chance to tie a game in which no Braves pitcher had surrendered an earned run.

The Braves were hopeful. The Phillies were terrified. With Williams on the mound, both the Braves and the Phillies were hostage to his weird luck. As Williams put it, "If something bad can happen on the baseball field, then it'll happen to me." With Otis Nixon at the plate in a clear bunting situation, the Braves' hearts sprinted as Williams fielded the ball and misplayed it. While Nixon raced to first, Williams bobbled the ball once, twice, then dropped it back on the ground. Both runners were safe.

After sitting out the 1992 season with a circulatory problem, Steve Bedrosian returned to the Braves in 1993. Pitching in 49 games, all in relief, Bedrosian went 5-2 with a 1.63 ERA.

It was now Jeff Blauser's turn to lay down a bunt, and Williams again broke with convention. He got to the ball quicker than any of the Braves thought possible, and even though he never got a proper grip on the ball, he threw to third. "I thought that [throw] was headed into left field," Blauser later said. Batiste caught it, though, stretching grotesquely to make sure the ball stayed glued in his glove, and nailed Blauser as he slid into third.

Williams, the Braves, and the Phillies then paused for a deep breath. Gant was waiting for the fastball and Williams was happy to oblige. It came at Gant at better than 90-mph, but he timed it perfectly, connected just right, and later said, "I thought I did what I had to do with the pitch." He hit it hard, but, unfortunately for the Braves, the ball was a line shot right into second baseman Mickey Morandini's glove. Morandini caught the ball for the first out, then stepped on second base before Nixon could even move. The double-play happened so fast, it was almost impossible to digest at first. Williams had survived. The Braves had lost Game Four, 2-1. It was ugly and terrifying, but the Braves cursed under their breath: That's Mitch.

In Game Five the Braves dug deep into their reservoir of October luck and seemed to find magic—again. They were trailing 3-0 going into the bottom of the ninth, but suddenly the Phillies' Curt Schilling lost the strike zone on Jeff Blauser and walked him. After third baseman Kim Batiste made yet another error on an easy doubleplay ball off Ron Gant's bat, manager Jim Fregosi turned to Mitch Williams, who was recovering from food poisoning and didn't have much of a fastball.

In the span of four batters, Williams allowed three singles and a sacrifice fly. Francisco Cabrera—who else?—tied the game with a pinch-hit single to center. Not even the next batter, Lemke, who had struck out twice in his first three at-bats, had trouble catching up to Williams' heater. He hit it perfectly down the left-field line, an angry line drive that landed four feet outside the left-field foul line. Suddenly, Atlanta-Fulton County Stadium

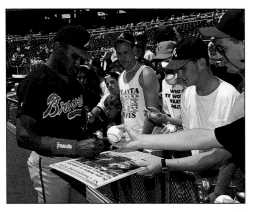

After setting Atlanta base-stealing records in 1991 and making the catch of the year against Pittsburgh in 1992, Otis Nixon finished his Braves career in 1993, hitting .269 with 47 stolen bases. Nixon was signed as a free agent by the Boston Red Sox in 1994.

went quiet, and Williams stood on the mound, rubbing up a new ball. Usually, such moments belong to the hitter. A long, angry line drive, even if it's a foul ball, is his way of telling a pitcher how lucky he was to survive, that his best fastball had just been timed and measured. Instead, Lemke said, "I told myself, 'One of the best closers in the game has you in a hole and you almost got out. Now you gotta start over.'" There was no celebration in the Braves' dugout. Lemke's foul ball was just that—a foul ball, another chance for Williams. So Williams broke off a mean slider, too vicious for Lemke to handle, and the Braves' infielder swung over it, later calling it, "an unbelievable pitch." One out later, and the Phillies were the ones high-fiving each other in the dugout, even though they should never have been forced to play extra innings. Suddenly, it wasn't the Braves who tied the game, 3-3, it was the Phillies who survived certain catastrophe.

It seemed like only a minute later that Lenny Dykstra was jumping on Mark Wohlers' fastball, hitting a massive home run to right-center that gave the Phillies a 4-3 lead. With their adrenaline reserves empty, the Braves had no response in the bottom of the tenth inning: forty-year-old journeyman Larry Anderson struck out Blauser and Ron Gant to end the game, and all around that quiet clubhouse, one could sense how weary the Braves had become, tired of the endless search for miracles. Even a half-hour after the game, several Braves were in the players' lounge, watching a replay of Dykstra's home run. A few sought refuge in the trainer's room or the weight

THE GREAT RACE

The Braves "High Five" has become a post-game tradition after an Atlanta victory. Clockwise from bottom left, Coach Jimy Williams, coach Jim Beauchamp, coach Clarence Jones, Greg McMichael, Greg Maddux, John Smoltz, Greg Olson, Ron Gant, Kent Mercker, David Justice.

room. No one had much to say. "Eventually, the close games start to take something out of you emotionally," Jeff Blauser said. "You ever been to Six Flags? They've got a ride there called the Ninja—it's an unbelievable roller coaster. You go straight up, and then a second later you're going straight down. I think it's fair to say that's how we felt."

Two days later, when the Series returned to Philadelphia, the Braves found that three years of stress had finally caught up to them. Despite having Greg Maddux, their Cy Young Award winner, on the mound, the Braves couldn't stop the Phillies from running out to a 6-1 lead in the sixth inning. The most damaging blows came from Dave Hollins, who hit a two-run home run in the fifth, and Mickey Morandini, who hit a two-run triple in the sixth. The Braves never made Tommy Greene uncomfortable, and afterward they were in the sad position of passing the torch to the younger, fresher Phillies. In a word, the Braves were burnt out.

"It's been three years, three long years and there are a lot of tired guys in here," John Smoltz said after the season ended with a 6-3 loss in Game Six. "I mean, when you're not just the favorite, but the heavy favorite, everyone is ready for you. Everyone attacks you. No one is afraid of you. It's not easy to keep playing like that, game after game, year after year."

Smoltz talked about the exciting summer, about 104 wins, about catching the Giants, then holding them off. After a while, it finally made sense: the Braves' playoff had been the final weekend of the regular season, sweeping the Rockies and ruining the Giants' hopes. How else to explain Atlanta's three straight losses in the 1993 National League Championship Series except to say the adrenaline was gone? In retrospect, it seemed Mark Lemke's foul ball in the ninth inning of Game Five cost the Braves the pennant. They were unable to mount another attack on the Phillies after that point—stunned after Lenny Dykstra's home run in the tenth inning and ineffective against Greene in Game Six.

The Braves loved the pressure and made it their ally for three straight years, which is why they were, intially, the overwhelming favorites to win the National League Championship Series. In fact, the Braves-in-five and Braves-in-six sentiment was so strong, so prevalent, even Phillies general manager Lee Thomas said, "I was starting to have some doubts in the recesses of my mind. I wondered if people knew something about my team that I didn't."

But before the game Lenny Dykstra was oblivious to the Braves' superiority, at least to their experience. Dykstra sidled up to a reporter and said, "Trust me, we're gonna win this thing." He was in the middle of the Phillies' first two-run rally, bouncing a single to right and later scoring on Darren Daulton's ground-rule double into the right-field corner. That was the first tip-off that Greg Maddux wouldn't be invincible, and that's all the Phillies needed to know. David Justice had no choice but to admit, "We just got outplayed." Terry Pendleton nodded and said, "You can look for all the reasons you want why we lost. The reason is in the other clubhouse. They played better in these six games."

The Phillies knew what life was like for the Braves in 1991—exciting and new, where any postseason game made for great drama. By 1992 the Braves came a little closer. By 1993 they had improved even more, but suddenly the Chop wasn't new anymore, the war-chant wasn't as much fun, and regular-season games were just a warm-up for October. By midnight, the Braves clubhouse was a sad, nearly empty place. Smoltz sat down to finish tying his shoes, realizing there was no need to hurry anymore.

"It was like we had to play perfect baseball all the time," Smoltz said. "It's going to be a frustrating off-season."

1993 NLCS program.

Wait Till Next Year

Bouncing back from the shock of losing to the Phillies in the National League Championship Series, the Braves came to spring training in 1994 with one iron objective: to win the World Series. To get there though, they would have to beat a new set of opponents, as the team had been reorganized into a new Eastern Division. With Major League Baseball realigning to create a Central Division in both leagues, Atlanta joined the Phillies in the East, and the Cardinals, Pirates, and Cubs moved to the Central Division. The Dodgers, Giants, Padres, and Colorado Rockies formed a four-team Western Division. In the American League, the Cleveland Indians and Milwaukee Brewers left the East for the Central Division, and the Texas Rangers joined the West Coast contingent—the A's, Angels, and Mariners—in the four-team Western Division.

A new round of playoffs would result from this reorganization. For the first time in baseball's history, a wild-card team could qualify for the postseason. That is, the team with the best record among the divisions' second-place finishers—known as the wild card—would be matched against the division winner with the best record in a best-of-five series. The other series would pit the remaining two division winners in a best-of-five, and the winners of each series would square off for the pennant in a best-of-seven.

The equation seemed complicated and cumbersome to baseball purists, who after twenty-five years were only starting to get used to two divisions and a League Championship Series. But the Braves didn't seem to have any need for wild-card berths, at least not in April when they won thirteen of their first fourteen games. By April 18, the Braves had already taken a five-game lead on

Tom Glavine (left) and Greg Maddux.

Kent Mercker, Fred McGriff, and Javy Lopez celebrate Mercker's no-hitter against the Dodgers, April 8, 1994.

THE GREAT RACE

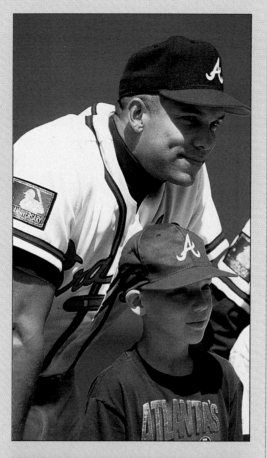

the East, as their new neighbors watched with understandable concern as Greg Maddux went 3-0, Kent Mercker threw a no-hitter against the Dodgers, first baseman Ryan Klesko hit four home runs, and rookie catcher Javy Lopez hit three homers with twelve RBIs. From the outside, there was every reason to believe that the Braves could be untouchable the rest of the summer and spend September warming up for October. After all, in that fourteen-game stretch, Atlanta outscored its opposition 91-36, including a 19-5 win over the Cubs that represented the most runs the Braves had ever scored in one game since 1966.

Still, there were signs as early as spring training that 1994 wouldn't be so kind to the Braves. For the first time since their ascent from last place, serious injuries plagued the starting lineup, beginning with Ron Gant. The muscular outfielder was the victim of a dirt-bike accident in the off-season that left him with a broken leg. In his place, the Braves were prepared to use Chipper Jones, a perfect choice since Jones had hit .325 at Triple-A Richmond in 1993, leading the International League in hits (174), runs (97), total bases (268), and triples (12). Jones was voted the Braves' Triple-A Player of the Year, and the fates seemed to be working in his favor. Unfortunately Jones, too, was struck down by injury, suffering a torn anterior cruciate ligament in his knee that cost him the entire season.

After their impressive 13-1 start, the Braves went on to lose nine of their next eleven games. Although they were still in first place, they allowed the Expos back into the race, and left April only two games ahead of Montreal. With a tight race looming for the rest of the summer, general manager John Schuerholz decided his lineup was imbalanced with too many left-handed hitters, and vulnerable to left-handed pitching. As a result, the team officially severed its ties with Deion Sanders on May 29, trading him to the Reds for right-handed hitter Roberto Kelly. The new center fielder promptly hit safely in eighteen of nineteen games between June 2-

Top: David Justice.

Bottom: Javy Lopez (center) in spring training.

25, and even though the Braves were 17-10 on the month, and at 48-28 overall, a full twenty games over .500, the Expos were still breathing down their necks—just one and a half games out of first place.

Obviously, this was going to be a war of attrition, not unlike the pennant races the Braves had endured in 1991 and 1993. But this time, there was trouble in the bullpen, as the relief corps blew five of eleven save opportunities in July alone. In past years, the bullpen had always produced at least one hero: there was Alejandro Pena in 1991, going eleven-for-eleven in save situations in September. In 1992, Jeff Reardon appeared in time to push the Braves into the World Series, and in 1993, rookie Greg McMichael was like an apparition. But in 1994 the bullpen was inconsistent, failing to convert on fifteen of forty-one save opportunities, and posting an ERA of over 4.00. Also, the injuries kept coming, as Jeff Blauser was bothered by a strained oblique muscle and Terry Pendleton was a victim of chronic neck and back ailments. On July 8, the Braves' hold on first place ended, as the Expos finally moved into a tie. Two days later, as the All-Star break arrived, Montreal beat San Diego, and as John Smoltz was losing, 6-1, to the Cardinals, the Braves were nudged into second place. Even though their won-lost record was still an impressive 52-33, the Braves had spent their last days alone in first place.

In the second half of the season, the Braves were only 16-13, as the Expos went 20-7. That allowed Montreal to open up a six-game advantage on Atlanta, although that hardly seemed to bother manager Bobby Cox. He reemphasized that the Braves' goal was winning the World Series, and with the wild-card route now available, slaying the Expos was no longer anyone's obsession. In fact, Cox said, "If it gets to be late in the year and we've already clinched a wild-card spot, I won't necessarily use everyone in my starting lineup to catch the Expos."

Cox never found out if his strategy would have worked because the major league season ended

THE GREAT RACE

on August 12, the casualty of a labor dispute. Despite intense negotiations between the owners and the Players Association, the schedule never resumed, and for the first time since 1904 there was no World Series. The Braves were in second place in the East, six games behind the Expos, and with a 68-46 record, had their best winning percentage of the season. Had the playoffs begun at that point, the Braves would have qualified as the wild card—2½ games ahead of the Houston Astros, who finished second in the Central Division—and would have opened the first round of the play-offs against the Expos. But all the speculation was moot, and the only certainties that remained from the 1994 season were a handful of impressive, albeit incomplete, statistics.

Greg Maddux went 16-6, and with a stunning 1.56 ERA became the first pitcher in history to win the Cy Young Award three straight seasons. Maddux also led the National League with 10 complete games and 202 innings pitched. Tom Glavine finished with a 13-9 record, and Steve Avery was 7-3. Most surprisingly, perhaps, was Kent Mercker, who, after throwing the third no-hitter in Atlanta's history, went on to a 9-4 record with a 3.45 ERA. Among the hitters, Fred McGriff placed fourth in the League with 34 home runs, along with his .318 average. David Justice hit .313 with 19 homers and Mark Lemke's .294 average was a career high. All that was missing from these numbers were the September and October performances, which will forever belong to the imagination.

Greg Maddux.

THE GREAT RACE

epilogue

No team in baseball has a longer history than the Braves. And for most of their more than 120 years of existence, they've been tied to the National League's whipping post. All that changed in the last four seasons, beginning with the miracle last-to-first summer of 1991. Since then, the Braves are 364-236—the best overall record in the big leagues, 27½ games better than the Toronto Blue Jays, who won back-to-back World Series championships in 1992 and 1993. The Yankees used to be baseball's role models for corporate efficiency, the Dodgers for franchise loyalty, and the Mets for clubhouse charisma. Now it's the Braves everyone wants to emulate.

In Greg Maddux, Tom Glavine, and

Steve Avery, the Braves have the three winningest pitchers since 1993. They have Fred McGriff, one of the National League's most dangerous home-run hitters; David Justice, owner of the sweetest swing; and, of course, they have the most dramatic stadium-wide chant to be found in all of baseball. With all the theater the Braves have provided these past four years, baseball fans nationwide really took notice of America's team and learned about its distinguished history.

Fans milling around outside Braves Field, Boston.

There was the dramatic 1914 World

Series, in which the lowly Braves, then from Boston, came out of nowhere to defeat Connie Mack's powerful Philadelphia A's in four straight games. Babe Ruth finished his career with the Braves in 1935, and Honus Wagner spent time in a Braves uniform on his way to the Hall of Fame. In 1953 the Braves moved to Milwaukee, where for thirteen years they would never endure a losing season. To many older fans, the Milwaukee period was the Braves' real Golden Era. Warren Spahn pitched his way to 13 twenty-win seasons, third baseman Eddie Mathews worked on his 512 career home runs, and of course, Henry Aaron, the soft-spoken infielder, got his first chance when Bobby Thomson broke his ankle in spring training, 1954. All three would eventually own a piece of baseball history.

Left to right, Fred Haney, Lou Perini, Warren Spahn, Don McMahon, and Hank Aaron.

The Braves made it to the World

Series twice while they resided in Milwaukee, beating the hated Yankees in 1957 and nearly repeating against them in 1958. There was a lull after that, and by 1966 the Braves belonged to Atlanta. It was Aaron, of course, who authored those early Atlanta years, chasing Babe Ruth all the way into 1974. That's when he finally became the game's all-time home-run champion, slugging No. 715, and finishing his career with 755. Ted Turner came along to purchase the Braves in 1976, and even though there was a Western Division title in 1982, the real excitement didn't begin in Atlanta until 1991.

Who will ever forget the way the

Braves caught and passed the Dodgers that summer, then beat the Pirates in a seven-game National League Championship Series? Or the way the Braves broke the Pirates' hearts again in 1992 with Francisco Cabrera's ninth-inning, Game Seven, RBI single. And although the Braves didn't make it past the Phillies in the 1993 National League Championship Series, the future looks as bright as ever. All you have to do is look across the street from Atlanta-Fulton County Stadium to the new Olympic Stadium now under construction.

At the conclusion of the 1996

Summer Olympics, the stadium will become the Braves' new home. With construction plans similar to Baltimore's Camden Yards, a trip to the Braves' ballpark will hold the promise of great seats for everyone, great scenery, great atmosphere, and great baseball. Especially great baseball. For that, the Braves practically own a patent.

statistics

Braves Batting Champions

Deacon White: 387 in 1877
Dan Brouthers: .373 in 1889
Hugh Duffy: .440 in 1894
Rogers Hornsby: .387 in 1928
Ernie Lombardi: .330 in 1942
Henry Aaron: .328 in 1956
Henry Aaron: .355 in 1959
Rico Carty: .366 in 1970
Ralph Garr: .353 in 1974
Terry Pendleton: .319 in 1991

Braves RBI Champions

Deacon White: 49 in 1877
John O'Rourke: 62 in 1879
Hugh Duffy: 145 in 1894
Wally Berger: 130 in 1935
Henry Aaron: 132 in 1957
Henry Aaron: 126 in 1960
Henry Aaron: 130 in 1963
Henry Aaron: 127 in 1966
Dale Murphy (tie): 109 in 1982
Dale Murphy: 121 in 1983

Rogers Hornsby displays Hall of Fame plaque, 1961.

Braves Home-Run Champions

Charley Jones: 9 in 1879
John O'Rourke: 6 in 1880
Hugh Duffy: 18 in 1894
Hugh Duffy: 11 in 1897
Jim Collins: 15 in 1898
Herman Long: 12 in 1900
David Brain: 10 in 1907
Wally Berger: 34 in 1935
Tommy Holmes: 28 in 1945
Eddie Mathews: 47 in 1953
Henry Aaron: 44 in 1957
Eddie Mathews: 46 in 1959
Henry Aaron (tie): 44 in 1963
Henry Aaron: 44 in 1966
Henry Aaron: 39 in 1967
Dale Murphy (tie): 36 in 1984
Dale Murphy: 37 in 1985

Braves ERA Champions

Tommy Bond: 1.96 in 1879
John Clarkson: 2.73 in 1899
Jim Turner: 2.38 in 1937
Warren Spahn: 2.33 in 1947
Chet Nichols: 2.88 in 1951
Warren Spahn: 2.10 in 1953
Lew Burdette: 2.71 in 1956
Warren Spahn: 3.01 in 1961
Phil Niekro: 1.87 in 1967
Buzz Capra: 2.28 in 1974
Greg Maddux: 2.36 in 1993
Greg Maddux: 1.56 in 1994

For the Record . . .

Baseball records are set not only by future Hall of Famers, but also by otherwise unheralded players destined to enjoy their "fifteen minutes of fame" during their playing days. Since the turn of the century, every decade of Braves franchise history has witnessed a player who fits this category of record holder.

"Big Jeff" Pfeffer highlighted an otherwise nondescript career when he pitched a no-hitter against the Reds in 1907. The "Miracle" Braves of 1914 were carried by the three-man rotation of Dick Rudolph, Bill James, and Lefty Tyler, but it was the unknown George Davis who threw a no-hitter against the Phillies during the Braves' stretch drive in September. In a dual performance that surely will never been approached again, Joe Oeschger and Brooklyn's Leon Cadore each pitched a major league record 26 innings in a 1-1 tie on May 1, 1920. The 1930s saw thirty-four-year-old rookie Jim Turner lead the National League in 1937 with a 2.38 ERA, 24 complete games, and 5 shutouts en route to 20 victories for the Bees. Three years later in 1940, Boston's Buddy Hassett tied a still-current National League record with ten consecutive hits over three games, while the Braves' Jim Tobin became the only major league pitcher ever to hit three homers in one game on May 13, 1942.

In the fifties, another Braves pitcher made the record books when Milwaukee's Max Surkont set what was then a major league mark by registering eight consecutive strikeouts in a game on May 25, 1953. And in that same decade, on April 12, 1955, Chuck Tanner became only the sixth major leaguer to homer on the first pitch he ever faced. Mack Jones, in a lineup with sluggers such as Hank Aaron, Eddie Mathews, and Joe Adcock, made headlines with his bat in his debut on July 13, 1961, when he tied a major league record with a four-hit performance. Buzz Capra won 16 games in 1974—more than half of his career total of 31—while leading the National League with a 2.28 ERA, but never recaptured his form after major shoulder surgery in 1976. Relief pitcher Rick Camp's shocking seventeenth-inning homer against the Mets on July 5, 1985, is recounted in detail in these pages. And thus far in the 1990s, Kent Mercker is the only Braves pitcher alongside the quartet of All-Stars in the team's rotation (Greg Maddux, Tom Glavine, Steve Avery, and John Smoltz) to hurl a no-hitter in his career. Mercker's no-hitter against the Dodgers on April 8, 1994, was preceded by his participation in a no-hitter against the Padres on September 11, 1991—the first combined no-hitter in National League history.

Chuck Tanner, 1955.

Left to right, Steve Avery, Tom Glavine, and Greg Maddux, 1993.

Braves Strikeout Champions

Tommy Bond: 170 in 1877
Tommy Bond: 182 in 1878
Jim Whitney: 345 in 1883
John Clarkson: 284 in 1889
Vic Willis: 225 in 1902
Warren Spahn: 151 in 1949
Warren Spahn: 191 in 1950
Warren Spahn (tie): 164 in 1951
Warren Spahn: 183 in 1952
Phil Niekro: 262 in 1977
John Smoltz: 215 in 1992

Braves Win Leaders

Tommy Bond: 40 in 1877
Tommy Bond: 40 in 1878
John Clarkson: 33 in 1888
John Clarkson: 49 in 1889
Kid Nichols: 31 in 1897
Kid Nichols: 32 in 1898
Dick Rudolph (tie): 27 in 1914
Johnny Sain: 24 in 1948
Warren Spahn: 21 in 1949
Warren Spahn: 20 in 1950
Warren Spahn (tie): 23 in 1953
Warren Spahn: 21 in 1957
Warren Spahn (tie): 22 in 1958
Warren Spahn (tie): 21 in 1959
Warren Spahn (tie): 21 in 1960
Warren Spahn (tie): 21 in 1961
Phil Niekro (tie): 20 in 1974
Phil Niekro (tie): 21 in 1979
Tom Glavine (tie): 20 in 1991
Tom Glavine (tie): 20 in 1992
Tom Glavine (tie): 22 in 1993
Greg Maddux (tie): 16 in 1994

index

The Aaron brothers, Hank and Tommie, 1962.

Curley, James, 41
Cy Young Award, 195, 211, 216, 236, 250

Daal, Omar, 239
Dark, Alvin, 76, 83, 84, 108, 240
Daulton, Darren, 242, 245
Davidson, Bob, 229
Davidson, Donald, 103, 143
Davidson, Satch, 158
Davis, Chili, 211, 212
Davis, Sammy, Jr., 158
Day, Ralph, 52
"Daylight play," 73
Deal, Charlie, 36, 42
Del Greco, Bobby, 108, 110
Detroit Tigers, 27
Dibble, Rob, 202, 227
Didier, Bob, 141–44, 146
DiMaggio, Joe, 161, 174, 191
Dittmer, Jack, 110, 111, 113
Division championships, 139–40, 141, 246
Doby, Larry, 76
Donatelli, Augie, 118
Dovey, George, 56
Dovey, John, 56
Downing, Al, 158–60, 161
Doyle, Paul, 145
Drabek, Doug, 204, 207, 208, 222–27
Driessen, Dan, 176
Duffy, Hugh, 26, 28, 29

Brett Butler, 1983.

Durante, Sal, 158
Durocher, Leo, 141, 153
Dyer, Eddie, 70
Dykstra, Lenny, 242, 243, 245

Easterly, Jamie, 160
Ebbets Field, 89
Egan, Dave, 66
Elliott, Bob, 70, 76, 78, 79
Elliott, Donnie, 236
Emslie, Bob, 41
Evans, Darrell, 154
Evers, Johnny, 37, 40, 44, 48, 49

Federal League, 37
Feeney, Chub, 170
Feller, Bob, 71–78
Ferguson, Joe, 158
Ferraro, Mike, 173
Forbes Field, 63
Ford, Whitey, 115–16, 118, 127, 128
Forest Citys, 22
Forsch, Bob, 182
Forster, Terry, 179, 189
Fregosi, Jim, 243
Frick, Ford, 93
Frisch, Frankie, 65
Fuchs, Judge Emil, 47, 50–63

Gaffney, James, 34, 37, 48, 56
Gagne, Greg, 211
Gant, Ron, 195, 198, 201, 204, 205, 211,
    215, 216, 219, 221, 222–31, 237, 240,
    241, 243, 248
Garber, Gene, 174, 176, 178, 182–83
Garr, Ralph, 157, 210
Garrett, Wayne, 143, 145, 147
Garrido, Gil, 144
Garvey, Steve, 193
Gaston, Cito, 231
Gehrig, Lou, 27, 55
Gehringer, Charlie, 37
Gentry, Gary, 145
Gilbert, Larry, 36, 44
Giles, Warren, 121
Gladder, Dan, 211–16
Glavine, Tom, 195, 198, 199, 202, 203–16,
    219, 220, 221, 224–33, 236–39, 242,
    250
Goetz, Larry, 97
Gold Glove Award, 191

The Mathews family, 1966: Left to right, Eddie, Virjean, Eddie Jr., Stephanie, and Johnny.

Bob Didier, 1969.

*Publicity shot for
the 1891 Boston
Beaneaters.*

Left to right, John Smoltz, Mark Grant, Tom Glavine, and David Justice display rally caps, 1991.

bibliography

Anderson, Dave. *Pennant Races*. New York: Doubleday, 1994.

Bibb, Porter. *It Ain't as Easy as It Looks*. New York: Crown, 1993.

Buege, Bob. *The Milwaukee Braves*. Milwaukee: Douglas American Sports Publications, 1988.

Carter, Craig. *The Sporting News: The Series*. St. Louis: Sporting News, 1988.

Charlton, James. *The Baseball Chronology*. New York: MacMillan, 1991.

Couch, J. Hudson. *The Braves' First Fifteen Years in Atlanta*. Atlanta: Other Alligator Creek, 1984.

Creamer, Robert. *The Babe*. New York: Simon and Schuster, 1974.

Creamer, Robert. *Stengel*. New York: Simon and Schuster, 1984.

Durant, John. *Baseball's Miracle Teams*. New York: Hastings House, 1975.

Durso, Joseph. *Amazing: The Miracle of the Mets*. Boston: Houghton Mifflin, 1970.

Hope, Bob. *We Could've Finished Last Without You*. Atlanta: Longstreet, 1991.

Kaese, Harold. *The Boston Braves*. New York: Putnam, 1948.

Musick, Phil. *Hank Aaron*. New York: Associated Features, 1974.

Onigman, Marc. *This Date in Braves' History*. Briarcliff Manor: Stein and Day, 1982.

Plimpton, George. *Hank Aaron: One for the Record*. New York: Bantam Books, 1974.

Reichler, Joseph. *The Baseball Encyclopedia*. New York: MacMillan, 1973.

Rosenberg, I. J. *Miracle Season*. Atlanta: Turner, 1991.

Sink, Richard. *Chop to the Top*. Cornelius, North Carolina: Tomahawk, 1992.

Thorn, John and Pete Palmer. *Total Baseball*. New York: HarperCollins, 1993.

Zack, Bill. *Tomahawked*. New York: Simon and Schuster, 1993.

acknowledgments

Many thanks to the people whose assistance made this book possible. To Kevin Mulroy, Kathy Buttler, and Rob Zides of Turner Publishing, for their patience and understanding. To Glen Serra of the Atlanta Braves; Dave Kaplan, Bill Madden, Fagei Rosenthal, all of *New York Daily News*; and Jay Horowitz of the New York Mets—your research was invaluable. Also, to Bill Goodstein, my attorney, and David Vigliano, my agent. To all of you, I owe you one.

Bob Klapisch

When Michael Reagan of Turner Publishing invited me to participate in this book, I had no idea where to begin. Editors Kevin Mulroy and Kathy Buttler not only steered me through the process, but provided invaluable ideas, assistance, and encouragement. Thanks also to Rob Zides, Lauren Emerson, and Dianne Joy.

Glen Serra of the Atlanta Braves gave hours of his time to help with research and verify its accuracy. The reference staff at the main branch of the Dekalb County Library also helped.

Special thanks to the Boston Braves Historical Association for the loan of a portion of their impressive collection of memorabilia. And to the hundreds of executives, managers, players, coaches, writers, and broadcasters I've gotten to know over the years, thank you. This wouldn't have been possible without the stories we've shared.

Pete Van Wieren

Warren Spahn.

picture credits

Allsport/Jim Gund: p. 228.

AP/Wide World Photos: pp. 55 (bottom), 68–69, 72, 78 (bottom), 88, 119, 122, 138, 145, 215 (top).

Archive Photos: pp. 64, 96, 114.

Archive Photos/Howard Muller: pp. 45, 161.

Atlanta Braves Public Relations: pp. 102, 134 (top), 135, 140 (bottom), 141 (bottom), 142, 143, 144 (bottom), 146, 147, 153, 157, 158, 159, 164, 167, 169, 171, 172, 174, 176, 177, 178, 179, 181, 182, 184, 186, 187, 188, 189, 191, 193 (bottom), 194 (top, bottom), 205, 215 (bottom), 224, 257, 262, 263, 264, 266, 271.

Atlanta Braves Public Relations/A. E. Babbitt: p. 183.

Atlanta Braves Public Relations/John Boccabella: p. 150.

Atlanta Braves Public Relations/Susan DeShazo: p. 192 (top).

Atlanta Braves Public Relations/Bob Johnson: pp. 154, 168 (bottom).

Atlanta Braves Public Relations/Charlie McCullers: p. 225 (top).

Atlanta Braves Public Relations/Bill Setliff: p. 195.

Atlanta Braves Public Relations/Tim Small: pp. 166, 170.

Atlanta Braves Public Relations/Walter Victor: pp. 222, 237.

Courtesy of William Bartholomay: p. 162.

Bettmann/UPI: pp. 27, 32, 40–41, 56, 58, 86–87, 103, 104, 106, 108–109, 111, 116–117, 123, 124, 128, 129 (top), 140 (top, center), 148, 151, 156, 261 (courtesy Dan Schlossberg).

Greg Crisp/TBS, Inc.: p. 243.

Scott Cunningham: pp. 175, 200, 203, 216.

Alan David: p. 234.

Phil Davis/Atlanta Braves Public Relations: pp. 198, 199, 201, 206, 207, 209, 210 (bottom), 220, 221, 226 (top left), 231, 239, 241, 244.

Art Foxhall/Major League Baseball Photos: p. 247.

Chris Hamilton/Atlanta Braves Public Relations: pp. 202, 208, 218, 223, 225 (bottom), 226 (top, center, bottom), 227, 238, 240, 242, 246, 248, 249, 250, 251.

Mark Hill/TBS, Inc.: pp. 144 (top), 190 (top), 193 (top), 233, 245.

Teryl Jackson/TBS, Inc.: pp. 211, 212–213, 229 (top).

Andy Jurinko: p. 70 (bottom).

Milwaukee Journal: pp. 92, 94–95, 112.

National Baseball Library & Archive, Cooperstown, N.Y.: pp. 2–3, 18, 20, 22, 24, 26, 27, 29, 30–31, 34, 35, 36, 38 (top), 43, 44, 46, 49, 50–51, 53, 54, 65, 67, 71, 73 (bottom), 83, 89 (bottom), 90–91, 97, 100, 101, 127 (top), 256, 265.

Newsweek: p. 160.

Frank Niemeir/*Atlanta Constitution*: p. 196.

Joe Sebo/Atlanta Braves Public Relations: pp. 6–7, 180, 190 (bottom), 214, 217, 230, 232, 258–259, 267.

Courtesy of Steven Tanhauser/J. Stoll: pp. 55 (top), 66 (bottom), 89 (top), 155.

The Sporting News: pp. 4–5, 21 (bottom), 28, 52, 61 (top), 66 (top), 70 (top), 73 (top), 74–75, 76, 77, 79, 80, 82 (bottom), 84, 85 (top), 107, 115, 118, 120, 121, 127 (bottom), 130, 132, 133 (top), 134 (bottom), 135, 136–137, 252, 254.

Sports Illustrated: p. 152.

J. Stoll/TBS, Inc.: pp. 17 (center), 78 (top), 91 (center), 137 (center), 141 (top), 168 (top), 192 (bottom), 210 (top), 212, 229.

Total Baseball, Michael Gershman: p. 48.

Transcendental Graphics, Mark Rucker: pp. 21 (top), 23, 37, 38–39, 42, 57, 60, 61 (bottom), 62, 82 (top), 85 (bottom), 94 (top), 98, 110, 129 (bottom), 133 (bottom), 168.

Ron Veseley: p. 204.

1995

World Series

Champions

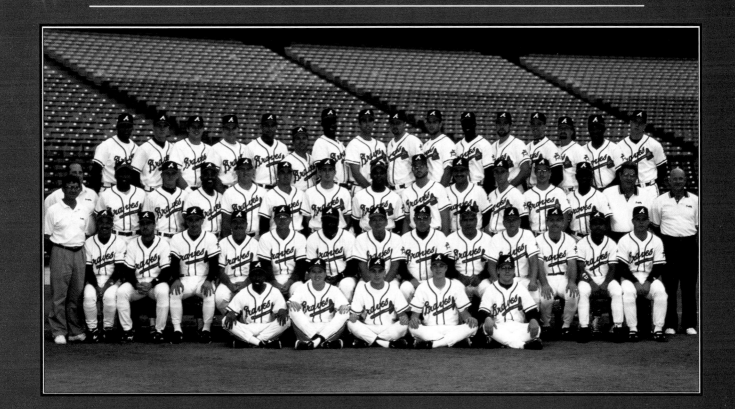

1995 world champs

22

*"Atlanta is a proud city, a dynamic city,
and now it's a World Championship city."*

—John Schuerholz

As 1995 spring training approached,

the labor dispute, which had shut down major league baseball in mid-August of 1994, was no closer to resolution. While the bickering continued over proposals on a salary cap, a luxury tax, and revenue sharing, owners decided that the game would go on despite the strike. Thus was born the most unusual spring training in major league history. So-called replacement players—major league never-weres and wannabes—populated the twenty-eight major league camps and played out a full spring-training schedule as opening day neared. The surreal atmosphere gave way to tragedy late in March when pitcher Dave Shotkoski was killed in an apparent robbery attempt during an after-dinner walk in West Palm Beach. On the Friday before

After a thirty-year wait, the Atlanta Braves celebrate a World Series title.

the regular season was to begin, however, a U.S. District Court issued an injunction against the owners, ordering them to restore the provisions of the expired collective bargaining agreement, at which time the players ended their strike. The two sides agreed to a shortened 144-game regular season, which would follow an abbreviated three-week spring training for the regular major leaguers. But the court order did nothing to relieve the growing number of financially strapped teams, which allowed the Atlanta Braves to make their first move toward strengthening their 1995 roster.

All-star center fielder Marquis Grissom was one of the three high-priced Montreal Expos dealt to other teams as "Spring Training II" began. The Braves made the winning bid, giving up outfielders Roberto Kelly and Tony Tarasco and a minor-league pitcher in exchange. In Grissom, the Braves now had the lead-off hitter they had lacked since the departure of Otis Nixon. Added to such mainstays as Fred McGriff, David Justice, Jeff Blauser, and Mark Lemke, and combined with talented youngsters such as Javier Lopez, Ryan Klesko, and Chipper Jones, Grissom gave the Braves as solid a starting lineup as anyone in baseball.

The true strength of the Braves, however, remained in their starting pitching. No one in baseball could match the potential of the quartet of Greg Maddux, Tom Glavine, John Smoltz, and Steve Avery. But questions remained as the delayed season-opener neared: Who would be the closer out of the bullpen? Greg McMichael? Mike Stanton? Mark Wohlers? Rookie Brad Clontz? Was the bench, populated mostly by rookies, strong enough?

To some fans, these questions didn't matter. Feeling betrayed by the seven-month strike, many stayed away as the 1995 season belatedly began. Only 24,000 showed up for the opening day game in Atlanta against the San Francisco Giants. Those who did return witnessed a promising start. The Braves pummeled the Giants, 12-5, and Greg Maddux picked up the victory. The winning ways continued for a week as Atlanta began the season with a 6-1 record and moved to the top of the National League East.

Reliable starting pitching and occasional splashes of offense kept the Braves above .500 through May, but the team gradually lost ground—to the Phillies and the Montreal Expos. By June 4, Atlanta had fallen to third in the division, five games behind the Phillies and two behind the Expos.

The bullpen had been the source of weakness. Manager Bobby Cox had found no proven closing pitcher available in trade, and so decided to try again with Wohlers in a June 5 game against Chicago. Taking a 7-5 lead into the eighth inning, Wohlers shut down the Cubs. It was just the second save for Wohlers in the past three seasons, but it earned him another chance, and he responded with a third save two days later.

Meanwhile, the Braves' starters were beginning to hit their stride. On June 15, Greg Maddux shut out Montreal. The next night, Tom Glavine pitched the first-ever shutout in Colorado's hitter-friendly Coors Field. Three days later, John Smoltz whitewashed the Cincinnati Reds. And something else was happening—the Braves found that their offense was developing a pattern of winning games in its last at-bat.

On June 28, David Justice hit a three-run homer in the bottom of the ninth to give Atlanta a 4-3 win over the Expos. On July 4, Jeff Blauser's run-scoring single in the bottom of the eighth lifted the Braves past the Dodgers, 3-2. The next night, Chipper Jones connected for a three-run ninth-inning homer, giving Atlanta a 4-1 victory over Los Angeles.

On July 6, Fred McGriff's run-scoring single in the bottom of the ninth beat the Dodgers, 1-0, and on the final day before the All-Star break, McGriff struck again with a three-run ninth-inning homer to defeat the Giants, 3-2. It gave Atlanta a nine-game winning streak and a four-game lead over Philadelphia as the All-Star break arrived.

By the end of July, Atlanta led the Eastern Division by eight full games. But the bullpen and bench still needed some fine tuning if the Braves were to be a true postseason force. On July 31, an overhaul began when left-hander Mike Stanton was traded to the Boston Red Sox, and two weeks later thirty-seven-year-old veteran pitcher Steve Bedrosian announced his retirement. The Braves reacquired pitcher Alejandro Peña, who had been a part of the Braves' "Worst to First" miracle of 1991, from the Florida Marlins. The bullpen now had the depth and quality that John Schuerholz and Bobby Cox wanted. To strengthen the bench, Atlanta claimed the Yankees' lefty Luis Polonia, who was on waivers, and made a trade with the Chicago White Sox for veteran right-handed hitter Mike Devereaux.

After going 19-10 in August, the Braves increased their lead in the East to fourteen full games over the Phillies. With the roster now set, it was no longer a question of if, but when the Braves would clinch the division title.

By September 11, the "magic number" was down to two, and it appeared that the Braves would clinch during a three-game series in Colorado. However, the Rockies were involved in a first-place battle with the Dodgers in the West, and they won the first two games of the series. When Atlanta held on for a 9-7 win over the Rockies on September 13, they exited Denver having secured a tie for the division crown.

It was while airborne on their way to Cincinnati that the Braves learned of the Phillies' loss to Montreal. The National League East title belonged to Atlanta.

In his second full season with the Braves, twenty-four-year-old Javier Lopez became the first Braves catcher to hit over .300 since Joe Torre in 1966. Lopez finished at .315, with 14 home runs and 51 RBIs.

Jeff Blauser, the Brave with the longest tenure, was plagued by injury throughout much of the 1995 season. Hitting just .211 and bothered by nagging leg and ankle ailments, Blauser was removed from Atlanta's World Series roster.

1995 WORLD CHAMPS

Winning an unprecedented fourth consecutive Cy Young award, Greg Maddux drew comparisons with baseball's greatest pitchers. Most scouts compared Maddux's pitching style to that of Catfish Hunter. Another called him "a right-handed Whitey Ford."

Second baseman Mark Lemke provided airtight defense up the middle, committing only five errors all season. This double-play relay nabs former teammate Ron Gant in the bottom half of the fourth inning of Game Four of the NLCS with the Reds.

Bobby Cox now had three weeks to get his team primed for postseason play, especially starter Steve Avery, who had been struggling. Since July 15, Avery had gone 2-8 with a 6.38 ERA. Some minor adjustments to his delivery and perhaps the absence of pressure quickly corrected the Avery skid. In his last three starts, Avery allowed only three runs and struck out 25.

The Braves had to wait until the final day of the regular season to find out that the Colorado Rockies, who clinched the wild-card playoff berth with a come-from-behind victory over the Giants, would be their opponent in the Division Series.

The first-round series was billed as a battle of Atlanta's pitching against Colorado's awesome power. The Rockies had hit a league-leading 200 home runs during the season and featured the second 30-homer quartet (Dante Bichette, 40; Larry Walker, 36; Vinny Castilla, 32; and Andres Galarraga, 31) in all major league history. The match-up would also test one of baseball's oldest questions: Which is better, to clinch early and get everyone some rest (Atlanta) or to get in on the final day and have momentum working for you (Colorado)?

The series began in Denver on October 3, with Greg Maddux facing Kevin Ritz (11-11, 4.21 ERA). The game entered the ninth inning tied, 4-4. With two outs and the bases empty in the top of the ninth, Chipper Jones connected for his second homer of the night, giving the Braves a 5-4 lead. Mark Wohlers

closed the door on the Rockies, and the Braves were one game up in the best-of-five series.

In Game Two, Tom Glavine blanked the Rockies over the first five innings, but in the sixth Larry Walker connected for a three-run homer to tie the score. Colorado took the lead in the eighth on a run-scoring double by Andres Galarraga off Alejandro Peña. But Atlanta had yet another ninth-inning comeback in them, led by Mike Mordecai, who delivered a pinch-hit run-scoring single, giving the Braves a 5-4 lead. An error by Colorado second baseman Eric Young led to two more runs, and when Mark Wohlers again closed the door on the Rockies in the ninth, the Braves were 7-4 winners, up 2-0 in the series. It was the twenty-seventh time that season Atlanta had won a game in its final at-bat.

On October 6 the series moved to Atlanta

for Game Three, and this time the Rockies prevailed. Home runs by Eric Young and Vinny Castilla, and tenth-inning run-scoring singles by Andres Galarraga and Castilla gave the Rockies a 7-5 win. The series now stood 2-1, Atlanta.

Game Four brought Greg Maddux back to the mound to face the Rockies' Bret Saberhagen. Colorado silenced the Atlanta crowd in the top of the third when Dante Bichette hit a three-run homer, making it 3-0, Rockies. But the Braves bounced back quickly, winning Game Four easily, 10-4, and winning the best-of-five series, 3-1. Their next stop would be the National League Championship Series against the Cincinnati Reds, who had swept the Los Angeles Dodgers, 3-0, in their first-round series.

The NLCS opener in Cincinnati featured the National League's two premier left-handers, seventeen-game winner Tom Glavine for the Braves against eighteen-game winner Pete Schourek for the Reds. The Reds led 1-0 going into the ninth, when again the Braves came back. Singles by Chipper Jones and Fred McGriff put runners at first and third, and when David Justice grounded into a force play, Jones tied the score, 1-1. The game went into the eleventh inning before the Braves broke the deadlock. With Fred McGriff at second and two outs, Mike Devereaux delivered a run-scoring single, giving the Braves a 2-1 lead. Brad Clontz was brought in to save the game, but he gave up a lead-off double to Thomas Howard, who advanced to third when Barry Larkin grounded out. Steve Avery replaced Clontz, but he walked pinch-hitter Lenny Harris, putting the Reds' runners at first and third. Enter Greg McMichael, who got Reggie Sanders to hit into a short-to-first double play, and the Braves escaped with a 2-1 win and a 1-0 lead in the series.

It was more of the same in Game Two. Both starting pitchers, John Smoltz and the Reds' John Smiley, pitched well, and both bullpens pitched out of numerous jams, sending the game into extra innings, this time

Blue Chip Rookie

The major league career of Larry (Chipper) Jones was to have begun in 1994. The highly-touted prospect had been moved from shortstop (his minor league position) to left field to replace Ron Gant, who had lost his job with Atlanta when he broke his left leg in an off-season motorcycle accident. But Chipper never even made it to opening day. While running out a ground ball in a March 18 exhibition game against the New York Yankees, he suffered a complete tear of a ligament in his left knee, putting him out for the season.

In 1995, Chipper was back, feeling, he said, "stronger than ever." He replaced Terry Pendleton, who had become a free agent and had signed with the Florida Marlins, at third base. Jones took to the position as if born to it, demonstrating the quick hands and strong throwing arm required to play third base.

Offensively, his ability to deliver in the clutch emerged on May 9, when he hit his first major league home run, a ninth-inning game winner against the New York Mets. He also led the Braves to wins over the Florida Marlins on May 20 and the Los Angeles Dodgers on July 5 with ninth-inning homers.

Jones finished his rookie season with a .265 average, a career-high 23 home runs (15 had been his minor league high), and 86 runs batted in, just one shy of the Atlanta rookie record set by Earl Williams in 1971. He was also one of the Braves' top postseason performers, hitting .364 with 3 homers and 8 RBI in fourteen games.

The Braves acquired Jones with the nation's first draft pick in 1990, but he was really Atlanta's second choice. "We came out winners there," said Braves manager Bobby Cox. "Chipper is the best athlete on the team. I really think I could play him anywhere and he'd be good. He's also a leader and a winner. He's going to be around for a long time."

Chipper Jones, rookie third baseman.

Maddux—The Master

By winning a third consecutive Cy Young Award in 1994, Greg Maddux secured a spot on any list of all-time pitching greats. But as the 1995 season progressed, the question being asked was: Has anyone ever had a better *four*-year stretch than Maddux?

At the All-Star break, Maddux was already 8–1 with a 1.64 ERA, prompting a national columnist to write, "Maddux is already a shoo-in to win his fourth straight Cy Young Award, but I'm not sure Cy Young could ever have won a Greg Maddux award."

By season's end, Maddux had reeled off a major league record of 18 consecutive victories on the road over two years, compiling an astonishing 0.99 ERA during that stretch. But the most notable name he passed in setting the record was that of Denny McLain, baseball's last thirty-game winner, but not a Hall-of-Famer.

Starting pitcher Greg Maddux.

The other names Maddux was matching were more impressive. Finishing the year at 19–2 with a 1.63 ERA, Maddux compiled the highest winning percentage (.905) of any pitcher in major league history, with twenty or more decisions (also in 1995, Seattle's Randy Johnson went 18–2). He led the league in earned run average for a third consecutive season, becoming the first National League pitcher to accomplish that since Sandy Koufax, who did it five consecutive seasons (1962–66). And by posting an ERA of under 1.80 for a second straight year (1.56 in 1994), Maddux matched a feat last accomplished by Walter Johnson in the 1918 and 1919 seasons.

With ten complete games, Maddux became the first National League right-hander to lead the league for three straight seasons in that category since Grover Cleveland Alexander in 1916.

Finally, Greg's 1.63 ERA was an incredible 2.55 below the league average of 4.18. No other pitcher had ever outperformed their peers by that margin, not even Bob Gibson, whose record 1.12 ERA in 1968 stood against a league average of 2.99.

Koufax, Johnson, Alexander, Gibson—all pitching legends—were now being matched or surpassed by the newest member of their exclusive club—Greg Maddux.

Unlike the others, Maddux does not blow hitters away with overpowering stuff—he gets them out with remarkable control and command of the four basic pitches. Asked to describe himself, the scholarly-appearing Maddux says simply, "I just pitch."

tied, 2-2. With Mark Portugal pitching for Cincinnati, the Braves loaded the bases in the tenth. With Ryan Klesko hitting, Portugal delivered a wild pitch, scoring Lemke and giving the Braves a 3-2 lead. After Klesko popped out, Javier Lopez launched a three-run homer deep into the left-field seats. The Braves were up 6-2. Mark Wohlers pitched a scoreless bottom of the tenth, and the Braves headed back to Atlanta, up 2-0 in the best-of-seven series.

Game Three in Atlanta saw two newcomers to postseason play become the heroes. Catcher Charlie O'Brien, playing in his first League Championship Series after ten years in the major leagues, broke a scoreless tie with a three-run homer off of Reds' southpaw David Wells in the bottom of the sixth. And rookie-of-the-year candidate Chipper Jones added a two-run shot in the seventh as the Braves,

Dwight Smith, a preseason free-agent signee, became the Braves' premier pinch hitter, delivering 16 pinch hits, just four shy of the Atlanta record held by Chris Chambliss. An accomplished vocalist, Dwight also sang the national anthem before Game Three of the NLCS.

1995 World Championship pin.

Outfielder Mike Devereaux, the NLCS MVP, solidified the Braves' bench after his late-August arrival, hitting .255. His game-winning hit in the bottom of the ninth on September 24 gave the Braves a league high of 25 wins in their final at-bat.

World Series MVP

Growing up, Tom Glavine was involved in both baseball and hockey, sports in which he excelled. "But we always seemed to come up short," says Glavine. "My mom kept telling me to stick with it, and one of these days 'you'll be the bride instead of the bridesmaid.' "

That day finally arrived for Glavine on October 28, 1995, when the crafty left-hander hurled eight innings of a one-hit shutout game as the Braves clinched their first World Series title in thirty-eight years. Following the game, Glavine was named Most Valuable Player in the 1995 Series.

The season had come full circle for the twenty-nine-year-old. As the team's player representative, Glavine had been on the receiving end of much of the fans' wrath during the eight-month players' strike. He was booed loudly when introduced on opening night and didn't seem to win back the fans' full support until August 10, when he not only outdueled Cincinnati's John Smiley in a 2–1 Atlanta win but also hit the first home run of his nine-year major league career.

Glavine finished the season with a 16–7 record and an ERA of 3.08, then pitched effectively in all four of his postseason starts, allowing only 5 earned runs in 28 innings.

Glavine said he tried to approach the final game of the World Series as just another game. "But it was hard," he added. "I was here in the eighties on some of those teams that lost a hundred games every year, and I knew what a World Series title would mean to this city. But I tried not to think about that and just go out and pitch my game."

When did he know that his stuff was at its best in Game Six? "In the very first inning," he answered. "I felt strong right from the start."

And at the end Glavine graciously accepted the MVP trophy, the one his mom always knew he would win.

Starting pitcher Tom Glavine.

behind Greg Maddux, coasted to a 5-2 win and a 3-0 lead in the series.

This put Atlanta on the verge of making history. Since the NLCS went to best-of-seven format in 1985, no team had ever swept the first four games.

The night of October 14 began ominously for the Braves. A knee injury caused David Justice to be scratched from the starting lineup; he was replaced by Mike Devereaux. As it turned out, fate could not have intervened more favorably. Game Four saw another tight pitcher's duel, this time between Steve Avery and Pete Schourek. The Braves were clinging to a 1-0 lead as they entered the bottom of the seventh. After Reds reliever Mike Jackson loaded the bases on a triple by Marquis Grissom and a pair of walks, a passed ball charged to catcher Benito Santiago let in a run, making it 2-0, Atlanta.

That brought up Devereaux, who promptly homered into the left-field seats, breaking the game wide open for Atlanta. That blow, plus Devereaux's game-winning hit in Game One, earned him Most Valuable Player honors for the Championship Series. The Braves won Game Four easily, 6-0, and pulled off an unprecedented sweep in the NLCS to claim their third National League pennant in five years.

It was time to play the waiting game again. The Braves would have a full week to prepare for the World Series. They did not learn whom their opponent would be until three nights later, when Cleveland ousted Seattle in the ALCS, four games to two.

Now baseball had the World Series match-up

(Left) After a disappointing regular season, Steve Avery rebounded with a win in Game Four of the NLCS and in Game Four of the World Series.

(Opposite) Charlie O'Brien, with Javier Lopez, gave the Braves a potent catching tandem—they combined for 23 homers and 74 RBIs.

that most fans seemed to want—the heralded pitching of Atlanta against the best-hitting team in baseball, the Cleveland Indians.

If the Rockies and the Reds were a stern test for Atlanta's heralded pitching, the Indians provided the final exam. Winner of 100 games in the 144-game regular season, Cleveland led all major league teams with a .291 batting average and 207 home runs, scoring an average of just under six runs per game. Seven members of the Indians' starting lineup hit .300 or higher, led by Albert Belle, whose 52 doubles and 50 home runs made him the first player since Stan Musial in 1948 to garner more than 100 extra-base hits in a single season.

But as Game One neared, the focus was on pitching—Atlanta's Greg Maddux against Cleveland's Orel Hershiser—in what the *Cleveland Plain-Dealer* called the "best game one match-up since 1968, when Detroit's Denny McLain faced Bob Gibson of the

1995 World Championship ticket.

Ryan Klesko, after hitting 23 home runs during the regular season, added three more in the World Series at Jacobs Field—becoming the first player in the history of the Fall Classic to homer in three consecutive road games.

1995 WORLD CHAMPS

World Series Odds and Ends

Marquis Grissom's 5 HITS IN TONIGHT'S GAME ARE A BRAVES' FRANCHISE RECORD FOR A POST-SEASON GAME

Marquis Grissom became the first National League player ever to pick up five hits in a post-season game, going 5-for-5 in Game Four of the Division Series with Colorado. The only other players to get five hits in a post-season game are Paul Blair in the 1969 ALCS and Paul Molitor in the 1982 World Series.

In winning the World Series, the Braves became the first franchise in baseball history to win the Fall Classic in three different cities: Boston in 1914, Milwaukee in 1957, and Atlanta in 1995.

Marquis Grissom set a major league post-season record with 25 total hits. Hitting safely in all fourteen postseason games, Grissom went 11-for-21 vs. Colorado, 5-for-19 vs. Cincinnati, and 9-for-25 vs. Cleveland. The previous record had been 24 hits by Boston's Marty Barrett in 1986.

Only ten players for the 1995 Braves were a part of the worst-to-first team in 1991: pitchers Steve Avery, Tom Glavine, Kent Mercker, Alejandro Peña, John Smoltz, and Mark Wohlers; infielders Rafael Belliard, Jeff Blauser, and Mark Lemke; and outfielder David Justice.

Atlanta pitching held Cleveland hitting to a combined average of just .179 for the six-game series—the second-lowest batting average ever turned in by a World Series team in a six-game finish. Only the 1911 New York Giants hit lower, batting just .175 while losing to the Philadelphia Athletics, 4 games to 2.

The one-hitter pitched by Tom Glavine and Mark Wohlers in Game Six was only the fifth in World Series history. The others were delivered by Ed Reulbach of the Cubs in 1906, Claude Passeau of the Cubs in 1945, Bill Bevens of the Yankees in 1947, and Jim Lonborg of the Red Sox in 1967. The Yankees' Don Larsen still has the only no-hitter in World Series history with his perfect game against the Dodgers in 1956.

Cardinals." Hershiser (16–6, 3.87) had never lost a postseason game, going 7–0 since he first hit the October stage with the 1985 Dodgers. Maddux, meanwhile, had a nine-game winning streak dating back to August 20.

On a cool night in Atlanta, the Indians found their bats even colder as Maddux hurled a two-hit masterpiece. Atlanta managed only three hits off of Hershiser but eked out a 3–2 win to go one game up in the Series. Rafael Belliard's suicide-squeeze bunt scored what proved to be the winning run, but it was Maddux who made the difference.

Cleveland manager Mike Hargrove called the Maddux effort "one of the best-pitched games I have ever seen."

In Game Two, another pitcher's duel unfolded between Tom Glavine and Cleveland's forty-year-old Dennis Martinez. Heading to the bottom of the sixth, the Indians held a 3–2 lead. David Justice opened the Braves' half of the inning with a single to left field. One out later, Javier Lopez drilled a Martinez pitch over the center-field wall, giving Atlanta the lead. Alejandro Peña and Mark Wohlers shut down Cleveland in the final two innings, and with the 4–3 victory, the Braves were up 2–0 in the Fall Classic.

Now the Series moved to Cleveland and its beautiful new stadium, Jacobs Field. Game

Three turned out to be a memorable battle. The Indians knocked Braves starter John Smoltz out of the game in the third inning, taking a 4–1 lead. But in the top of the sixth, a solo homer by Fred McGriff made it 4–2, Cleveland. In the seventh, Ryan Klesko's home run cut the Indians' lead to one run. The Indians scored off of Kent Mercker in the seventh to make it 5–3, but in the eighth, the Braves rallied for three, taking a 6–5 lead on a run-scoring single by Mike Devereaux.

Cleveland tied the score at 6-6 in the bottom of the eighth on a run-scoring double by catcher Sandy Alomar, and the game went into extra innings. By now, both managers had their closers on the mound, and neither Mark Wohlers nor Cleveland's Jose Mesa would give in. With both pitchers working well beyond their usual one inning, the game entered the bottom of the eleventh—still tied.

The Braves brought in Alejandro Peña, who tried to pitch despite painful back spasms. It didn't work. Carlos Baerga led off with a double to center, and after Albert Belle was intentionally walked, Eddie Murray lined Peña's first pitch into center field, scoring Baerga to give the Indians their first victory in a World Series since 1948.

In Game Four, the pitching returned to the spotlight. Atlanta's Steve Avery and Cleveland's Ken Hill were deadlocked 1–1 after six innings. But in the seventh, with one out, Marquis Grissom walked. Luis Polonia then doubled into the gap in right-center, scoring Grissom and giving Atlanta a 2–1 lead. A walk to Chipper Jones and a passed ball moved the runners to second and third. Fred McGriff struck out, but David Justice followed with a two-run single, giving the Braves a 4–1 lead.

By the ninth inning, the Braves were leading 5–1 and gambled that Mark Wohlers, who had pitched 2⅔ innings the night before, could give them one more inning tonight. He couldn't. Manny Ramirez led off the bottom of the ninth with a home run to left and Paul Sorrento followed with a double.

The only fresh arm in the Atlanta bullpen belonged to Pedro Borbon, who hadn't

pitched in three weeks. Bobby Cox called for the seldom-used left-hander, and the son of former Cincinnati relief ace, Pedro Sr., borrowed a page from his father's book. Borbon struck out Jim Thome and Sandy Alomar and retired Kenny Lofton on a line drive to right, notching his first save since May 18. Now the Braves were one win away from the championship.

With Greg Maddux fully rested for Game Five, the Braves entered their final night in Cleveland confident and with high expectations. A telling banner proclaimed "not in our house," and for one of the few times all season, Maddux was ineffective. Albert Belle

Pedro Borbon (upper left) strikes out Colorado's Mike Kingery in Game Three of the Division Series. He did not pitch again until Game Five of the World Series, when he recorded a dramatic save.

Alejandro Peña (lower left) returned to the Braves just before the postseason roster deadline. After missing nearly two full seasons due to elbow surgery, Peña averaged better than a strikeout-per-inning in the closing weeks.

(Opposite) Shortstop Rafael Belliard begins a short-to-first double-play in game four of the Division Series with Colorado. Counting his 1990 season with Pittsburgh, Belliard has gone to postseason play five consecutive times.

Bobby Cox became the forty-first manager in major league history to win more than 1,000 games. At year's end, he was thirty-fifth on the all-time list with 1,115 victories.

connected for a first-inning two-run homer, Jim Thome and Manny Ramirez delivered back-to-back run-scoring singles in the sixth inning, and Thome added a solo homer off of reliever Brad Clontz in the eighth. Orel Hershiser kept the Braves at bay for eight innings, and Jose Mesa was just good enough in the ninth as Cleveland held on for a 5–4 victory. The Series would head back to Atlanta with the Braves now leading 3 games to 2.

On the off day before Game Six, David Justice stunned the media and Braves officials when he went on an unsolicited verbal rampage against Atlanta fans. "They'll probably burn our houses down if we don't win," said Justice. "They're not behind us like the Cleveland fans, who were standing and cheering even when they were three runs down."

The crowd for Game Six responded by booing loudly when Justice's name was announced in the starting lineup and when he came to the plate for the first time in the second inning. But the booing chorus quickly became a cheering choir when Justice led off the bottom half of the sixth inning with a dramatic home run over the right-field wall for the only run of the night.

Tom Glavine, meanwhile, was pitching one of the greatest games in World Series history, limiting the powerful Indians to just one soft single over eight innings. Mark Wohlers came on to pitch the ninth and quickly retired Kenny Lofton on a pop foul caught by Rafael Belliard. Paul Sorrento followed with a fly ball to center. Two down, one to go. When Marquis Grissom caught Carlos Baerga's drive to left-center field, a thirty-year dream finally came true—World Champions!

No longer would the Atlanta Braves be called "the Buffalo Bills of baseball." No longer would Atlanta be a city without a world championship team.

A two-day celebration concluded with a parade down Peachtree Street before an estimated 650,000 spectators. "Our fans," said David Justice, "have definitely proven me wrong. They are the best."